Venom
Of
Asps

Meira bat Erachaim

ISBN: 1499200110
ISBN-13: 978-1499200119

Dedicated to the people of Israel and Palestine.
Not so much to their leaders.

CONTENTS

INTRODUCTION

My father was a diplomat. I grew up in a house where politics, history, social issues were frequent topics of conversation. I do not recall a family dinner where we did not address the political issues of the day. We lived in a place where social injustice was the law. My parents made no effort to shield their children from the wide world of discrimination and intolerance around us. On the contrary, they made sure that we understood what those with power were doing to those without.

Neither of my parents was ever especially religious when I was a child. They tried not to break most of the rules and always showed reverence for the traditions. They always made it clear to their daughters that how deeply we pursued our own religious paths was entirely up to us. We were exposed to disparate traditions and encouraged to investigate other faiths. We were always told that God is for everybody, regardless of how they pray, or even if they never pray at all, and that there is absolutely nothing wrong with people who have their own gods or reject religion altogether.

I learnt from an early age to talk about a wide variety of subjects with a wide variety of people. The last thing my parents wanted was children who could only relate to and be comfortable amongst people completely like themselves.

Society tells us that politics and religion are not to be discussed in polite company. Most people are fairly set in their opinions and not likely to change them when hearing other opinions. Discussion can easily turn to arguments. In some circles arguments are required. There used to be a time when you could discuss politics online. Those days are over. People still rant and rave about their opinions, of course, but there is no discussion. That would require actually listening to what the other person has to say. Why do that in a day and age where anybody with a different opinion is obviously either crazy or stupid. Or both.

There were flaws in my childhood. As there are in everybody's. My opinion is that moving from one place to another as frequently as we did was probably not ideal. I have no hometown and only vague memories of the city in which I was born. I generally consider Cape Town my hometown and I did not even live there until high school.

But living in a handful of countries on half of the planet's continents has given me an appreciation for how similar people are, and how differently we express ourselves. People who expatriate themselves and their families develop a necessary respect for other cultures and ideas. Those who do not or cannot tend to become disgruntled and unpleasant to be around. But for most people, living in alien cultures is a great way to preclude any xenophobia or bigotry.

My religious beliefs began in my childhood before I rejected pretty much everything I was taught. It was only after I moved to my current home, perhaps the last home I shall ever have, that I returned to those beliefs. I am the last person whom anybody would call a religious zealot but I care more about my faith now than I ever have.

My political beliefs have evolved greatly over the years. As the daughter of somebody who can ambiguously be described a former bohemian I was quick to dissent from her nonconformist views. As a teenager I often took opposing views for the simple purpose of having opposing views. But the more I saw of the world the more I opened myself to some of my mother's opinions whilst always retaining the option of rejecting others. My religious views may have come full circle but my political opinions have meandered in more of a serpentine pattern.

The end result, though hopefully this is not

the end, is that I have strong opinions and beliefs but also the confidence in those views to listen to opposing opinions and beliefs. There are some subjects in which I very much believe what I believe and will fight to the death my right to express it but I take no issue with those who just as strongly believe whatever they believe. I think perhaps the world might be a healthier place if we could all tolerate each other a little more. Even those people who you know are completely wrong.

I know the internet would absolutely be a healthier place.

WASTED SEED
ON THE GROUND

Where do I stand politically? That is a good question. The answer depends on whose definitions you use.

In the South Africa of my youth I was considered radically liberal by the white establishment because I vehemently opposed apartheid. Most of the Jewish community protested apartheid. Probably because we know how far discrimination can go. Apartheid was horrible but it could have easily led to even worse.

Black South Africans thought I was conservative because I opposed the militants and their terrorist tactics. I always thought Gandhi had the right idea. Nelson Mandela eventually agreed but he started out with a terrorist organisation. His achievements in later years are incredible but his early years should not make anybody proud.

I was progressive to the coloureds because I thought they should be treated equally, something not even most blacks favoured at the time. My first lesson in my homeland's racial problems came at an early age from a group of black children who disapproved of my friendship with a coloured girl.

South Africa has changed dramatically since then. There is still plenty of racism and political corruption but at least the majority race is in charge of the racism and corruption. Now I am considered liberal by the people who used to think me conservative because I disagree with their policies of racism and corruption.

The people in charge have changed but my views have not. I still believe that everybody should be treated equally. The people in charge, whether white, black or whatever comes next, seem to believe that their race is above all the others. Racial superiority in a country as culturally diverse as South Africa is never going to work out.

On Wednesday 22 April 2009 the people of South Africa once again rubber stamped the African National Congress into office and elected the racist, sexist, homophobic and corrupt Jacob Zuma president.

I despise Jacob Zuma. I despise him because he hates white people, and that is the kind of thinking this country needs to finally be rid of. I despise him because he hates women. I do not know how he can have so many wives and still think so little of women. I do not believe you can effectively govern a country if you consider half of its people inferior.

I despise him because he advocates violence against homosexuals, unmarried pregnant women, anybody who does not fit his idea of an acceptable religious adherent. I do not want him to be president because he is the epitome of corruption within a party that has elevated corruption to high art.

In another life the African National Congress were the kind of party people could admire. Though it started out as little more than a terrorist organisation it evolved as the conflicts that created it changed. The people who led and followed wanted more than power. They stood for something greater than themselves. Their cause was truly just.

Today the African National Congress are all that is wrong with political parties. They use their power to hurt the people whom they are supposed to help. Money meant for relief programmes somehow always ends up in ANC bank accounts. Legal charges against prominent party members somehow always get dismissed.

Corruption became so bad that Thabo Mbeki authorised a national agency to combat corruption and organised crime. The Scorpions, as they were called, were so successful that ranking ANC members were actually being convicted of their crimes. This led to the abolition of the Scorpions. This freed the ANC to continue to accept and receive bribes, launder money, kidnap, rape, murder.

But the good people of South Africa will continue to vote for the African National Congress just as an abused dog will kneel before its master. The ANC brought South Africa out of apartheid. More or less. There were a lot of other people and groups involved but ANC leaders generally give themselves all the credit.

There is a loyalty within South Africa to an ideology and purpose that has long since passed. Defeating the corrupt white leaders is no longer a major issue. Now it is the corrupt ANC leaders who need to be shown the door. But even the mere suggestion by any white person that any ANC leaders are corrupt brings charges of racism. No white politician will ever bring down the ANC. It will require a black politician from within or from another party. Unfortunately the current climate of corruption within the ANC makes it extremely difficult for any honourable leader to emerge.

ANC members speak of the party of Nelson Mandela just as American Republicans speak of the party of Abraham Lincoln, even though neither party is anything like it was when those men were in office. The ANC of today is not Mandela's ANC. People seem to think it is and that is why they still vote ANC. That was the party that tore down apartheid. That is a pretty big deal. But that ANC is most definitely not today's corrupt bully ANC.

American Republicans call their group the party of Lincoln that ended slavery. Lincoln's party did. Today's Republicans did not. But Lincoln died long before people started to use him as their figure head. There was nothing he could do to stop people who do not believe what he believed in using his name.

Nelson Mandela was used as the ANC standard as soon as he went to prison. He had every opportunity to speak out against ANC corruption and abuse after he left office. The fact that he never did is his greatest failure. And soon it will be illegal for anybody to say so.

Times change and organisations evolve, especially after the apartheid and slavery that those parties resisted are long gone. But the people in charge often let their followers believe that they are still what they used to be. That only pops up occasionally with the Republicans but it is absolutely essential for the survival of the ANC.

When Jacob Zuma wrested control of Mandela's party and forced Thabo Mbeki from office, much of Mbeki's cabinet resigned and many of his supporters broke from the ANC. I think that is a step in the right direction. The best hope for defeat of the ANC is if factions break away and form an effective opposition.

Presently the Democratic Alliance under Helen Zille are the leading opposition party but the ANC have always successfully labelled it as the party of whites, despite the fact that the majority of DA members are black.

The first thing ANC leaders do whenever the DA win more seats is to scare the most ignorant amongst us into believing that the DA will bring back apartheid. As if a party of mostly blacks would ever advocate such a thing. As if it was even legally possible. The Democratic Alliance bringing back apartheid is as likely as the American Democrats bringing back slavery. Facts rarely matter when you are dealing with a corrupt regime that will do anything to stay in power.

The world watched South Africa toward the end of apartheid. Europe wondered if the blacks would take over and kill all the whites. Asia wondered if the blacks would take over and restore trade agreements. Africa wondered if the blacks would take over at all. When apartheid died the world went back to worrying about other distractions. The ANC were free to grow as corrupt as their greed would allow without anybody outside of Africa noticing.

Eventually the world started watching South Africa again. Only this time it was for the FIFA World Cup. China was able to hide many of its problems during the 2008 Olympics but the ANC were not powerful enough to camouflage the country's poverty and crime from the television cameras.

For fifteen years the ANC were able to rule with most of the world not really paying much attention. Suddenly people noticed again. This time the ANC could not claim to be the heroes. Their corruption and incompetence was front page headline news.

Until the World Cup ended. Then the world went back to not paying any attention. If international news outlets use a pyramid chart to determine which areas of the world are newsworthy then Africa is definitely at the bottom. After all, it is only the second largest continent in the world. Surely whatever the people of Europe and North America are doing must be more important. And when people say North America they obviously mean the United States. And sometimes Canada.

Jacob Zuma is not the most corrupt president in the history of South Africa because he is black. And I do not call him corrupt because I am white. He is the most corrupt president in the history of South Africa because the people allow him to be. His race is only relevant in that only a black man can be elected president in today's climate. My race is only relevant in that the ANC say that whites only call their party corrupt because we are white.

That might be a valid point were it not for the millions of black who have been calling the ANC corrupt for years. This should be difficult for the ANC to counter but they simply claim that all DA supporters are white and therefore any criticism against the ANC is racist. The saddest aspect to this is not that they resort to such an outrageously false rebuttal but that so many people in South Africa actually believe it.

Jacob Zuma does not simply line his pockets while the people of his country live in poverty. That is pretty standard throughout the world. As is his building political support with bribes and extortion. Getting out of legal troubles by bribing judges is not especially impressive either.

What bothers me the most is how he treats the people of South Africa as his subjects. He seems to fancy himself a king rather than elected representative of the people. He thinks the people are there to work for him and the country's treasury is his personal bank account.

Jacob Zuma has six to eight wives and at least twenty children with thirteen different women. This would normally sit in the none of our business category. Except that the people of South Africa have to pay to support many of these wives and children. The president's family have always got a free ride. Some people object to this practice. Most simply do not care. But past presidents had one wife and children with that wife.

Jacob Zuma marries women at the drop of a hat and makes his subjects pay for their elaborate lifestyle while a great many South Africans live in poverty. He then claims that he cannot publicly declare his assets, as required by law of all presidents, because he has too many wives and children to keep track. And, my favourite part, polygamy is illegal in South Africa.

The ANC AIDS programme's motto is "one boyfriend, one girlfriend". The people of South Africa are routinely told to limit sexual partners, use condoms, abstain from extramarital sex, embrace monogamy, commit to marriage. The leader of the ANC does none of these things. He refuses to even use condoms whilst raping women with AIDS. Yet he and his supporters see nothing wrong with doing as they say and completely ignoring what they do.

The ANC say that Jacob Zuma's personal life is not a matter of state. But in a country with one of the worst AIDS records in the world, tribal superstitions that sex with virgins cures AIDS, widespread violence against women, it seems to me that a president who engages in extremely high risk behaviour and has a violent hatred of women makes his actions a matter of state.

Jacob Zuma, when elected president in 2009, promised to serve only one term as Mandela had. In 2013 he announced his candidacy in the 2014 elections.

What I like about my homeland are the people, the food, the scenery, the music. And the climate. Cape Town has some of the best weather on the planet. What I do not especially care for is how inept the African National Congress have become.

The ANC started out as a violent terrorist organisation but by the time they were allowed to participate in the electoral process they had renounced violence and were simply a minority party made up of the majority. Their first elected president is somebody of whom the entire continent is proud. People have called Nelson Mandela our Gandhi. I do not think that is such a bad comparison.

Thabo Mbeki will never be as beloved as Mandela but I think he did a pretty good job. He was who pretty much every African country turned to for diplomatic answers and he was good for the economy. You could be proud of living in the country even if you disagreed with his politics.

Jacob Zuma is somebody of whom very few people are proud. Partly because only his most blind supporters can argue that the country is better off now than it was before he took power. Partly because Jacob Zuma is a corrupt asshole.

As a corrupt asshole he has never been the favourite of editorial columns and cartoonists. Or he has been their favourite since they point out what a corrupt asshole he is so often. Being an asshole, he likes to sue anybody who criticises him. His favourite action is defamation of character, which is ironic as he has shown very little character. Being a corrupt asshole, he likes to use the government to attack anybody who criticises him.

The list of his government abuses against the women he has raped and those who investigate his corruption is long and tedious. Now we can add to that his attempt to censor a work of art that most people would have never heard about had he not tried to censor it. Since he had to go through the courts to close down a gallery where a painting that he did not like was on display, and since the courts took too long to bow down to his will, he had some of his thugs go into the gallery and destroy the painting.

The Spear by Brett Murray is, or rather was, a portrait of Jacob Zuma looking like a Soviet propaganda poster of Lenin. Except that Zuma in this portrait had his penis hanging out of his trousers.

Destroying original works of art in the internet age does nothing to keep them out of millions of computers. Now that Zuma's henchmen have destroyed the real thing, even more people will see digital copies.

I have no proof that Jacob Zuma was responsible for the painting's damage. I would not be at all surprised if it was really just a publicity stunt. I suppose he could sue me for defamation of character. That is the kind of thing he would do if he knew I existed. But to Jacob Zuma I say you did worse to yourself years ago than I ever could.

And in case I forgot to mention it, you are a corrupt asshole.

Now the African National Congress government under Jacob Zuma has decided that enough is enough. Zuma has been investigated for corruption, bribery, extortion, rape so often in the last ten years that something must be done if he is to remain in office.

He has sued more than a few news agencies for over sixty million rand but they keep printing stories about him. He has appointed several government lawyers to investigate the media. When that failed to stop them he hired private "security" firms to dig up as much dirt on newspaper editors and TV producers as possible. That also failed to stop the media from reporting about a powerful political leader who seems to think that what he does with state money is nobody's business.

I obviously do not like Jacob Zuma. He is as corrupt as can be and from what I can tell he is a fairly terrible human being. But I do agree that some of the editorial cartoons against him were a bit much. Even if the president is an asshole there should still be some respect for the presidency. But I also agree that if you cannot take the criticism then you should not be president. The opinions against him in the media have been flattering compared to some of the things said about American presidents and British prime ministers every day.

Since the Zuma government cannot stop the media legally they have decided to change the laws. The Protection of Information bill, dubbed the Protection From Information bill, will make it illegal for any news agency, or anybody really, to publish any information that any state agency decides they should not be able to publish. This will make it illegal for any newspaper to publish any story that anybody in the government does not want published.

That is the exact opposite of freedom of the press. But it does not stop at the press. As a citizen I could be arrested for writing something that they do not like. Like saying that Jacob Zuma is a corrupt asshole, for example.

Article 2.16 of the 1996 Constitution of the Republic of South Africa states that "everyone has the right to freedom of expression, which includes freedom of the press and other media". The Protection of Information bill would dissolve that.

Obviously this bill is terribly unconstitutional. The kind of people who take these things to court are already preparing to do so. I have a certain amount of faith that they will win. But that faith is tempered with the knowledge that the current government is controlled by corrupt assholes. Jacob Zuma and his friends have bribed and manipulated the courts many times already. Without his quid pro quo cronies Zuma would have been jailed many times by now. And they would never hold the high offices they now have.

The good news is that pretty much everybody who is not part of the government is against this bill. Helen Zille has spoken out against it many times. Obviously the media oppose it. Desmond Tutu spoke out against it. I disagree with him often but I agree completely when he calls this bill insulting. It is insulting to the people who risked their lives, and the people who lost their lives, to make this country free. It is insulting to those of us who were too young to really do much for freedom but still remember how little freedom there was. It is insulting to future generations who should know only freedom.

Even Nelson Mandela spoke out against it. Though not directly. And his message was more diplomatic than Tutu's. This was a perfect opportunity for Mandela to finally hold the ANC accountable. But he failed to do so. He was 93 years old when this bill was introduced. He earned his retirement. But I would have prefered that he spoke out against ANC corruption back when he was able to speak.

When I lived in the United States I could not be liberal because I oppose abortion but I could not be conservative because I oppose capital punishment. Both issues that I think have nothing to do with conservatism or liberalism. An abortion is a medical procedure, not a political statement. And letting the state execute people is neither conservative nor liberal. It is barbaric.

American courts cannot force convicted tax evaders to work as IRS agents because that would be considered cruel and unusual punishment. But it is ok to kill somebody. In the United States you have to favour killing criminals, babies or some group or another.

I think the arguments on both sides about taxes are just as stupid. Americans bitch and moan about having to pay taxes like it is going out of style. They either fail to realise or simply do not care that they have some of the lowest tax rates in the world. Republicans will tell you that five percent of their income is too much. Tell that to a Frenchman. Democrats will tell you that taxes would be lower if Americans stopped making so many bombs.

It all baffles me. I live in a country that makes lots of weapons. We also have an excellent educational system, stable infrastructure, thriving businesses, medical treatment for everybody. We can do this because every one of us pays more in taxes than any American. And we all understand that this is how these programmes are funded. We gladly pay taxes to help the less fortunate amongst us and would never consider forcing the richest to pay for everything. We are socialist when it comes to helping our fellow man and rabid capitalists when it comes to acquiring wealth.

When I lived in California I fit in with the film snobs because of my education and training. The adrenaline junkies liked my willingness to try almost any physical outdoor activity. But I never agreed much with either crowd's politics.

They loved me in Alaska because I could do what they considered a man's job, often better than the men, and because I am a woman. With the low female to male ratio there any woman can be very popular. But I disagreed with many of their political views. American political attitudes are different from most countries I have been to anyway. Even the most liberal Americans are generally centre right to the rest of the world.

I used to spend a lot of time at message boards. Too much time. In the beginning it was fascinating to me how easy it was to talk to people from all over the world about any number of subjects. You could get on your computer, day or night, and add your two shekalim to any discussion about anything.

I saw this as a vast improvement over chat rooms since it did not make any difference who else was online at the time. When I lived in

Alaska I used chat rooms and the time difference with everybody else meant that I missed most of the action. Message board discussions could span days, months, even years.

Then somebody decided that a free exchange of knowledge and ideas had to be moderated. Whenever you get a group of people together to talk about anything, somebody is going to decide that they are in charge. Sooner or later the people who put themselves in charge will want to control the course of the conversation.

I do not doubt that moderators are a necessary evil at many message boards. Some people simply cannot behave civilly. Especially if nobody knows their name and you cannot see their face. Anonymity is like alcohol. It turns mildly annoying people into narcissistic dicks.

But sometimes people can get together and talk about things without resorting to hostility. I am a member of such a message board. Nobody attacks anybody for having a different opinion and everybody seems genuinely interested in what others have to say. Is this not the point of a message board? Why participate if you are not interested in any voices besides your own? Places where everybody tries to yell the loudest do not make any sense to me. If you are yelling the loudest that only means that you cannot hear anything.

My chief complaint to the moderator at the one civil message board that I know about, and I have told him this several times, is that he tries to control the conversations. But you cannot control conversation. It goes where it wants to go. It is like going to a party and the host has everything planned out by the minute. Now it is time to do this, now it is time to do that. I think moderators should get involved when people are threatening each other with physical violence. But when a civil discussion does not exactly match the intentions of the opening post, leave it alone.

So I spend more time at political message boards. Those discussions almost always veer off road. But apparently you cannot have a political discussion without self appointed experts who all know what is best for everybody. Sometimes those people make those places far more entertaining than they ever would be without self righteous ranting and raving. Sometimes those people are just sad.

I have been following American politics for years, and it always fascinates me how people who basically agree on most things can be the most vociferous with their national dialogue. Whoever is president at any given time is characterised as the epitome of evil by the opposition but anybody who dares criticise their leaders should be shot as a traitor.

The easiest and most recent examples are the people calling Barack Obama both communist and fascist. These people elevate themselves to the highest levels of patriotism. After all, Thomas Jefferson once said something that can vaguely support their position if you interpret it a certain way. These same people were also quite clear that any criticism of George Bush whilst he was president was nothing less than treason.

You will see the Jefferson quote, "The tree of liberty must be refreshed from time to time with the blood of patriots and tyrants" at every neohippy meeting and rally. Apparently Barack Obama is supposed to be the tyrant and the neohippies are the patriots.

But some people were not especially fond of George Bush when he was president. That quote could easily apply to him. Except that even the idea of violence against Bush and his regime would have been treasonous and un-American. The office of the president is sacrosanct. Whoever holds that office should always be respected whether you respect the man in it or not. Unless the other side is in charge. Then you can storm the castle and murder the bum.

Using quotes out of context from somebody who died two hundred years ago is probably not the best way to advance your political opinions. I would doubt that Thomas Jefferson was calling a five percent tax increase instead of a three percent increase tyranny. His idea of a tyrant was likely an officer of the king who could take away your life, destroy your farm, rape your wife, enslave your children without any cause or court order.

Patriots in his world were people who kissed their homes and families goodbye and faced probable death and horrible suffering at the hands of the most powerful military in the world. These were people who sacrificed and suffered for their ideals. I do not think that putting a tiny black mustache on an Obama picture is really in the same league.

But since Thomas Jefferson, who thought religion had no place in government, who called war abhorrent, who was an active member of the lamestream media, is now the ensign of modern American conservatism, let us look at another of his conservative quotes.

> *"I hope we shall crush in its birth the aristocracy of our monied corporations which dare already to challenge our government to a trial by strength, and bid defiance to the laws of our country."*

I do not think you will see that one any time soon at any neohippy rallies. That sounds more like Ralph Nader than Bill O'Reilly. I think it is also far more relevant today than the tree of liberty quote. But I like the irony of people who think that climate change is a hoax wanting to nurture trees.

I am not saying that American liberals are not also hyperbolic hypocrites. Their catchphrases and bumper stickers can be just as stupid. I just never see them quote Alexander Hamilton. It would be strange if they did since Hamilton was far more conservative than Jefferson. Thomas Jefferson was a card carrying liberal lunatic compared to Alexander Hamilton.

Today's American liberals criticise George Bush as coming from an aristocratic family whilst still praising John Kennedy's Camelot. They said that Bush was unfit to be president because of his past drug use after excusing Bill Clinton's. Then they said that Barack Obama's drug use was in the past and not relevant.

Barack Obama's less than one term as a senator was good for hope and change whilst Sarah Palin's less than one term as a governor was dangerously inexperienced since she would be an old man's heartbeat away from the highest office. That has got to be more crazy stupid than conservatives quoting a liberal founding father. And it was the liberals who drew George Bush as a monkey long before anybody drew Barack Obama as a monkey.

Go anywhere that any Americans are talking politics and they will all say that "spin" is a bad thing. Yet they do it themselves all the time.

Americans love to complain about gas prices. Even when it is less than half of what most of us are paying. There was a collective hissy fit when prices went from two dollars per gallon to three dollars. I was paying about eight dollars at the time.

But they were comparing themselves with themselves in the past, not with others. When Americans say that they have the highest prices in the world they really mean the highest in their vicinity. Obviously prices will be higher than they were ten years ago. If they are not then consider yourself very fortunate indeed.

Now that prices are high by their standards

conservatives blame Barack Obama whilst liberals point out that the president cannot do much to influence international market fluctuations. Both sides spin it in their own little way. When George Bush was president, liberals blamed him for high prices whilst conservatives pointed out that the president cannot do much to influence international market fluctuations.

It is not that they all lack any self awareness. It is that they are stuck on the spin cycle. Liberals will tell you that Bush caused the high prices by invading a few Arab states that supply very little oil to the United States. Conservatives will tell you that Obama caused the high prices by refusing to rape Alaska. And also that he is a fascist communist.

Is any of that true? Of course not. The president of the United States cannot decide what other countries do with their oil. And the United States gets twice as much oil from Canada as it does from all Arab states combined. But the spin makes for better arguments.

Many Americans cheered when Osama bin Laden was killed in 2011. Some people said that was in poor taste. Osama was a bad guy to most of us. He was a terrorist. That used to be considered a bad thing. He was responsible for the murder of thousands of people. Sane people would not mourn his death. But openly applauding the murder of a fellow human being is a bit much for some.

My personal view is that people can cheer

his death as much as they want. He was evil. Plenty of people are vilified and characterised as evil but he truly was. I did not applaud his death but I do not mourn him either.

Many Brits cheered when Margaret Thatcher died in 2013. Some Americans said it was all in poor taste. Maggie was a bad person to many. She was not a terrorist by any stretch of the imagination. But one could argue that she was responsible for the deaths of hundreds of people. Though I doubt she ever ordered anybody to strap on a bomb and blow up children.

I will not mourn her death. She was the leader of a country with which I have no special connection. I reacted to news of her death in the same way that I reacted to the death of Roger Ebert. Neither was a particular surprise.

Ariel Sharon finally died in 2014. I say finally because he was not especially active his last few years. The doctors were trying to keep him alive at the end but my personal point of view is that after eight years in a coma it might be time to move on. I can see where his family did not want to let him go but when you are in a persistent vegetative state there is little reason to stay alive. If recovery is not an option and you will spend the rest of your life in a coma then what is the point.

There were mixed reactions at his death. It surprised nobody. Most people are pretty amazed that he lasted as long as he did. Some will mourn him deeply while others moved on a long time ago. He was one of those people that most either loved or hated. I think he was an important military commander but only an average politician.

Arab terrorists praised his death, of course. He was a Jew, after all. Some predictably called his death a punishment from God. It seems queer to me that when an old and sick Jew dies it is Israel's fault but when an old and sick Arab dies it is Israel's fault. I also have to doubt that God is on the terrorists' side. A better argument could be made that God took Sharon out of power because Sharon unilaterally pulled Israel out of Gaza and was planning to do the same in Judea and Samaria.

The people who said that rejoicing in Thatcher's death, or even Osama's death, was in poor taste were silent when it came to rejoicing in Sharon's death.

Even some Palestinians who might not be considered terrorists were seen rejoicing in the streets when they heard about Ariel Sharon's death. I do not think Sharon was the best prime minister in the history of the world and I will not mourn him but I have to wonder what is wrong with people who rejoice at another's death.

Ariel Sharon was no friend to terrorists but he did more than anybody else to take Israel out of Gaza. You would think that would make the people who wanted Israel out of Gaza happy. Obviously it only made them angry. Terrorist activity from Gaza increased dramatically as soon as Israel left. Maybe the terrorists wanted Sharon to stick around.

Maybe they are not praising his death but giving thanks that his family's long suffering is finally over. That might be unlikely.

Ariel Sharon was prime minister when I moved to Israel. I found it hard to label him at first because I was still looking at Israel the way people outside of Israel try to define it. He was very conservative in some ways and very liberal in others. It all makes sense to me now but he seems like an odd character when everything is BBC black and white.

In some ways I miss having Sharon as prime minister. But it is right that he is no longer on the political scene. A lot has changed since he was in charge. From my point of view the worst thing about Sharon's stroke, aside from the eight years in a coma, was that Ehud Olmert became prime minister. I never missed that guy once he was gone. I definitely will not mourn his death whenever that occurs.

A glaring difference between Sharon and Thatcher on one end and Osama on the other, other than the democratic elections versus terrorism, is that one of them was the active leader of his groups whilst the other two had been out of power for a number of years. I can see rejoicing when Thatcher and Sharon left office. Both were controversial leaders. But there seems little point in gloating at their deaths. If you think they were terrible leaders who ruined your country, fair enough. But they stopped doing that a long time ago. Dying changed nothing.

Americans, those people who were called

gauche when Osama died, rejoiced when Richard Nixon resigned. I do not remember any of them cheering when he died in 1994. Perhaps we could learn something from our backwoods cousins.

As my grandfather always used to say, "Wenn man nichts Nettes zu sagen hat, soll man den Mund halten." To which my grandmother would respond, "Ich will mich dazu nicht äußern." They were a fun couple. And I think there is a reason you do not see many older people talking online.

When their generation wanted to relax and unwind they would take long walks in nature, read and write poetry, paint and draw. Their greatest minds cured diseases and split atoms. My generation relaxes by staring mindlessly at TV sets and video games. The greatest minds of my generation created Twitter and porn addiction.

What I think happened was that whilst dumbing down our leisure activities and educational pursuits we have hampered our ability to simply talk to each other on a human level. When you talk to machines more than people it is too easy to ignore that there is a person on the other end of your machine. By dehumanising the method of our conversations we have taken the humanity out of what we say. I think that the more we scream at each other online the more we will start doing it offline. That will not lead to anything useful.

Thomas Jefferson also said, "A coward is much more exposed to quarrels than a man of spirit."

In China I was ultra conservative because I am not all that keen on communism. Some of it sounds good in theory but there has never been a communist country in practice that was not a dictatorship. China simply traded the brutal totalitarian emperors for brutal totalitarian party chairmen.

The best thing about the system is that the state will help out anybody in need. Under the right circumstances. The old saying that people are starving in China simply is not true. The food is far too inexpensive and people who cannot afford it get government assistance.

One of the worst things about the system is that too many people live hopeless lives. So much potential is wasted because there is little opportunity for individual success. It is no wonder the alcoholic rates are so high.

The Dalai Lama took a trip to Taiwan in September 2009. This was an interesting thing. To me at least. He says he went to pray for victims of the latest typhoon and offer spiritual guidance to whomever wanted it. Taiwan has a lot of Buddhists so you would think that he would be very popular there. Imagine a Buddhist popemobile driving up to a stadium and lots of old ladies crying and clutching crucifixes. Only without the crucifixes.

Except that the Dalai Lama in Taiwan is a very political situation. China does not especially like him. What with their stranglehold over Tibet and the annoying way he thinks Tibet should be free. China also thinks that it owns Taiwan. Except that it does not. Sort of.

The People's Republic of China, which we shall call China because that is what it is called, is ruled by a single party. Not a democracy by any definition but getting more capitalist every day.

The Republic of China, which we shall call Taiwan to avoid too much confusion, is ruled by a mostly two party system. It is a genuine democracy and very much capitalist. China, the real China, used to be the Republic of China and ruled over China and Taiwan. When Taiwan was not ruled by Japan. We shall simply call Japan Japan.

When China became the People's Republic of China, Taiwan became the sole Republic of China. China claimed ownership of Taiwan and Taiwan claimed ownership of China. Eventually Taiwan dropped that claim. With China's nuclear weapons and the largest military in the world, Taiwan realised that it was never going to happen.

Now half of Taiwanese want an eventual reunification with China if there is ever a less totalitarian government in China, and the other half want recognised independence. This is the main difference between the two parties in Taiwan.

And you thought your country's politics were divisive.

The Kuomintang currently run the government in Taiwan. They are the party who want to reunify with China. Someday. The Democratic Progressive Party are the party who want unadulterated independence. The DPP invited the Dalai Lama to Taiwan. The government in China, the People's Republic of, do not particularly like the DPP. They love the KMT, which is ironic since it is the KMT whom the Communists fought for control of China.

What is truly ironic is that the Chinese government takes sides in every Taiwanese election, always favouring the KMT, when they claim that Taiwan is part of China. If Taiwan is part of China then why is China even acknowledging these illegal elections?

There are plenty of other questions. If Taiwan is part of China then why does Taiwan have its own currency, passports, legislators, infrastructure, visas, economy? The Dalai Lama got a visa from Taiwan to enter Taiwan, not from China. When I lived in China I needed a Taiwanese visa to enter Taiwan and a Chinese visa to return to China. And I had to exchange currency. They did not seem like the same country to me.

You have to give China credit. They declared that anybody who favoured Taiwan would be completely shut out of China. If you recognise Taiwan then China will not recognise you. So most of the world recognises China over Taiwan.

China is basically a dictatorship. Taiwan is a democracy. But most of the freedom loving democracies of the world favour China. Only a few tiny countries that most people could not find on a map officially recognise Taiwan. And the Vatican. These are countries that China does not care about. South Africa used to recognise Taiwan but switched to China when the African National Congress took over. The United States recognised Taiwan for almost seventy years. Probably longer than anybody. But they switched to China just like everybody else.

Why would countries that claim to champion democracy and even fight in wars for the struggle of democracy over dictatorship choose to side with a dictatorship over a democracy? China has 1.3 billion customers. Taiwan only has 23 million. And Taiwan would rather buy Japanese products than yours.

Cash trumps democracy any day.

So when the Dalai Lama goes to Taiwan he is flipping a giant bird to China. And what upsets China upsets the world. If we keep upsetting China we might have to get our poisonous food and toys from somebody else. I am looking at Haiti.

In Israel I am considered liberal because of my views on Palestine. The fact that I call Judea and Samaria Palestine tells you something. The only reason I do not fly the AH-64 is because I do not want to kill Palestinian civilians. But I consider it a beautiful aircraft. I would be very happy if I could fly it all day without shooting at anybody. But nobody is willing to pay me for that. I firmly belive in Israel's right to defend its soil but not at the expense of its soul.

My economic views are more conservative but there is little difference between conservatives and liberals here when it comes to the economy. All the major parties in most elections want to lower taxes and increase government assistance. They merely disagree on the specifics.

I would love to see Tzipi Livni as prime minister, Benjamin Netanyahu as finance minister, and Ehud Barak as defence minister but that will never happen. That would be an incredibly powerful coalition. But the opposition would be weak and useless.

Tomorrow we vote in a new Knesset and prime minister. The top three contenders are the usual suspects, Kadima (Tzipi Livni), Likud (Benjamin Netanyahu), Avoda (Ehud Barak). Likud are expected to take the most seats, making Netanyahu prime minister again. Kadima will likely come in second, making Livni the opposition leader. It is a role she has never played and I am not convinced that she will play it well.

As usual, Shas are expected to win enough seats to almost guarantee that they will be part of the next coalition government. Perhaps if they did not have such a long history of fraud and corruption then I would not have such a problem with that.

The big surprise in this election, as much as you can be surprised by predictable outcomes, is that Yisrael Beiteinu are expected to take Avoda's number three spot. This does not bode well for us rational types.

Yisrael Beiteinu are the leading anti Arab party. Their motto is "More Jews in, more Arabs out". It really is. This is not me trying to make a point. Their peace plan is to ship all the Arabs out of Israel, regardless of whether they are citizens or not or how long they have been living here, and expand settlements in disputed territories. Call me crazy but I do not believe such a course of action would bring about much peace.

Just before the election the big issues promised to be the economy and security. Then we invaded Gaza. All the leading candidates supported the invasion but Benjamin Netanyahu was quick to point out that it would not have been necessary if we had never left Gaza in the first place. The peace that everybody in the world told us would come as soon as we left Gaza turned out to be almost constant rocket attacks.

Maybe that is what the International Community think of as peace. As long as Israel is not fighting anybody what difference does it make if people are killing Israelis. Fighting is only bad when Israel does it.

Benjamin Netanyahu was already favoured to win and Gaza only helped him more. Ironically for the people of Gaza. They would be much better off with Tzipi Livni but their almost constant rocket attacks are almost guaranteeing Netanyahu's election. This is a clear case of the terrorist leaders in Gaza voting against their own best interests. But then terrorist leaders are never the most rational people.

Now the only campaign issue seems to be security. The economy is still heading downhill but more people are concerned about being wiped off the map than wiping out their debt.

Kadima are the most likely to reach deals with Palestine and that is why they will likely lose to Likud. Kadima's big strategy under Ariel Sharon was to pull out of Gaza. The theory was that removing any Israeli presence in Gaza would bring peace. That failed miserably.

Everything Benjamin Netanyahu said would happen has happened. That is one of the reasons he will probably win. He is a bit of an asshole but he was right. Tzipi Livni is nice. Some think she is too nice. Even worse, her concessions to the terrorists have only brought more violence from terrorists. The funny thing about terrorists is when you give them an inch they still want to kill you.

There have been some complaints about how ugly the campaign has been but it is pretty tame compared to some other countries. We simply cannot compete with the level of personal attacks in the American and Zimbabwean elections. Those people accuse each other of the worst things they can imagine. And unlike recent "democratic" elections in Gaza and Zimbabwe, none of our candidates have been tortured or killed by opposing factions. Or by anybody else.

Not so much as a beating or kidnapping. This election has been pretty boring.

"There have been tyrants and murderers, and for a time they seem invincible. But in the end they always fall. Think of it. Always." Mahatma Gandhi.

For quite a while now some people in Arab states have been using this quote against Israel. As anybody who reads Arab media knows, Israel is the mighty oppressor and all Arab states are the poor downtrodden. Except when they say how big and strong they are and how weak and small Israel is.

I am pointing it out not to rub in anybody's face but because I have always found it ironic. Israel is the only democracy in the vicinity. Our leaders cannot be dictators because they are never in office long enough. The prime minister with the longest tenure served for only thirteen years. And not consecutively. Nobody else even comes close. A few served less than three years. It is hard to build up an oppressive regime in under three years.

Hosni Mubarak was the dictator of Egypt for twenty nine years. The Assad family has controlled Syria since 1970. Jordan's Abdullah has been king since 1999. His family has sat on the throne since Jordan broke away from the Ottoman Empire. Saudi Arabia has been ruled by the Saud family for as long as it has been Saudi Arabia. The country is named after them. Qatar has been ruled by the Thani family since the 1800s. Kuwait has had the

Sabah family since the 1700s.

There have been more than a few famous dictators in modern Arabia. By contrast Israel's Golda Meir was a strong Iron Lady but she was no more a dictator than Britain's Margaret Thatcher. Thatcher is still a divisive figure in the United Kingdom but you have to be completely hyperbolic to call her a dictator.

Then the inevitable happened in a few Arab states, beginning in 2011. People always tire of dictators eventually. Especially when the economy is bad.

Hosni Mubarak resisted the revolution in his country for as long as he could. Eventually he stepped down to avoid being taken down by force, which would have obviously led to his death. He made a deal that led to a mock trial that appeased the angry masses. He was sentenced to life in prison, and after the people were satiated, that sentence was very quickly reduced to house arrest.

The people of Tunisia had already kicked out their dictator a month earlier. Zine ben Ali had been in power for twenty three years and was forced into exile in Saudi Arabia.

Yemen's Ali Saleh agreed to step down after thirty four years upon condition that he not be imprisoned or executed. Muammar Gaddafi never wanted to make a deal. He was killed by revolutionaries after forty two years as Libya's dictator.

Mohamed Morsi became one of the few democratically elected leaders any Arab state has ever had, and the first democratically elected leader of Egypt. He was removed a month later in a military coup, one of the Arab world's favourite ways of elevating dictators.

There were serious protests in Lebanon, Iraq, Algeria, Sudan but the dictators in those states were able to prevent outright revolutions or civil wars. The protesters in Saudi Arabia, Bahrain, Djibouti, Somalia were silenced by their dictators. The dictators of Jordan, Oman, Kuwait, Morocco appeased protesters with minor government changes whilst retaining the full power of their dictatorships.

Syria's dictator refused to step down or make any kind of deal. He chose an all or nothing approach. The civil war has been in full force since March 2011 and has killed at least 200 000 people, with well over 4 million homeless, 3 million refugees in neighbouring states, and at least 150 000 missing. Bashar al Assad knows that he will die if he loses the war. Which he will sooner or later. He might win this particular civil war but he will be deposed eventually. Whoever takes him down will almost certainly kill him.

Sooner or later they all fall. There was once a time when people thought the European monarchies would last forever.

I cannot say that I agree with any of the protesters regarding the United States. Many people are upset by the lack of American intervention in these conflicts. But if they stepped in to help any of the dictators then they would be accused of setting up puppet governments. Again. And the United States cannot afford to invade another Arab state, even diplomatically. But if they do nothing and the dictators stay in power then they are accused of helping a dictator stay in power. Again. They cannot win either way.

I cannot agree with the Israeli government's support of the status quo. Egypt and Jordan have formal relations with Israel so I can see not wanting to upset the cart in those states but I do not think that Israel should support dictators even if doing so is in our temporary interests. We have seen how horribly such shortsighted diplomacy works out for the United States.

On the other hand a power vacuum in an Arab dictatorship is rarely a good thing. When dictators are forced out, who forces themselves in? The coup in Egypt can just as easily happen in any of the other states.

I would like to see every Arab state become an actual democracy. Some have argued that at least a few of those states would likely elect extremely conservative religious leaders. That is almost certainly true but once people get a taste of democracy they will have a hard time blindly doing whatever they are told. They will all eventually learn that they control their government, rather than the other way around. That almost always leads to more information and better education. Informed and educated people are far less likely to wage holy wars against their neighbours.

I am convinced that the Arab world will have democracy in some form or another sooner or later. I am hoping for sooner.

Much has been made of the riots in England.
Not so much because some poor and
uneducated people are upset with their lot in
life. The have nots have been giving the haves
headaches for millennia. But because we, and
by we I mean the International Community,
want to see England as a civilised country that
brought us such eternal cultural highlights as
Shakespeare, The Beatles, those Carry On
movies.

The two billion of us who grew up in current
or former Commonwealth countries are told to
see England as a bastion of all that we are
supposed to hope to be. Even Americans, who
got out long before anybody thought to include
Imperial subjects in the same sentence as
British subjects, have an umbilical fascination
with England. Even more so in some respects.

I have never met an African, Indian,
Australian who follows the goings on of the
British royal family with as much vicarious
interest as do some Americans. Africans have
Mandela. Indians have Gandhi. Australians
have the Bee Gees. I guess Americans need
something to fill the void that TV simply
cannot offer.

But I am seeing too many people try to
compare the British riots with the protests in
Arabia. The Arabs are not looking for senseless
looting and burning their own neighbourhoods.
There is an aspect of that but it is not their
main point.

Most Arabs are an oppressed people. Some

of them seem to have had enough and want a taste of democracy. The hooligans in England already have democracy. They may say that they are oppressed but they can always vote their way out of it and even work their way to a higher station if that is truly what they want. The Man can keep you down in a democracy but not nearly as much as people keep themselves down. In an Arab dictatorship you have far fewer options.

Now the world is hearing about protests in Israel. Some people who do not know what they are talking about want to tie it into the Arab protests. But that is like comparing apples and fizzy bubblech. Israel already has plenty of democracy and freedom. The fact that a protest in Israel takes place at the same time as protests in Arabia does not make them equal. It is not even such a great coincidence that they are happening at the same time.

I will let you in on a little known secret about Israelis. We protest as much as the French. Raise VATs and we protest. Lower the national pension and we protest. Privatise Bezeq and we protest. It is not a secret around here.

But amongst the International Community who only know what their TVs tell them it is a startling revelation.

But nobody compares with Africans when it comes to protests and riots. We protest lack of democracy, lack of food, lack of shelter. We have race riots, housing riots, student riots, unemployment riots, police riots, sports riots.

Our protests range anywhere from bloody massacre to surreal farce.

When I was ten years old we had a democracy protest where the police tried to disperse the crowds with purple dye in water canons. It failed miserably and started the Purple People Power movement. Instead of the divisions between black people, white people, coloured people, everybody was united as purple people. And the purple shall govern.

The fourth United Nations World Conference Against Racism was scheduled for April 2009 in Geneva, Switzerland. Israel, Canada, Italy, the United States quickly announced that they would boycott the conference. Australia, France, Denmark, the United Kingdom announced that they might boycott the conference and eventually did.

The conference is sometimes called Durban II because the previous one was held in Durban, South Africa. Durban was a good location because the first conference in 1978 mainly focused on apartheid. And Durban is a good place to hold a conference. It has year round mild weather, great beaches, the Mile, plenty of surfing, plenty of great food. If you are thinking about holding a conference on racism then Durban is the way to go.

The first Durban conference in 2001 did not go entirely as planned. Israel and the United States left the conference once it became clear that some Arab states wanted the final text to be riddled with anti Israel language whilst completely ignoring racism in Arab states.

Much of the European Union threatened to leave when talks about slavery and colonialism in Africa centered on reparations. In the end the final declaration criticised racism whilst going to great pains not to criticise any specific country or government where racism is a problem.

It is ironic that an international conference on racism and xenophobia cannot succeed because the participants are too racist and xenophobic. Instead of coming into it with an open mind to discuss these problems, too many of them have an agenda of hate against some other country or ethnic group. If they are only looking to criticise one group or another while considering themselves sacrosanct then what is the point.

As usual something that likely started out with the best intentions was politicised until it became functionally impotent.

Much to nobody's surprise Mahmoud Ahmadinejad's speech at Durban II upset a lot of people. All of the European Union delegates walked out during his speech. It made for some dramatic television. What is surprising is that Ahmadinejad seemed surprised when they walked out. He has always been a shrewd politician. I would have assumed he expected this reaction. Indeed I assumed he only made such a divisive speech to elicit such a reaction. He was facing a reelection at the time and such stunts always played well to his constituents.

It is possible that he got overconfident. Since Israel was not very popular immediately following the invasion of Gaza and since Israel and the United States boycotted the conference long before it began and all of the Arab states remained, Ahmadinejad might have thought he could say whatever he wanted and be cheered a hero. I hope that he is not that naïve. Arab leaders hate Ahmadinejad almost as much as they hate Jews.

The final conference declaration says nothing about Israel. It does not declare that freedom of religion is hate speech as some of the Arab delegates wanted. In the end Iran and the Arab states did not get what they wanted. Aside from a few publicity stunts there was nothing that the countries which boycotted the conference feared. It would have been better if they were there and after Ahmadinejad's speech Elie Wiesel gave his own speech. That would have made Ahmadinejad look like a complete idiot. Not that such a thing takes much effort.

There is an irony in letting Mahmoud Ahmadinejad make a speech at a conference on racism. I wonder if it was lost on the delegates. Then again the United Nations described the conference as a "shining example of what the UN is supposed to do best: unite to combat injustice in the world." How is that for irony?

There are generally three points of view when it comes to Iran developing nuclear weapons. One is that it must not be allowed to happen under any circumstances. Another is that it probably will happen and there is not much we can do about it. A third option is that it is a good thing. I doubt very many people outside of Iran and a few Arab states agree with this one. Which is a little ironic since Iran has never had the best relationship with most Arab states.

For the sake of discussion I am assuming that Iran is trying to make nuclear weapons and not simply peaceful nuclear energy. It is not much of a stretch since pretty much everybody else assumes the same thing. The only people who believe the energy story have either lived their entire lives under totalitarian dictatorships and know better than to question their leaders or are under the utopian impression that people are generally good no matter how much hate they preach.

There are some who say that Iran has every right to nuclear weapons. Plenty of other countries have them. Iran should be able to defend itself. But from whom? The United States and Soviet Union built bombs to defend themselves from each other. As did India and Pakistan. China built bombs as a reaction to American and Soviet bombs. But even today China has relatively few warheads.

North Korea is supposedly building bombs to defend itself from the United States. This is a bit of a stretch, especially since their current weapons are weak and their missiles inadequate, but there are thousands of American soldiers pointed at their southern border. Israel may or may not have nuclear weapons, wink, nod, but there are very real threats to Israel all within rocket range.

The greatest threats to Iran in the past sixty years were from Iraq and the United States. Iraq is not a country they should worry too much about these days. Nobody needs nuclear weapons to defend themselves from today's Iraq. The United States is more of an ideological threat than anything else. They simply have no reason to invade Iran short of a hostage situation or nuclear proliferation.

Most of Iran's Arab neighbours do not trust Iran farther than they can throw it, especially Saudi Arabia and UAE, but I would be gobsmacked if any of them invaded in the near future.

Iran sees Israel as a mortal enemy but the feeling is most decidedly not mutual. Mahmoud Ahmadinejad can rattle his sabre all he wants but we all know that only Ali Khamenei can authorise war. Khamenei is not the biggest fan of Israel either but he seems to understand that getting himself and his government killed is a terrible way to keep his dictatorship going. Israel simply has no reason to invade Iran short of a hostage situation or nuclear proliferation.

This is why some people feel it is best to let Iran build their bombs. They are not an especially suicidal people. Just as the Americans and Soviets never annihilated each other it is assumed that Iran would never attack a country that could wipe their regime off the map.

Ron Paul said that he does not care if Iran builds nuclear weapons. Back when people cared what Ron Paul said. The United States and Soviet Union had more than enough to destroy the world several times over and nothing ever came of it. Therefore, I assume he assumes, nothing bad will ever happen if anybody else has nuclear weapons.

Some people think that is stupid. And I agree. The United States and Soviet Union were ruled by committees. No one person ever had absolute authority. Enough people had to agree before you could go completely crazy.

Dictatorships do not follow that rule. Had Kim Jong Il wanted to launch missiles into Japan nobody in North Korea could have stopped him. Short of a clandestine bullet to his head.

Khamenei probably does not want to die just now but how will he feel when he is on his deathbed anyway? And what about his eventual successor? Nuclear warheads do not go away with a change of government.

Other people think it is probably best that we simply invade Iran now before it is too late. That probably would solve the nuclear issue. Israel and/or the United States could take out Iran's facilities with a few quick airstrikes and some sabotage on the ground. But that would only cause other problems.

As hard as it may be to believe, some Arab states are just waiting for any excuse to attack Israel. It is crazy but true. Even though most of them are not big fans of Iran they would suddenly develop an intense solidarity with their Persian cousins. And the United States simply cannot afford to alienate even more Arab states. There are too many potential customers.

Then there is diplomacy. That is often a good thing. Diplomacy eventually brought Jordan on the side of peace. Leaders who are willing to talk to each other are often less willing to attack each other. More wars end in diplomacy than victory.

But Iran is doing exactly what North Korea always did. They say they are not building any weapons and then say they will destroy their weapons. They agree to let inspectors inspect and then they change their minds. They agitate to the point of sanctions and then agree to whatever lifts the sanctions. Only to carry on as soon as everybody is appeased. You cannot have meaningful negotiations with compulsive liars who are just yanking your chain.

My point of view is that Iran probably will not attack Israel with nuclear weapons any time soon. But I hate it when American leaders say that. If for no other reason than American leaders have the luxury of being nowhere near Iran's launch trajectory.

It is not a matter of theoretical curiosity for some of us. I like to think Iranian leaders are sane but if they are not then I and my entire family could be killed in an instant. That is completely unacceptable. To me at least. I know some sociopaths would dance in the streets. I am not at all willing to be collateral damage just to satisfy somebody's definition of political correctness.

If the rumours can be believed then Israel has between one hundred fifty and three hundred fully functional nuclear warheads ready to go. That is more than enough to turn Iran into a radioactive rubbish heap. That is really the only thing that makes me believe that maybe Iranian leaders will use a little common sense.

But a very important factor to consider in the appeasement or attack debates is that Iran has a long history of supplying some of the most violent terrorist organisations the world has ever known. Iran might not be trigger happy when they are held accountable but what is to stop them from supplying nuclear weapons to some of their murderous terrorist buddies. I have heard a lot of people say that Iran would never use nuclear weapons but I have never heard any of these people acknowledge that Iran sells weapons to terrorist groups.

Israel would have to respond to a nuclear attack. But without clear proof of who is responsible the response would most likely be aimed at Iran and Syria. This would lead to a very large and very deadly nuclear war between more than a few countries. The United Nations would likely do nothing since they are largely impotent anyway, and the United States would be stuck between Iraq and a hard place without any real proof. No American president is going to use weapons of mass destruction as an excuse to invade another Arab state any time soon. Even Persia is off limits.

This scenario does not bother some people. The death of a few million Jews is a fun time to some. Even if that means killing a few million Arabs. Terrorists are more than happy to kill their own in order to kill somebody else.

But somebody might want to consider another consequence. Not only would millions of people be killed but thousands of years of priceless history would be lost. The most important sites to Judaism, Christianity, Islam would likely be destroyed. People who kill in the name of their religion rarely care about other religions but they might want to think about how it would affect their own. All of those buildings that people riot over would be ash.

The good news is that people would stop fighting over the land since it would be unlivable for the next twelve thousand years, and the world would have no choice but to find alternative fuels. Radioactive oil cannot be refined and it pretty much kills anybody who tries to work with it.

Terrorist organisations are not concerned with how they will be viewed by history. They do not care if they are seen as the good guys or bad guys. They do not worry about sanctions. They do not bow to international pressure. And they are more than willing to kill themselves to achieve their goals.

Most countries with nuclear weapons will never use them against anybody. Even Iran and North Korea are debatable. But I have absolutely no doubt that the terrorists friendly to Iran would use any weapons they had in a heartbeat. This should scare people awake far more than anything Mahmoud Ahmadinejad, Benjamin Netanyahu or anybody running for America's presidency could ever say.

Iran may or may not ever attack us. But their friends absolutely will.

Does that answer the question?

LIKE CRIMSON CURTAINS
SLOWLY RISING

"The prisoner issue is an emotional one for Palestinians after decades of conflict with Israel. Palestinians generally view them as heroes, regardless of the reason for their imprisonment. Israelis mostly view them as terrorists." The Guardian.

This "regardless of the reason for their imprisonment" is the closest I have seen from the international media admitting that these "heroes" are murderers who targeted schools and hospitals.

"The Palestinians have now abandoned an undertaking to refrain from applying for membership of various

> *international organisations; a step*
> *which displeases Israel and the*
> *Americans."* BBC.

The BBC often go to great pains to avoid saying that any Arab dictator ever did anything wrong. "Abandoned an undertaking to refrain from applying" rather than simply saying they did what they agreed not to do. "A step which displeases Israel and the Americans". It is not a massive violation of an agreement with Israel and the United States; the only countries on this planet that are keeping Palestine alive. It is merely displeasing.

> *"There is an identical twin of this*
> *plane. It has been sitting in a*
> *hangar in Tel Aviv, Israel, for the*
> *past couple of months. There was a*
> *shell-game played with this*
> *aircraft. It was in the south of*
> *France, and then they moved it*
> *down to Israel. Speculation is that*
> *there was some sort of false-flag*
> *plan afoot, perhaps another planes-*
> *into-buildings deception like 9/11."*
> Press TV.

This is about how Israel made that Malaysia Airlines flight go missing. It is easy to dismiss stories like this as the rantings of crazy people. But the more the crazies rant the more people listen. The narrative used to be that all terrorists were bad. Now some are bad and some are good. Depending on whom they murder. Someday terrorist will be a positive designation.

> *"Palestinians want an independent state in Gaza, the West Bank and East Jerusalem - lands captured by Israel in a 1967 war."* Reuters.

This is always my favourite. I see this all the time. Israel took this land away from poor innocent Jordan. The international media always ignore a few key points. What prompted Israel to "capture" this land from Jordan in 1967? Why was it under Jordan's control? Was it considered an ancient Palestinian homeland whilst under Jordan's control? What country was it part of before Jordan captured it? Anybody who cannot answer these basic questions, which are not at all subjective, is not in the least bit qualified to discuss this issue.

I live in a world where terrorists from repressive dictatorships are given equal standing from the international media as the democratically elected representatives from a progressive liberal democracy. This same international media would never label al Qaeda and the United States as equals. Or Tamil Tigers and Sri Lanka, PLA and India, Taliban and Afghanistan, FARC and Colombia, Shining Path and Peru, DHKP and Turkey.

All of those countries are the good guys whilst the terrorists who blow people up are the bad guys. Most will agree that strapping on a bomb and blowing people up makes you the bad guy. Unless you blow up Jews. Then you are an oppressed minority, despite being part of the overwhelming majority ethnic group in the region.

As we all know, minority groups are the good guys and majority groups are the bad guys. Yet all of the terrorist examples above are minority groups in their countries and they are the bad guys compared to that country's majority. Israel, the bad guy, is the minority surrounded by a rather hostile majority of good guys. Maybe, just maybe, being in the minority or majority does not automatically make one right or wrong.

American liberals support homosexual rights, women's rights, minority rights, abortion rights, gun control, high taxes, science, education, whilst they oppose capital punishment and religious law. They rabidly defend liberal political candidates who say and do crazy things whilst rabidly attacking conservative candidates who say and do crazy things. The same is true in other "western" countries. Although the terms "liberal" and "conservative" do not necessarily apply.

Arab dictatorships and terrorists generally want to kill or at least arrest homosexuals, kill or subjugate women, kill or at least subjugate minority groups, kill anybody who has an abortion or any doctor who performs one. They love guns, have little to no taxes, frown upon science and education, especially if girls want to get involved. They absolutely love capital punishment and religious laws, and rabidly oppose any open dissent in countries where free speech is blasphemy. Liberals would not be very happy living in the average Arab state.

Israeli homosexuals, women, minorities have all the same rights as everybody else. Abortion is rare but legal, guns are very hard to get, taxes are very high. Israel is one of the world's leaders in medical research and technology, and environmental science. Israel spends a greater percentage of its GDP on science and technology than any country in the world. Education is open to anybody and everybody. There is no capital punishment or religious laws. The state does not demand that anybody keep kosher and does not give a rat's tuchas if you honour Shabbat or not. I would argue that there is more freedom of speech in Israel than in the United States. Liberals flourish in Israel.

Yet American liberals, and often their equivalents in other "western" countries, support Arab terrorists and oppose Israel.

Aaron Sorkin has compared American conservatives with the Taliban. That is fairly extreme. But American conservatives actually agree with Arab dictatorship positions more than they agree with Israeli positions, albeit in a far more moderate form. Michele Bachmann says some crazy shit but the fact that she is allowed to speak in public shows that American conservatives are not the Taliban. And I would doubt that she has ever advocated throwing acid on a girl's face. Yet American conservatives support Israel over these terrorists.

How does this make any sense? Has the international media mantra of Israel bad, terrorists good actually conditioned Americans to hate Jews in order to love Arabs? This would be odd when you consider that most Americans completely ignore the international media when it comes to any criticism of American actions.

Also, and this might only be a minor point, the typical Arab terrorist would gladly sacrifice his own life to kill as many Americans as possible. The typical Israeli would not sacrifice so much as a bagel to kill an American. Israeli citizens and Arab terrorists might be equals in the eyes of the international media but there is a pretty big difference when it comes to our definitions of right and wrong.

I was very much on Palestine's side before I came to Israel. Then I lived here and saw what it was really like as opposed to what the international media told me it was like. The more I saw people rationalising the murder of Jews, and open support for terrorists, the more I started to support Israel.

Pretty soon terrorists will be like pirates. Everybody will love them and their madcap adventures. But pirates were murderers, rapists, kidnappers, thieves. In pirate movies the British Navy are the bad guys and the pirates are brave heroes who sing and dance.

Now I am not only protecting my family from people who would willingly kill their own families to kill people they hate. Now I am protecting my children from people who would willingly kill their own children to kill people they hate. I am not even a mother yet but I cannot imagine any circumstance where I would want to kill my own child just because I hate somebody's religion or culture. I cannot imagine that it would ever be possible for me to hate any race or religion that much. I realise that racism is all the rage right now but how can hating others ever take precedence over protecting your own children?

Not only do these people hate Jews so much that they think all of this is reasonable, and they are willing to rationalise any horrors that terrorists commit against Jews, but they even take their hate a step further and complain that "the Jews" control the international media. If The Jews control the international media then I can only wonder what their devious master plan must be.

Israel is a very small country. I have a globe of the world and I can barely see Israel. Globes are far better representations than maps. Look at a standard map of the world. Africa is the same size as Greenland, even though Greenland is actually about the size of Algeria.

Israel is about the size of New Jersey with a million fewer people. It is smaller than China's smallest province, 海南, with a million fewer people. It is twice the size of Lebanon but much smaller than its other neighbours. Syria is nine times larger than Israel. Egypt is fifty times larger with seventy million more people. Israel takes up just 0.01% of the Earth's surface.

Israel is very liberal compared to its neighbours but relatively conservative compared to Europe. The modern state has always had universal suffrage. Women and some minority groups cannot vote in Egypt, Syria, Jordan, and terrorist controlled parts of Lebanon. Israel is the only democracy as far as the eye can see. Lebanon is almost a democracy but leaders have to belong to specific religious organisations. Egypt and Syria are basically dictatorships, and Jordan is a constitutional monarchy but the king has far more power than monarchs in Britain or Thailand.

Marriage law in Israel is conservative and largely archaic but any marriage legally performed anywhere in the world is recognised in Israel, regardless of gender, religion, race.

Israel's neighbours have laws against interracial marriage, interfaith marriage, and none of them will recognise a homosexual marriage under any circumstance. Homosexuality itself is illegal in Egypt, Jordan, Lebanon, Syria. Homosexuals serve openly in Israel's military and government. Tel Aviv is home to the largest gay pride parade in Asia. Homosexuals face honour killings in Syria and Egypt. There is no such thing in Israel.

Speaking of killing, 17 British serial killers have murdered somewhere between 332 to 453 people. Depending who you ask. 24 Australian serial killers have murdered 134 to 194 people. 83 American serial killers, including a few cannibals, have murdered 943 to 3288 people. There have never been any known serial killers in Israel.

But what about the terrorism? Israel is a dangerous place, you say. About 1533 Russians have been killed in Russia by terrorists since 1995. In that same time period 1924 Pakistanis have been killed in 42 separate terrorist attacks in Pakistan, not including military engagements. 2218 Indians and 3432 Americans have been killed on their own soil by terrorists. How many Israelis have been killed in terrorist attacks since 1995? Less than 1200. Three times as many Americans have been killed by terrorism. You are more likely to be shot in New York than Jerusalem.

Natural disasters kill far more people than terrorism anywhere in the world. Floods alone kill more people than terrorism. Israel does not have floods. Deadly earthquakes are rare. Typhoons and famine are unheard of. Tsunamis are theoretically possible but none have hit Israel for seven hundred years.

Israel is ranked number 8 by life expectancy according to the United Nations, just below Sweden. Only the people of four European countries, Japan, Hong Kong and Australia generally live longer than Israelis. Egypt is number 106, between Peru and Georgia. The United States is number 38, just below Cuba.

There is very little reason for the rest of the

world to pay attention to or even care about what happens in Israel. The so called human rights violations in Israel simply cannot compare to things that happen every day in countries like China, Saudi Arabia, Afghanistan, the United States. Waiting at a checkpoint for a few minutes to enter Israel is not nearly as bad as being tortured or having body parts cut off. It always amazes me when people call checkpoints a human rights violation with a straight face.

The United Nations has passed 120 resolutions criticising Israel in the last sixty years, including calling zionism racism, telling Israel that it cannot choose its own capital, and attacking Israel's capture of Eichmann.

There has never been a single UN resolution condemning any terrorist organisation or the countries that support them when they have launched rockets at Israeli schools and hospitals or sent in suicide bombers to murder Israelis. There have been quite a few resolutions condemning Israeli military attacks against its neighbours but not a single resolution against those neighbours condemning their attacks on Israel.

There have been five UN resolutions condemning the genocide in Darfur, and none called the genocide in Rwanda genocide until it was too late. The UN was too busy condemning Israeli checkpoints to recognise the millions of people who died in Africa.

There are wars all over the world while Israel is currently at peace. People elsewhere are murdered, raped, robbed by the minute. Israel has one of the lowest crime rates in Asia. And Asia is not as small as the international media would have you believe. There are actually more than a few people living there. People in New Jersey are four times more likely to be murdered than people in Israel. According to the World Health Organisation. Israel's per capita murder rate is comparable to most of Australia. Except Northern Territory for some reason. That is twice as high as New Jersey.

Somewhere around 300 000 people die in traffic accidents in China every year. Official numbers are hard to come by since China goes to great lengths to keep that information to itself. Where is the international media coverage? Some say that China has a much higher population than anybody else so naturally there will be more deaths. But only a very small percentage of Chinese people drive cars.

There are somewhere around 4000 traffic deaths each year in South Africa. China is large but not 75 times larger than South Africa. As China's economy grows and more people buy cars the per capita rate will explode.

The American death rate per capita by car accident is almost three times higher than Israel, according to the World Health Organisation. I would never classify Israelis as safe drivers but that is what the figures say.

Israel has very little oil and few natural resources. Unless you are in the United States,

China, India or Europe we probably do not trade with you on any considerable level. Nothing Israel does will affect your life.

Yet if a single Arab dies near Israel's borders you will hear about. But you probably will never hear about an Israeli death unless it is a blood bath. If Israel drops a single bomb anywhere it is on the news. But how often do they mention the thousands of rockets that are fired into Israel?

If seven Turks are killed by the IDF then CNN goes into overkill. Did they ever mention the five Israelis who were killed by Turkish police just before that? How about the four Israelis who were killed by Palestinians just a few months before that? One was nine months pregnant. Her paramedic husband found her body whilst responding to the call. I do not remember any international outrage or protests over that. The International Community were silent. When was the last time you heard about Kashmir, Cyprus or Tibet? They are all oppressed/liberated by countries much larger, stronger, richer than Israel.

Why the overwhelming disparity? The easy answer is racism. Israel is the only predominantly Jewish country in the world. And I think the last five thousand years have shown how too many people fear Jews. Israel has been very successful and that just annoys some people. It is the 151st largest country in the world but is 28th by GDP per capita. And some of the most powerful countries in the world are friends of countries that want nothing short of the complete destruction of Israel.

The convoluted answer is that Israel is the big bad guy whilst Palestine is oppressed. If that is true then why do I never see complaints against Jordan, Syria, Egypt, and other states that are oppressing Palestine? Why is nobody protesting Egypt's blockade against Gaza? Or even Palestine's blockade against Gaza? If the blockades are a crime against humanity then why is absolutely nobody complaining to Egypt and the Palestinian Authority for their blockades?

The International Community have complained no end that Israel has troops in Judea and Samaria. This is land that was owned by Israel before Jordan invaded and took over, and where many Israelis currently live. Iran and Syria have troops in Lebanon and Palestine, where no Iranians or Syrians live. Why is that never mentioned on the BBC?

The International Community will tell you every day that Israel does not let Palestine be free. But they have never complained that the Arab League have blocked every effort by Israel, the United States, and several European countries to make Palestine a sovereign state.

Even if everything the Arab League say about Israel was true it would not explain why Israel gets more media coverage than China, Russia, Britain, Spain, or other countries that oppress smaller neighbouring territories. In what parallel universe is Israel a bigger human rights violator than China or Saudi Arabia? You can be executed five minutes after your predetermined trial in both countries. You cannot be executed in Israel.

I have been reading in the American media about how horrible Israel is for giving birth control to Ethiopian refugees. I did not read about it in the Israeli media because it is not a news story. Some people escaped persecution in Ethiopia, fled to Israel, and some of the women were given the same birth control that they were taking whilst in Ethiopia. It is simply not newsworthy.

Unless you can somehow take a story of Israel taking in refugees and turn it into a crime against humanity or racial profiling or sexism or whatever you want it to be. Israel takes in refugees and lets them become full members of society rather than houses them indefinitely in refugee camps or turns them away. I think that is a good thing. Israel is a very small country. There really is little room. But we know why it is bad to turn away people who will probably be imprisoned and murdered in their homelands.

The United States takes in more immigrants. But they have about five hundred times more land. No democracy in the world except Andorra has a higher percentage of immigrants than Israel. And Andorra is about two thousand times smaller than the United States. Israel is about forty percent immigrant. Unless you want us to control Palestine. Then that number gets much higher. The United States has a paltry ten percent immigrant population. That is nothing. I do not know why they think Mexicans are taking over. Tiny Andorra is eighty percent immigrant.

The complaints about giving the Ethiopians birth control seem to be coming solely from Arab media. American media report whatever bad things Arab media report about Israel because the Americans want to appear fair and balanced. Journalists in other parts of the world have a saying, consider the source. I do not think current American journalists know what that means.

Right now there are some really bad things happening in the Arab world. A lot of people are dying. And most of it could be easily prevented. The American media have to report it because a lot of people are dying. It is news when dictators kill off huge chunks of their own people. But the American media do not want to appear biased against Arab states. They do not mind talking about dictators in Myanmar killing a bunch of their own people but Arab leaders killing Arabs makes them uncomfortable. In American eyes, Arabs are the poor downtrodden. It is perfectly acceptable to talk about Europeans or Jews killing them but not when they kill each other. It is not the sort of thing a liberal media is supposed to talk about. It goes against the narrative.

The easiest way to balance out your liberal guilt of reporting Arab on Arab death is to tell everybody how bad Israel is. Since, in the international media's eyes, the opposite of Arab is Israeli. Either they do not know that many Israelis are Arab or, more likely, they want to ignore the fact. If you say anything negative about any Arab state then you have to say something negative about Israel. This is the journalistic equivalent of music critics who always have to mention the Rolling Stones whenever they mention The Beatles. Unfortunately for the international media, Israel is not killing off a bunch of Arabs at the moment. What is an infotainment journalist to do?

Enter the Ethiopians. The Arab media reported that some Ethiopian refugees were forced to take birth control. Then some of the Ethiopians themselves said that it was not true, and the Arab media decided that about half of them were forced to take birth control. The numbers given in the initial reports would have had to include all of the men as well as the women. I cannot imagine why Israel would give men birth control. Probably for some nefarious Jewish plot.

The story could easily change again next week. Modern journalists might not have noticed but Arab journalists are usually not known as friendly toward Jews.

"We believe it is a way to prevent pregnancy among women in the community," said one Arab leader in between chants of "death to Israel". No shit. It is birth control. That is what it is supposed to do.

Some are arguing that this particular

method of birth control has not been fully sanctioned by the Food and Drug Administration. The FDA is an American organisation that has no authority in Israel or anywhere else in the wold. I am not sure why we should care what they think about any particular drug. Did they approve thalidomide?

I do not know if this drug is good or bad but I know that it is available in Israel and that Israelis use it. If it is bad then it should be removed. But giving it to the Ethiopians had nothing to do with the drug itself, other than it is what they were already using in Ethiopia.

I suppose somebody could argue that the Catholic church does not like any form of birth control. But these Ethiopians are not Catholic. Neither are most Israelis. Or most Arabs. I would doubt that the pope has any opinion on the subject, all things considered. By the time there is a new pope there will be some new international outrage directed at the sneaky Jews.

But why are the big bad Israelis giving these refugees any kind of medication at all, you might ask if you were an American journalist. Because, unlike the United States, Israel provides basic health services to incoming immigrants, no matter where they came from. That is part of all that evil communist universal cover you keep hearing about. Some of the refugees were likely given asthma medication. But you will not hear about that because nobody can think of a way to turn it against

Israel.

Something the international media are not bothering to report is that Israel and Ethiopia have a long history of cooperation. Some Arab states have complained about this but it exists nonetheless. Israel has airlifted thousands upon thousands of Ethiopians to Israel. Operation Solomon evacuated fifteen thousand people alone. This is not a country that hates Ethiopians.

Americans like to think that they have a monopoly on melting pots. But many countries on this planet have racially heterogeneous populations. Canada and Australia are as much rainbow nations as America. And they each have twice as many immigrants as a percentage of population. The original rainbow nation, South Africa, has eleven official languages. The United States does not even have one. The American media routinely engage in sampling bias, either intentionally or, more likely, from basic nescience.

Israel is full of Jews. We are a race but we are also black, white, everything in between. To say that Israelis do not like blacks is like saying that New Yorkers do not like Italians. Israel is also full of Arabs. Some are Jewish, some are Muslim. Many are Christian. Some are black and some are white. Israel also has a large Indian, east Asian, African population. We have rainbows up the tuchas. And every single person is entitled to birth control. Assuming they are women. Some people might hate Jews enough to call that gender discrimination but I doubt that Israel will be giving birth control pills to men anytime soon.

It is probably much easier to simply report that Israel is one race and that we all hate anybody else. But that would be like saying that Arab states are all one race and that Arabs hate everybody else. How many American journalists would be willing to report that? After all, that would be fair and balanced.

After several years of various civil wars, revolutions, coups in Arab states somebody decided that Israel needed another fabricated controversy attached to it. The initial attempt to blame the "Arab Spring" on Israel failed miserably as soon as it all started. Something had to be done.

Then American actress Scarlett Johansson did an advertisement for an Israeli beverage company. Clearly she was looking for trouble. In the interest of full disclosure I will point out that I am not much of a Scarlett Johansson fan and I think that SodaStream sucks. I thought she was better before she became an action star. Something happens to them after they do action movies. Remember when Liam Neeson was a real actor?

The whole SodaStream concept is queer to me, though I do appreciate the environmental aspects of their organisation. If you want a carbonated beverage then you should buy a Pepsi. Making your own is like making your own helicopter. It might seem a good idea at the time but it will not fly.

After Johansson started filming adverts, her

friends at Oxfam complained. They did not have the balls to drop her but they were more than willing to complain about her despite all the work she did for them. Apparently they hold firmly to their convictions up to the point of not trying to upset celebrities too much. So Johansson dropped them.

Up to this point I do not particularly care. What any celebrity advertises is none of my concern. What got my attention were the calls to boycott SodaStream and close down its factory.

The narrative is pretty simple. SodaStream is an Israeli company. Therefore it is evil. It has a factory in Ma'ale Adumim. Therefore it is evil. Ma'ale Adumim was part of the British Mandate land handed over to Israel. Therefore it is the new historic ancient Palestinian homeland.

If that does not make any sense, ask people who want to return to the 1967 borders why they refuse to even consider the 1948 borders. I know the answer to that one but sometimes it is amusing to see how they rationalise Jordan's invasion and occupation of land whilst decrying Israel's control of land it owned before Jordan invaded the first time.

What all the liberal peace activists who love human rights and favour brutal Arab dictatorships over a liberal democracy with human rights fail to realise, or more likely fail to care about, is that closing the Ma'ale Adumim factory would put about one thousand Arabs out of work. SodaStream may be an

Israeli, ie evil, company but it pays those Arab employees Israeli wages and gives them Israeli benefits. No Arab company in Judea and Samaria pays anything close or provides evil socialist health cover.

Israeli companies are also forbidden by law and common decency to murder homosexuals and treat women as property. Closing the factory would be bad news for any homosexuals or women working there who do not want to be murdered property.

Can anybody tell me why none of the liberal peace activists who love human rights ever comment on how the Palestinian Authority treat homosexuals and women? I have never heard any plausible explanation for this. Or even an implausible explanation. They simply ignore how much their heroes ignore peace and human rights.

Closing the factory would also cause unnecessary unemployment in a time and place that would not benefit from even more unemployment. And even if a few of those thousand people could find other jobs they would likely make far less money and work in Arab working conditions. If you think that all Arabs are oil millionaires driving their racing cars up sand dunes then you should join the liberal peace activists who love human rights and are equally as clueless.

And closing that factory would virtually guarantee a United Nations resolution condemning Israel for closing a factory and putting one thousand Arabs out of work. There would be a separate resolution against Israel after any former factory employees are murdered by their Arab dictators for being women or homosexuals. Or any former employees for being "traitors". The Palestinian Authority loves to execute "traitors". I would think that liberal peace activists who love human rights would be against that. But I would be wrong.

Why do human rights advocates hate the Arabs of Judea and Samaria so much? I cannot say. Perhaps for the same reasons that other Arabs seem to hate them so. I can understand hating the Arabs of Israel. After all, they live with a bunch of Jews. But is their hatred of Israel truly strong enough to condemn all Levant Arabs? Time will tell.

Anybody who wants to boycott Israel either knows that damaging Israel's economy is very dangerous for Yosh Arabs or is too caught up in their academic indignation to see how much Israel provides to Judea and Samaria. Or they simply have no idea what is going on here. And if you want to boycott Israel and any Israeli companies then I sincerely hope that you also want to boycott all of the Israeli technology that is in your computer, Israeli medical technology and research that is in your hospitals, Israeli weapons research and technology that is used by your military.

If you want to boycott all things Israeli then you might want to think twice about receiving modern medical treatment, getting an eye exam, using your computer, flash drive or the internet, using your GPS, ordering items from any company that has automated warehouses, that next plane trip, eating food grown on large industrial farms.

Boycotting Israeli technology would be as difficult as boycotting cheap Chinese crap. It is everywhere.

I do not believe that Americans are highly suspicious of Israel. I think most Americans know very little about Israel. They know what their TVs tell them, which is neither fair nor balanced. This is true of most subjects in the United States. They fixate on buzzwords like "fiscal cliff" and "sequester", which used to have a different meaning not all that long ago, and not think about any more detail than fits in the average TV news broadcast.

As with any issue about anything these days, Americans divide themselves between Republicans and Democrats. If one group supports something, the other will automatically oppose it without giving any thought as to why. If Barack Obama likes creamy peanut butter then Republicans will praise chunky. Since Republicans support Israel, Democrats automatically oppose.

Ask a Democrat why they do not support Israel and they will talk about "stolen land", which is ironic if you know basic history, and "human rights abuses", meaning foreigners cannot enter Israel without papers. I never hear them complain about Arab states treating women like property, castrating girls, executing homosexuals and children, controlling the press, and any number of actual human rights abuses. If any European state did all of this, Democrats would scream loud and clear. If Israel did this, Democrats would want to nuke us.

Look at Arab politics. No women's rights, no homosexual rights, no minority rights, no racial equality, no free press, no free speech, no separation of church and state but plenty of religious persecution, public executions. These are not things Democrats would support at home.

Look at Israeli politics. Equal rights for all citizens regardless of race, gender, religion, sexuality, a free press, free speech, no capital punishment, separation of church and state, very few guns, environmental activism, lots and lots of government, lots of hippies. This is Democratic paradise.

Yet Democrats favour ruthless dictatorships over a liberal democracy because we have settlements. Is that crazy or is it just me?

When I say liberal media I am talking about media that is relatively free to report whatever they choose, as long as it does not interfere with their corporate owners' interests. Liberal media is quite different from media in countries like Saudi Arabia and North Korea, where they report what they are told to report by the state. I am most definitely not talking about the American definition of liberal media, wherein paranoid types see a mass conspiracy to brainwash people to a liberal political perspective within the American definition of politically liberal. When an American uses the word liberal it generally has nothing to do with the meaning of the word liberal.

I suppose I also might as well point out as long as we are here that when I deride the Arab media, which are mostly controlled by the state, I am not attacking the average Arab. Just as when I deride the American media, controlled by corporations, I am not attacking average Americans. This is difficult for some people to fathom but it is possible to criticise an aspect of a country's society without hating everybody in that country.

What is reported in Arab media has nothing to do with what the people think or feel. It is more about what they are told to think and feel. What is reported in American media is also less about the people and more about what consumer goods they are told to buy. Israeli media was never like Arab media. It has been free since the Ottomans left. Sadly, it is moving closer to the American model every day.

Former American president Jimmy Carter is considered an elder policeman of the world. In this position he has announced that Israel, and more specifically the Benjamin Netanyahu government, is completely to blame for all of the problems with Palestine.

I used to defend Jimmy Carter. He used to say things that made sense. I do not think he was America's worst president. But whatever inside of him that made him a weak president has now made him a weak elder statesman. I always thought people were supposed to get more conservative with age. Is that not what Winston Churchill said.

When Carter got the Democratic nomination in 1980 he caved in to the more liberal wing of the party and adopted their platform. This made it very easy for Ronald Reagan's conservative movement to take control. Had Carter remained the conservative Democrat that he used to be he might have won that election.

Jimmy Carter has been a very vocal opponent of capital punishment for most of his life. But when he was a governor he signed a bill into law that established the death penalty in Georgia. He said that the bill was going to pass no matter what he did so he might as well sign it.

Carter has always opposed abortion but chose to ignore the issue whilst president since most of his party does not agree with him. He has spoken out against it after leaving office but kept quiet when people were actually listening to what he had to say.

Jimmy Carter is often used by the United States as an international monitor in elections in other countries. It is not his fault but any country in the world should be insulted when Americans tell them how to count votes.

The international media generally ignore much of whatever Carter has to say about any given issue. He is no longer a world leader and he has never been an especially exciting TV guest. But every word he utters condemning Israel is front page news.

Benjamin Netanyahu is not the most liberal prime minister that Israel has ever had. But he has publicly supported the two state solution, as has every Israeli prime minister. He has said that there should be a sovereign Palestine, as has every Israeli prime minister. No Palestinian leader has ever recognised Israel's right to exist. Arab leaders want all or nothing. They will not even talk about preventing their terrorists from murdering people without massive concessions and appeasement from Israel.

Israel supports no terrorist groups and simply wants to exist. Israeli leaders will and have come to the table without a single precondition. Arab states are dictatorships that often treat their own people like property. Israel is a liberal democracy. Yet people like Jimmy Carter never blame any Arab leaders.

Barack Obama once went to Israel with all of the pomp and circumstance that such a visit entails. He brought with him two Boeing 747s, four Sikorsky VH-60s, two armoured limousines, three secret service SUVs, separate vehicles for medical personnel and communication, two Boeing C-17s to carry everything, lots of secret service, all of the people to fly and drive all of the vehicles, all of the people who hover around him wherever he goes and must have some job other than being seen with the president. He might have brought his dog. I cannot say.

When Paul McCartney came to Israel in 2008 he arrived by private jet and brought maybe three or four bodyguards. The Israeli promoters of his concert provided private security and land transportation.

One could easily argue that Paul McCartney is not a head of state. That is quite true. But I think the world would suffer far more if something untoward happened to Paul McCartney than to Barack Obama. Obama has a long queue of people waiting to replace him. McCartney is irreplaceable. I would also feel much worse if Paul McCartney were killed in my country than I would about any political assassination. Either would convince people who know nothing about this place that it is one big exploding sandbox but had Paul died here we could never live it down.

Much to the surprise of the international media both McCartney and Obama survived their trips to Israel. The rest of us never even considered otherwise until we were told by outsiders that we are supposed to always assume that everybody who comes here is in danger.

A more important difference between the two is that I saw Paul McCartney perform. It was a very good show and the only time I did not have to make any special plans to see him. I paid very little attention to the Obama visit.

What I find disappointing is that every single time an American leader comes here they have to go to Judea and Samaria and/or Jordan and Egypt. They all buy into the false notion that giving equal time is necessary. If they visit Israel without visiting any Arab state then some Arab leaders will complain rigorously. Yet they can go and have gone to Jordan or Egypt without coming here without our leaders mentioning it. I have never heard of Germany complaining about an American president's visit to France. Those of us in democracies do not complain about such things.

Paul McCartney played here without making any attempt to play in any Arab state. That was probably more about money than anything else but I like that he never bowed to pressure. I never heard about a single Israeli complaint when he played Abu Dhabi in 2011.

I was at the Paul McCartney concert and I can still tell you what songs he sang. I did not watch Barack Obama's big speech and only saw bits and pieces on the news. McCartney sang about jets and calico skies on a warm evening after a very nice day for a picnic. He also sang "Back in the USSR" in a country with more than a few people who were tortured and persecuted by the Soviet regime. But none of us are perfect.

Barack Obama said that his daughters are very much like some Palestinian teenagers he met. He said that Palestinian youth are just like American and Israeli youth. Even though every American reality TV programme tells us that this is not at all true.

Let us ignore that the random people any American president meets on any given trip are carefully selected beforehand and are not at all randomly plucked off the street. While Barack

Obama was saying that any lack of peace is Israel's fault because we build houses, he and his flag were being burnt in effigy on the streets of Palestine by more than a few young Palestinians who objected to his visit to a country that they want wiped off the face of the Earth. While the American was lecturing Israelis about being nicer to our neighbours, some of our neighbours were firing rockets at our children.

I wonder how many bombs Obama's daughters have strapped on.

When Barrack Obama was young and his heart was an open book he used to say live and let live. You know he did. But now that this ever changing world in which we're living makes him give in and cry he says live and let die.

Some day people will likely abandon political correctness, or the parameters of it will change. Whether this happens before the international media change their narrative or because of it remains to be seen. Arab despots might want to consider how they will be portrayed once infotainers abandon their efforts to ignore any Arab crimes against humanity. Until then we can expect a litany of Israel's misdeeds and silence about Arab states and their support of terrorist organisations.

If Arab dictators were East Asian or black Africans you would hear an endless stream of their crimes. If most Israelis were not Jewish you would never hear about Israel on the nightly news at all.

WORLD LEADER
PRETEND

This Has Nothing to Do
With Andy Kaufman

On 20 July 1969 mankind penetrated the maidenhead of outer space and came on the moon. Neil Armstrong and Buzz Aldrin fertilised the surface of the moon whilst Armstrong moaned, "That's one small step for a man. And when I say small step I am of course referring to my diminutive penis". And like all men, they left a big mess.

Or did they?

We all saw *Capricorn One* where Sam Waterston and Barbra Streisand's husband tried to convince everybody that Elvis is dead.

Or did we?

Americans often claim they invented

democracy and freedom. This is false. France or Greece invented democracy and African and Pacific Island countries where women could walk around bare chested invented freedom.

But one thing history and the truth can never take away from America is that they put a man on the moon. They are the first, and so far only, country to ever accomplish something that is really pretty impressive when you consider the primitive technology of the day. I think this is their greatest achievement.

People complain about the United States all the time. Sometimes rightfully so. Sometimes not so much. I lived there for a brief period so I feel this gives me the right to have an opinion of the Land of the Free.

But since the United States has made it their business to make every other country their business then I think we all have the right to have an opinion. Most of the world seems to have an opinion about my country and we have likely never invaded you or told you what to do.

Few people have any opinion of Lesotho for some reason.

If the United States wants to be the biggest movie star in the world then it is going to have to accept some bad press from time to time. But one complaint against the United States that I find absolutely unacceptable is this queer notion that landing on the moon was not all that important. This was the defining moment of the twentieth century. Like it or not the Americans were the only people who could do it.

Ironically, Neil Armstrong's original line was supposed to be "Here I come to save the day".

American Idol

American president Barack Obama began a large scale public relations campaign during his first year in office wherein he wanted to convince the people of Israel and several Arab states that he had all the answers to peace. He boldly announced during his Obamania Tour that not only would there be peace in our lifetime but that there would be peace during his administration.

Good luck with that.

Barack Obama inherited a famously unpopular war in Iraq, a mostly ignored war in Afghanistan, a crippled economy, massive debt, a soiled popular image of his country. While running for president in 2008 he promised change. Not necessarily change for the better but change for the sake of change. I guess after eight years of George Bush any change could not be bad.

So what changed during his first year in office? Washington was still sharply divided politically. It was just a different party in charge. Party politics were as alive as ever, if not more so. And things would only get worse.

Political appointments were still made to friends and cronies. But probably not any of Obama's father's friends. Even his first defence minister was the same. The man in charge of

Bush's unpopular war was now in charge of Obama's unpopular war. The president and vice president still said stupid things and Bill Clinton's exploits still overshadowed his wife's accomplishments.

That's not change. That's more of the same.

Barack Obama's top priority should have always been to do whatever he could to assist the economy. Ask anybody. But instead he concentrated on the same bizarre health cover debate that made Hillary Clinton the most hated woman in America years ago and probably cost her the presidency years later. I sincerely cannot say why so many Americans care more about insurance companies than they care about their fellow Americans but I question Barack Obama's judgement if he thought the same shitstorm that hurt the Clintons would not hurt him.

Many Americans have been living in fear for a long time. If somebody who knows how to play to their fear screams that Barack Obama wants to kill granny then they are going to go with fear over reason. They have been comically afraid for years that somebody in a towel will blow up the local Walmart.

Now they are rightly afraid that they could lose their jobs at any time. Without a job in America it is easy to become one of those homeless people they hate so much. This is not the ideal climate for the president to tell Americans that he wants to spend even more money to kill granny and turn America into Russia. For, as anybody who watches Fox

News knows, he is the reincarnation of Joseph Stalin and Karl Marx's love child.

And then he decided to bring peace to the Middle East by giving interviews to television stations. Somebody should have told him that most people in the Middle East do not worship the TV the way his people do. More Americans can name the *Pop Idol* winners than their own political leaders. It is seen here as diversionary entertainment, not a companion and mentor. We do not believe everything every crackpot on TV tells us. We mostly just listen to our religious crackpots.

I do not believe that most leaders here really care what Barack Obama thinks. He is not a king or emir. His position is temporary. Any agreements and plans he makes can be undone by his successor. Those leaders will sell him oil and buy his weapons and launder their money in his financial institutions, when the economy is good, but they will never see him as an equal.

Barack Obama might know a lot about whatever he knows a lot about but I doubt he has a clue about what is going on in the Levant. I have never met an American who fully understands the situation. It took me years to grasp it and I live here. I probably still do not fully understand.

Most people oversimplify whatever argument fits their opinion. Dismantling settlements will not appease Palestinians any more than disarming Iran will placate Israel. This is not tit for tat schoolyard bickering. There are intrinsic fundamental differences between several countries that live uncomfortably close to one another. No American president can change that whether he is the great black hope or the harbinger of communism.

TV crackpots said that if the American government cannot manage car trades then they cannot manage health cover. I say that if Obama cannot negotiate a truce between people of his own culture and temperament then he certainly cannot negotiate with people he does not understand.

But if he wants to take Netanyahu to Camp David for a few years, he has my full support.

Barack Obama was awarded the Nobel Peace Prize in 2009. As the kids would say, WTF? What specifically has Obamania done for world peace? Or even American peace?

As far as I can tell he was a senator for half a term before becoming president ten months before the award. As a senator he did not vote for the wars in Iraq and Afghanistan. Probably because that vote took place before he was a senator. Is not voting for something because you were not in office a good enough reason to get the Nobel Peace Prize?

As a president he has yet to end the wars that he did not vote for or against. He has said that he will end the wars sooner or later. Are empty campaign promises that everybody knows are empty campaign promises good enough to get the Nobel Peace Prize?

The Nobel Peace Prize is supposed to be the most prestigious award given to people who do the most for world peace. But there are many reasons to take it far less seriously than it takes itself. In 2007 it was given to Al Gore because he made a movie about climate change. It was not a bad movie but I have seen better. Even if it were the best climate change documentary ever made would that make it worthy of a Nobel Peace Prize? Maybe the Chemistry Prize.

The big rumour is that it was given to Al Gore instead of Irena Sendler, a woman who literally saved people's lives. This is only a rumour because the Nobel committee does not tell anybody who their choices were.

In 1994 it was given to Yasser Arafat. A peace prize was given to a known terrorist. Arabs worship him in the bizarre way that Americans worship Ronald Reagan. But Reagan probably never told anybody that if they strapped on a bomb and blew up some children they would be awarded with sex slaves in the afterlife. As far as I know. I am not a Ronald Reagan expert but it does not seem like the kind of thing he would have done.

Some people want to soften Arafat's image now that he is dead. As often happens when people die. But when he was alive he called on his people to do everything legal and illegal that they could think of to kill every last Israeli man, woman, and child. That is the exact opposite of peace in my opinion.

But I cannot say any of this without somebody arguing that Israel did this and Israel did that. Israel built houses and has the audacity to defend itself from bombs and rockets. If you can ignore your hatred of Jews and/or Arabs for a second and look at it objectively, should a terrorist leader be given the Nobel Peace Prize?

At no point in time was it ever given to Mahatma Gandhi. Any organisation that gives a peace prize to Yasser Arafat and ignores Gandhi has serious issues. Part of the problem is that the committee that decides these things is appointed by Norway's parliament and mostly made up of former members of parliament. There is no way it will not be political under those circumstances.

As soon as it becomes a political decision then it ruins the entire idea of a prestigious international award for world peace. You have politicians giving it to organisations they favour such as the United Nations and IAEA. Pretty soon they will just generically give it to the United States or European Union for some bullshit reason.

Barack Obama got the award before he even served a full year in office. By the end of his second term will there be anybody in the world who truly believes that he deserved it?

I like watching American election campaigns. Not because I particularly care about who wins but because I am interested in the circus process and how it has evolved over the years. I did not care much for the 2008 presidential election because it lasted about as long as a congressional term in office. That is change I do not believe in. In my country you can go on holiday when they announce an election and come home after it is over.

I have never cared about British elections. They have all been pretty boring as long as I have noticed. The expected winner always does, except maybe when John Major won.

But sometimes boring is good. American elections are usually a series of sensationalised blunders. Americans are always saying they voted for the lesser of two evils, and the winner is usually whoever made the least embarrassing mistakes. The only American style British election I can think of was 1997 when Tony Blair could name the most Spice Girls. Until now.

Party leaders now have to deal with televised debates. I feel sorry for them. Winning an election on TV relies more on canned acting and good hair than leadership. If you have ever watched *Pop Idol* then you know why that is a bad thing.

Richard Nixon was more qualified to be president than John Kennedy in 1960. He took his work more seriously and earned everything he had, as opposed to Kennedy's sense of entitlement. Kennedy was barely younger but looked much younger, and he was far more comfortable in front of the camera. He probably won because of the televised debates. Jimmy Carter was much younger than Gerald Ford and had a full head of hair at the time. Ford was winning the election until they went on TV together.

When Carter was the incumbent he was

winning until he went on TV with Ronald Reagan, a former actor. Reagan won in a landslide. Michael Dukakis lost to the first George Bush largely because he seemed distant on TV. He was also a hairy Mediterranean immigrant's son running against a Connecticut WASP from a political dynasty.

The first Clinton was a generation younger than the first Bush and looked a lot better on TV. He was more charming and more articulate. Women wanted to sleep with him. And many did. Nobody wanted to sleep with George HW Bush. Clinton easily won. Barack Obama looked young, charming, articulate, nonthreatening. John McCain looked old, crippled, sometimes mean. Who did you expect to win.

The exception to this rule is the 2000 election between George Bush Jr and Al Gore Jr. They were about the same age, both had good hair, both came from wealthy white powerful families. But Bush was going to win that election even if he went on TV and sang "Yankee Doodle" on a washboard. Fixing the vote helps.

If the British follow the Americans, and they usually do, Gordon Brown is in Barney. Nick Clegg has the hair, youth, speaks a million languages. David Cameron looks like a prime minister, went to all the right schools, is related to royalty. Gordon Brown is the old man, partially blind, he is from Scotland, and every time I see him I wonder if Terry Jones will play him in the movie. Terry Jones is a funny man but I would rather vote for Palin or Idle.

Then Gordon Brown took the election fully into American territory. He did the kind of thing Joe Biden does every day and it became a media frenzy. CNN replaced their 24 hour Iceland volcano coverage with 24 hour Gaffegate coverage. Then CNN demonstrated a complete lack of self awareness by producing a report wondering if the media were spending too much time on something so trivial.

History books will show that instead of losing on the issues Brown lost because he does not understand microphones. I am sure that Gerald Ford knows how he feels.

> *"Americans decide, but their choice will change all of our lives forever."*

Once again the Americans are taking a few years to pick a new president. Or the same one. I am guessing that they will pick a new one.

I am going to ignore how annoying it is that it takes them so long to hold elections. France held elections in April, run offs two weeks later and François Hollande was sworn in a week after that.

Our 2009 elections were in February. About a week later Benjamin Netanyahu was asked to form a coalition. A month later he was prime minister. It would have been faster had Tzipi Livni been able to form a coalition. I still think she would have been a better prime minister.

Americans do it differently. Barack Obama started campaigning in February 2007. He was elected in November 2008 and took office in January 2009. It takes them two years to get a job that lasts four years.

I suppose I am not going to ignore it. Hindsight is 50/50.

What bothers me is how much I have to read about their elections. I do not technically have to read it but when something is in front of me I tend to start reading.

I am not American. I am not now nor have I ever been an American citizen. I do not plan on becoming one. Nobody in my family is in any way American. I lived there for a few years and have a mild interest in their goings on, the way you might occasionally think about that crazy uncle that nobody ever talks about.

But when they vote for presidents, legislators, and sometimes governors I have to hear about it. Do they hear about our elections? Very little. Do they hear about elections in your country? Probably not. Unless you live in Britain.

Why do their media not obsessively cover our elections? Because we are in different countries. Why should they care that some guy they have never heard of is running against some other guy they have never heard of. Just tell them who won and that is good enough. Most of the time for most of the countries in the world they do not even mention the winner. Who is the current president of Suriname? Do any Americans care?

Most of the people on this planet simply cannot live the isolationist lifestyle that

Americans enjoy. Most of us have more neighbours. They are all around us and we have to deal with them. Americans can bully their three neighbours any way they want.

The good news is that by not living in the United States I do not have to watch the endless stream of campaign advertisements. We hear about what is going on but we do not have to deal with the redundant rhetoric and hyperactive hyperbole.

Even better news is that their choice will not change my life forever. It will likely have no effect on my life whatsoever. They call the American president the leader of the free world but he could not even lead a dog parade around here.

Israel is being mentioned a lot in the current campaign. But Israelis know that the candidates are only using us to score points. We can tell the difference between bullshit and sincerity. Mostly because we hear enough of our own bullshit during our own elections.

Looking in from the outside I do not think most Americans can tell the difference. There seems to be a large segment of their population that will believe absolutely anything that anybody with their same political views says. That sounds crazy but I truly believe it to be true.

From my point of view it makes no difference who wins their election. Do Benjamin Netanyahu and Barack Obama hate each other? Would Netanyahu and Mitt Rmoney be friends? Who cares. Israel and the

United States are allies. The personal opinions of our temporary leaders are irrelevant.

Israeli prime ministers from David Ben-Gurion to Benjamin Netanyahu had a wide variety of opinions. American presidents from Harry Truman to Barack Obama did not entirely agree on all of the same things either. Yet Israel and the United States have remained allies. Democracies do not change allegiances every time they change governments.

I do not expect Obama to lose because I want Romney to win. I do not care who wins. I think it will be a case of Obamania losing more than Romney winning. Incumbents rarely win when the economy is so bad.

On the other hand, Americans generally think that Democrats are a better choice when the economy is bad. It took somebody as charismatic as Ronald Reagan to beat a very unpopular Jimmy Carter, and things were pretty bad at the time. It was much easier for Jimmy Carter and Bill Clinton to beat Gerald Ford and George Bush. If the Republicans had nominated somebody more interesting than Romney they would win easily.

I might have been wrong about my Romney prediction.

> *"Mr Speaker, Mr Vice President, members of Congress, distinguished guests, and fellow Americans."*

I have been following American politics for years. When I lived there I saw Americans with a wide variety of opinions. They would argue with and debate each other about anything. But as soon as I stated an opinion they would all suddenly become united. It is one thing for an American to criticise an American point of view. It is another entirely for some foreigner to have an opinion.

Barack Obama campaigned to end the war in Iraq in 2008. The Democrats campaigned to end the war in 2006. Both could have ended it immediately. It took nine years to get American soldiers out of Iraq. George Bush can and should get all the blame for putting them there but Obama and the Democrats need to take some blame for keeping them there.

Democrats and Republicans are equally as willing to send soldiers into war. It is the best way they know of to protect American corporate interests. Yet neither party cares about those soldiers after they leave the military. Barack Obama offered a "proud salute" to soldiers when they finally left Iraq and called them a "generation of heroes" but gave them the finger once they got home. Who would let heroes live on park benches?

I do not see how the United States is safer or more respected around the world now than it was before invading Iraq and Afghanistan. Iraq was never a threat to the United States. But keeping American soldiers in an Arab state for nine years has given them even more enemies. The reason people like Osama hated you to begin with is that you lingered in Arab states after pushing Iraq out of Kuwait.

Killing terrorist leaders does little to stop terrorists from hating you. Lieutenants are easily replaced. Momentum may be all it takes to win an American election but it has little to do with fighting a holy war. Nine years is endless to Americans. Thousands of casualties are unacceptable. But your enemies are prepared to fight and martyr themselves generation after generation. This war will not end in your lifetime.

But I do think that Obama should get the credit for killing Osama. George Bush's inaction let him get away with murder for ten years.

The United States was the most powerful country in the world for a few generations. But those days are almost over. People will debate and study why it fell out of power for several more generations. I think the main reason they will no longer be the world's dominant power is their complete inability to give a shit about their children. Americans talk about children. They have laws that supposedly protect the children but most of them seem more focused on punishment than protection.

A country that truly cares about children does not have one of the worst educational systems in the developed world. The United States has some pretty good universities but they also have high schools that graduate children who cannot read. The educational system seems to be the enemy of most politicians. And people actually vote for politicians that hate education. Children and their schools are always the first to lose funding whenever there are budget cuts. People who care about their children would not do that.

There is no guarantee of health cover for children. In fact, many Americans are fighting very hard to make sure that children are not covered. And some of the food they serve their children in school cafeterias and at home should be considered child endangerment.

Past generations of Americans were innovative and successful because they got a decent education, were fed healthy food, were taken care of. The current generation is unhealthy and undereducated. Dumbing down the children will not lead to adults who develop new technologies and medical advancement. Without positive changes future generations will make North Korea look good. When the next generation of Americans can only write in Internet English then you are screwed.

Most of the developed world invests in education. We all realise that today's children are tomorrow's adults. The United States either does not understand this basic truth or does not care. No politician wants to invest in tomorrow if it will cost money today.

Any society that does not care about its children is doomed to fail.

Americans used to be told that if they worked hard they could own a home and save money for the future. I do not think this exists in America anymore. Nobody works at one place their entire adult life. Pensions are no longer enough to keep you and your wife healthy and happy for the rest of your days. Even when they are not embezzled. A single income today cannot sustain a family. One job is not enough for a house, two cars in the garage, higher education for the children.

This American dream exists in many parts of the world. But Americans have let their corporations and the politicians they own take it away from them.

Americans are proud of their past accomplishments. Some of which are rightfully boastworthy. Landing on the moon was pretty impressive. But they also used to have strong leaders who could get things done and whom most Americans supported. Even when the power shifted from the Roosevelt-Truman Democrats to the Eisenhower Republicans there was broad public support. None of that is true today. The political climate is too divisive for anybody to ever support a politician from the other party.

Many Americans love to complain about taxes. Yet they have some of the lowest tax rates in the world. Their state sales taxes are much lower than most of our VATs. Their income tax rates are nothing compared to some European countries.

But most Americans want lower taxes, especially for the rich. Because they think that they will be rich someday and they do not want to lose any of that theoretical money. But if the rich pay less then the poor have to pay more. That is basic math.

Or they could simply cut more from the

education budget until nobody understands basic math.

Americans are losing jobs to countries like China and India. Not only are those countries making more things that people buy but they are also preparing their younger people for the workforce and giving businesses a reason to work there.

The cost of living in the United States is much higher than places like China and India. You can easily hire seven Chinese to do the same job as one American. Anybody who went to any business school will tell you that seven workers are more productive than one. Chinese workers do not demand overtime pay, sick days, paid vacations. Chinese workers do not have unions. They are willing to work in horrible conditions that most Americans simply would never accept.

China also has a lot of potential customers. They have a billion more people and a much smaller variety of goods on their shelves. For all that communist talk their government is a whore for capitalism. They love decadent western money. And Chinese people love to shop. They are very materialistic and see having more crap as a sign of success. Any American corporation can easily make more money in China than in the United States.

American products are very popular in some countries. Chinese people had to get on waiting lists to buy American watches a gencration ago. Now you can go to any of a million shopping centres. American products are often seen as status symbols.

But most Chinese do not distinguish between something that was genuinely made in America and some bootleg piece of crap that says it was made in America. People happily buy counterfeit products as long as they are similar to the real thing. American officials can keep the counterfeits from entering the United States but there is nothing they can do about it being sold elsewhere.

Korean products are more popular in East Asia than ever before. Do not count on Koreans to be as excited about American goods as they used to be. It is becoming more and more fashionable throughout Asia to buy Korean. The Philippines used to love all things American. Currently it has moved on to an unhealthy obsession with all things Korean. And inexplicably, K-pop, Korean popular music, is exploding all over East Asia.

Barack Obama once said that he would "go anywhere in the world to open new markets for American products". That is funny because American corporations will boycott entire countries if they are less profitable than their neighbours.

There are more American products in China than Taiwan because China will not let you sell to both, and they have far more customers. The result is that Taiwan buys more Japanese and Korean products.

American corporations that sell in Israel are banned from most Arab states. Over 300 million Arab customers are more profitable than 8 million Israeli customers. Especially when American corporations rarely do well in Israel. The result is that the Israel market is basically closed to Americans.

There was a time when the United States was a leader in research. That is not even close to true today. Even with all of their military conquests they spend very little money on advancing technology. Most of their money seems to go to whomever has the most influence with their leaders.

There was a time when the rest of the world looked to the United States and France to find the cures to diseases. Now far more medical breakthroughs come from Germany and Israel. Even China and India devote more time and energy to medical research.

Some Americans seem to have an idea that advancing anything in the medical field is bad. Medical cover would make you a Soviet style communist dictatorship and medical research is a direct insult to God. There is something fundamentally wrong with this.

I live in a country that has almost no oil and not enough natural gas. Even with all the debates in the Knesset. We cannot buy oil from Canada because that all goes to the United States. We cannot buy oil from our Arab neighbours because they are not exactly our biggest fans. Instead of invading everybody, we are investing heavily in other sources of energy. I live in one of the "greenest" cities in the world. One of the reasons it is so green is that more cars run on nontraditional fuel than anywhere else.

It would not take much for the United States to go into rehab and recover from its oil dependency. But when you are a recovering addict you have to stay away from the dealers and not be tempted by their sweet shiny oil.

Barack Obama has said that the United States is just as popular in the world as it used to be. "Anyone who tells you otherwise doesn't know what they're talking about. That's not how people feel from Tokyo to Berlin, from Cape Town to Rio."

If you want to be an American president you cannot say that China will be number one pretty soon. But from what I have seen people around the world are not too impressed with the United States lately. The people of Cape Town do not worship you. Not even close. Japan is still grateful for all that post war aid but they have moved on with their lives. Even the Philippines has found new friends.

But Barack Obama is correct that the United States still has financial influence over the rest of the world. When their economy sinks it hurts the rest of us. Our money is still too connected to their money. That is slowly changing. The next time they have a big depression it will not matter to most of us. We will all be watching the Chinese yuan.

Maybe I do not know what I am talking about. Or maybe I talk to more people outside of the United States far more than most American politicians. I seem to talk to funny sounding foreigners every day.

American immigration policy has always seemed queer to me. The country was bought, stolen, and built by immigrants. Almost all Americans are descendants of immigrants. Yet many Americans have a deep xenophobia of all things foreign. They also seem to think that their country is overrun with immigrants when only about ten percent of their population was born elsewhere. That is nothing compared to places like Israel and most Arab states. Even countries that nobody wants to fight over like Switzerland, Canada, Australia have a larger percentage of immigrants.

The British also do not seem to care much for immigrants, and they have an even lower percentage than the United States.

> *"As long as we're joined in common purpose, as long as we maintain our common resolve, our journey moves forward, our future is hopeful, and the state of our Union will always be strong."*

This obligatory patriotic ending to Obama's big speech only points out some of the reasons they are having so many problems just now. They are not working as a team. They do not have each other's backs. Unless knives are involved. They do not rise up to challenges the way they used to. Nobody is willing to sacrifice anything for the greater good. They do not have a common purpose. They have multiple agendas that do not work well together.

Americans think that America will always be on top. That makes sense. The British, Spanish, Romans, Persians, Chinese all thought the same thing, But a basic truth of world domination is that it will always be temporary. You can control the world if you really want to. But you cannot control it forever.

That is change you can believe in.

But something did change in America when Barack Obama became president. And I am not talking about all that newfound hope. American protesters always used to be the liberals for as long as I have been paying attention. If my newspapers can be trusted. The people who marched on Washington were always the longhaired hippies, dirty treehuggers, homosexuals with their insidious agenda, and those plain looking women who expected equality. According to conservatives. It was every conservative's sacred duty to look down on these liberals and laugh at their misguided naïveté. Protest in America? That is the purview of traitors.

But then the conservatives got together and said yes we can. Now they are the protesters marching on Washington with unintentionally funny signs. I guess love it or leave it only applies when your side is on top.

What are all these hippie conservatives protesting? They seem to like this tea party idea. If you do not like paying taxes then have a tea party and wear 18th century hats. My sisters and I used to wear funny hats when we had tea parties but I do not remember talking about taxes. The real Boston Tea Party protested the British Parliament's taxation of American goods without representation. Today's Americans have representatives. Choosing not to vote in your elections is not the same as not having any representation.

Another favourite of the hippie conservatives was to disrupt those town hall meetings as much as possible. I like a little anarchy as much as anybody but a little foresight tells you that your representatives will simply stop showing up if those town hall hooligans are allowed to continue. Instead of getting them to do what you want you will only get them to ignore you and everybody else even more than usual.

Then there is Joe Wilson. Anybody remember that guy? He was lauded and vilified for calling his president a liar. And then he became famous for it. For about fifteen minutes. I had never heard of him before. Had you?

Barack Obama has been called a lot of things. The reason Joe Wilson got attention was because it happened in Congress. Is this really the first time somebody in Congress was rude to the American president? I think somebody in the Knesset has called every Israeli prime minister a liar. Have you ever watched the British Parliament? They act like teenagers debating their favourite video games.

The main thing the neohippies started protesting was health cover. They do not want to be communists. And who can blame them. I am not sure if anybody ever told them that most of the countries in the world that have universal health cover are not communist. And I have never seen a single American point out that what they are really debating is health cover, not health care.

Most Americans seem to think their health care is the best in the world. Even though the World Health Organisation says that it is ranked 72nd and the most expensive in the world. Israel is 40th. That is not so great either but we did not have to go communist to get cover. Neither did the top 35 countries on the list.

And yes, I recognise the irony of somebody who holds passports from countries that historically do not care what the United Nations says quoting a UN organisation.

Jimmy Carter says the neohippies are racist. Carter has been saying a lot of stupid things recently. Today's hippies will say that he has always been saying stupid things but this one is almost as bad as his apartheid comments. Way back when Barack Obama was only a candidate for president I predicted that anybody who criticised him would be labelled racist. I am sorry to see that my prediction has come true.

I live in the country that not only controls the world but is also responsible for all of the world's problems. According to some very racist people. It is also the least racist place I have ever lived.

I have no idea what it is like to be a black

African living in America but I know exactly what it is like to be a white African living in America. I lived in California. The melting pot of America's melting pot. I was surrounded by whites, blacks, Latinos, Asians, Jews, Christians, atheists, people with real breasts, and actresses. With so much diversity you would assume there would be harmony. At least for the sake of peace. California was one of the most overtly racist places I have ever been.

But California is not America. I also lived in Alaska. There is a large indigenous population there but I lived and worked amongst mostly white Christian males who mostly did not care what religion I practised or where I was born. Race was never an issue. Gender was. But that is probably because there were too few women and most of the men suffered from chronic horny.

Racism in America has been well documented. Something you probably do not hear much about is racism in China. I cannot say how many times I have heard people say that it is because China only has one race, when in fact there are over fifty different ethnic groups. But they are all what most of us would call Chinese. China is also a depressingly racist country.

Americans talk about Korean video store clerks in Los Angeles that do not service black customers and are appalled. They should go to China. I cannot count how many times I walked into a shop or restaurant and heard

"沒有" before the door even closed behind me. With the Chinese hand signal for 沒有, either arms or index fingers crossed, this clearly meant that I was not welcome. Not because they ran out of whatever they sold but because my skin was white.

I saw plenty of discrimination in China because of my skin colour and gender but China is the only place I have never been discriminated against because of my religion. I find that ironic since China is the only place I have ever lived that does not profess religious freedom. I heard plenty of derogatory remarks about whites and women but nothing about Jews. And this is a place where the word for pig, "豬", sounds just like "Jew".

Chinese people are serious believers of yin/yang. Most of them are very friendly. And most are very racist. They will not necklace or lynch you. Most will never do anything violent toward you. But every Chinese I have ever met seriously believes that their race is superior. China, 中國, means Middle Kingdom. They literally call themselves the centre of the world.

Where Chinese racism is subtle, South African racism is grand mal obvious. I grew up under one of the most racist governments of modern times. That is not something of which I am proud. What I am proud of is how we turned it around without revolution or civil war and how quickly most people put the pain of the past in the past.

Black Americans can learn something from South Africa. Black South Africans were not second class citizens. They were not citizens at all. You could have been born in South Africa just like all your ancestors as far back as anybody knows but if you were black then you were not a citizen. They suffered indignities and humiliations like no living black American has ever seen.

But when they finally took charge they did not kill all the white people or even treat whites the way whites treated them. They extended their hands and asked for peace. Slavery in America was a horrible thing. But it is over. You were never a slave and that white guy looking at you funny never owned any slaves. Playing the victim never gets anybody anywhere.

I am not black so too many black Americans will say that I do not get it. I am Jewish. I grew up in South Africa. I get it. I have seen too many Jews play the victim.

The Shoah was the worst thing humans ever did to each other as far as I am concerned. But I was never in any death camps. I have never been tortured and murdered. I never had to live through any of that. Most of us have loved ones who did and there are still many survivors who could justifiably play the victim. But they are the people who never do. I have never seen a single survivor play that card. It is always those of us a generation or two removed who do that.

And my people were slaves, too. But that was also a long time ago. I have never felt that Egyptians were keeping me down. I have never used Egypt as an excuse for my failings. Somebody once told me that Egypt does not count since there are so few Egyptians in the United States. That is telling, but even more important is the fact that there are plenty of Egyptians around here. I see the descendants of the people who enslaved my ancestors just as much as any other group that has been wronged by another.

If you want to open a dialogue and advance race relations you have to acknowledge that whatever group you identify with is capable of bearing and inciting racism. It is not all black and white.

Obviously some people hate Barack Obama because he is black. But is that really why so many neohippies are protesting communist health cover? Were they racist when they rejected Hillary Clinton's health plan? Or was that sexist? I do not remember Jimmy Carter speaking out then. Does that mean Jimmy Carter is a misogynist?

I saw a homemade neohippie sign that read "I'll choose how I die/no communist healthcare". I wish I had a picture.

I did not realise that Americans get to choose how they die under their current health care system. No wonder they do not want to change it. I would love to be able to choose how I die. Unfortunately we have universal health cover for all citizens, Jewish, Arab, rich, poor, employed or not. So I shall just have to take death as it comes.

After watching the "debate on health care" I

have concluded that some Americans do not have a very high opinion of other countries. They also do not seem to know anything about the rest of us.

They used to point to Britain as a horrible example of universal health care. They knew somebody whose uncle had to wait five years to get an operation and died. Now it is Canada. Now they know somebody whose uncle had to wait six months to get an operation and died. At least that is better than Britain.

Neohippies have many arguments against universal health cover but they all fall flat from my experience.

Socialised medicine requires long wait times.

The longest I ever waited for a medical appointment was to see a gynecologist in California. And even when you have an appointment you still have to wait an hour before you actually see anybody.

I can go to a doctor right now in Israel if I want. I do not need an appointment and I would likely wait less than fifteen minutes.

I do not remember it taking long to see a doctor in South Africa at all. Once you have an appointment they are pretty good at seeing you on time.

There was no waiting in China but I was a foreigner. Foreigners are treated differently. Locals usually have to wait longer in bigger hospitals once they are there but it is easy to make an appointment for the next day.

They saw us immediately in Switzerland but

we were children and my mother was hysterical.

Alaska was very quick but that was an emergency. Follow up visits required longer waiting. I had one appointment for two weeks after I left the country.

Socialised medicine provides substandard care.

Americans seem to think their health care is the best in the world. The United Nations strongly disagree. I can go either way in my experience. It was actually pretty good in Alaska. The doctors knew what they were doing and the nurses were great. It would have cost me much less money in China but would the care have been better? In a large city hospital I think it would have. Especially for a foreigner. Probably not in a small village.

The quality of care in China depends on the type of hospital. The large city hospitals are comparable to anything in Europe. The small village clinics are very different from what I am used to but in some cases the care is even better. You just have to be more open to another perspective. But some things just cannot be fixed with roots and herbs.

My very limited experience in California was worse than Alaska. Those were the laziest doctors I have ever seen in my life. You see them for five minutes and pay far more than you would anywhere else in the world.

I think Israeli doctors are the best. There could be doctors somewhere in the world who do a better job but I have not experienced them. Israeli doctors care more about their patients than playing golf. Fortunately nobody in Israel cares about golf.

South African doctors were always very good to me and the nurses exceptionally caring. There is a certain work ethic you find in Africa that is lacking in much of the world. Those nurses look at their patients and not the clocks. But I was always white and employed. Black South Africans have different stories.

We got great care in Switzerland as far as I know. I did not have much to compare it with at the time. I do remember one particular doctor annoying me with his condescending tone. I was a child, not an idiot. But I think that is more to do with cultural attitudes than health care. Swiss children are probably pampered more than African children.

Why should those who work support those who do not?

Why not? Do you really hate people that much?

I have never seen this attitude outside of America. Most people seem to like their fellow countrymen. Americans will see a mentally disturbed person lying in the street and tell him to get a job. Surely not all of them but there is a selfish attitude that pervades the culture. There are a million reasons somebody might not have a job. They are not all lazy.

There is a famous story about a man complaining about homeless people. "Only in California do you see homeless people getting a sun tan in the streets." And the response is,

"Only in America do people see a man lying in the street and think he is working on his tan."

But if you do not want your tax dollars to pay for another's health cover then why do you allow those same tax dollars to pay for another's police and fire services? Do American fire departments ask if you have cover before they water your house? Do American police ask to see a wage statement before stopping a robbery? Do the people in American prisons all have prison cover? I bet some of them do not pay any taxes at all. Why should hard working Americans have to pay for lazy people to enjoy these services?

The government cannot manage car sales, how can they manage health care?

Are American police agencies, fire departments, prisons managed by private companies? Some prisons are. How is that working out? Do Americans believe their government is incompetent? If they do then why do Americans keep voting for the same politicians? Why do so many Americans hate America so much? This is what Americans will ask any foreigner who has an opinion about the United States.

Health care in most of the world is managed by doctors and hospitals. The state simply regulates what the fees are and helps pay for everything. Insurance companies are usually strictly limited in what they can bill and who they must cover. The government is not in charge of anything. They just make sure everybody is covered and keep us from being bankrupted by medical fees. Is that really such a bad thing?

If the government manages health cover they can see your medical records.

But it is acceptable to record your phone conversations?

Benjamin Netanyahu has never looked at my medical records. How do I know? First, he does not care. He has other problems. Second, he does not have access to anybody's medical records. The state subsidises insurance companies who in turn ensure that medical fees are paid. The hospitals keep the medical records.

What country has a better health care system than America?

Most of them. If you had the best health care in the world you might have a point. But you are not even close.

Leaving that aside, this debate is about cover, not care. The communists want to make sure that all Americans are covered. Even poor people, children, old people, people with preexisting conditions. Is that really such a bad thing?

Socialised medicine leads to communism.

When has this ever happened?

I have actually lived in a communist country. The health care was pretty good. The cover was great. You need permission to travel but nobody is perfect.

How many communist countries are left in the world? Other than China they are pretty small and not much of a threat to your way of life. If the Viet Cong were going to invade the streets of America it would have happened by now. I think it is time to stop being afraid of the communist menace. You are much more likely to be killed by terrorists. But saying health cover leads to terrorism would not play well.

I suspect Israel, South Africa or Switzerland will likely not be communist any time soon.

Socialised medicine will kill your grandparents.

My grandparents have lived with socialised medicine for over sixty years and they are still very much alive. They get extra cover in Israel because of their age. They would probably be denied cover in America because of their age. Which would be more detrimental to their health?

Israel has the best health care system of any country in which I have ever lived. Everybody has cover, regardless of religion, ethnicity, income, sexuality, political persuasion, age, preexisting issues. We are covered by what can loosely be called insurance companies that are funded by the state. This is paid for mostly by our taxes and our employers. Those who do not pay taxes are still covered. Nobody here seems to have a problem helping out those who need it.

Our taxes are much higher than some of our oil rich neighbours to the south but not nearly as high as France, and our health care does not cost nearly as much as America's. Much of those taxes go to research and innovations that are shared with and used all over the world. Most people seem to be satisfied with the system as is.

When I complain about taxes it is mostly because I am a victim of timing. The new tax laws offer great exemptions for new immigrants that were not in place when I settled here, though I am still immune to some taxes. They are lowering the tax rates for everybody but the VAT is still high. My health cover costs about 25 Israeli shekels per month. That is about 5 euros.

The only thing my sister paid for when my nephew was born was a special room. She could have had a room for free but they were willing to spend the extra seven euros and get a room with a nice view. All the medical supplies and personnel fees were covered as were all of my nephew's childhood immunisations and treatments. Not to mention the stipend. The state of Israel will actually pay mothers to have their babies.

Another sister's husband was in a car accident a few years ago. If you have ever seen the way Israelis drive then you will not be surprised. He paid for nothing out of tax except a procedure that was not covered because it was new and experimental. It is covered now. Everything was successful and it cost him less than 200 shekels or about 35 euros.

My grandparents are getting older and have a longer list of medical issues than they used to. There is nothing serious but once you reach a certain age you take a lot more medications. They see their doctors regularly and get all the tests. They take enough pills between them to bankrupt an uninsured American. They pay nothing out of tax for all their medical services. They are treated like people, not bank accounts.

I get occasional bouts of bronchitis. It is nothing serious and I never have to pay for any medical expenses. And when I take days off work I still get paid for time missed. It is good to have communist cover.

My experience with South Africa's modern health system is limited. I mostly lived there during apartheid and cover and care were very different than they are today. It used to be that the best care was saved for whites. Now it is about income. People with money use private cover whilst everybody else uses public cover. Most of the TV adverts are about insurance cover. The public system is in dire straits, mostly because of AIDS. Health care in South Africa would be completely different if AIDS were eradicated.

But the private system is very good. I had some residual medical issues after Alaska and got nothing but great care. But I was white, employed, and had private cover. Care has improved greatly for all blacks but it helps if they have money.

I lived in China at the end of SARS. It was mostly gone but many people still wore surgical masks in public. Bird flu was and still is a problem but they say people can only catch it from birds and I have never been in the habit of handling birds dead or alive.

China's health care system is a complicated combination of traditional and modern medicine. With so many people living in such a wide range of environments I suppose there is no easy way to cover everybody. But everybody is covered, even foreign workers and tourists. Most of it is paid by the state and all of that money comes from a very convoluted tax system.

What the patient pays depends on the medical issue, the size and location of the hospital, and where the patient lives. A poor farmer who gets stabbed with a pitchfork and goes to a local clinic for herb treatments pays nothing. A business executive with an ulcer who goes to a modern hospital in a large city pays much more. But a majority of the fees are covered for everybody regardless of the situation and even those who pay a larger percentage pay very little by European standards.

I was in a scooter accident when I lived in China. If you have ever seen the way Chinese drive then you would be surprised that anybody is still alive. It was not that serious but it aggravated a previous injury. I lived in a small village with a small clinic that used mostly traditional medicine. Everything would have been almost free but I insisted on modern medicine in a big city hospital.

The transportation was completely free. I got all the x-rays, tests, drugs I wanted from doctors who spoke decent English and still paid almost sixty yuan. That was about six euros at the time. When the modern medicine was doing nothing for me I went to the small clinic and got the free herbs and roots. They worked much better. I never had any faith in acupuncture until I actually tried it.

Health insurance is mandatory for everybody in Switzerland. It covers most medical situations with patients paying a small percentage of the charges. I assume most health care is paid by taxes but I know almost nothing about Switzerland's current tax system.

We used to go to Switzerland a lot when my grandparents lived there. My sisters Ellie and Ria, and I were treated for pneumonia during one visit. It started in South Africa but we did not know what it was until later. We only had coughs and Ellie had a low fever when we went. Today it would be harder to fly to other countries but back then nobody thought twice about coughing children on a plane.

Ellie got it first but it never got too bad. Maybe because she was older. Maybe not. Ria started coughing before I did and she had it the worst. Maybe because she was younger. Maybe not. We all saw the doctor but she was the only one who spent any time in hospital. Dara never got anything.

I think we were at least partially covered with Swiss insurance through our parents and grandparents. Our grandparents were citizens and lived there. Our parents and Ellie were citizens who lived abroad. Ria and I were not citizens, and lived abroad. I do not know how much the system has changed since then but treating three children and hospitalising one was not very expensive. It probably would have been more expensive if we were adults. Not that it mattered. My mother was worried to death about Ria and would have spent everything we had to treat her if necessary. Not that I am complaining. Any parent should be willing to do that. Fortunately we were in a country with socialised medicine so it could never come to that.

My introduction to America's controversial health cover system came at university. Health insurance was compulsory for students. I had to pay the usual school and housing fees, plus health insurance, a special fee for foreigners, and taxes on top of all that. Everything was taxed. I think they even taxed my student visa. California's tax code is second only in labyrinthe complexity to China. I spent more than fourteen thousand dollars on insurance in California, more than everywhere else combined. And I never really used it.

The most time I ever spent in hospital was in Alaska. Fortunately my health cover was provided through my employer. But it was never enough. Taxation in Alaska is far lower than California but I had to pay more for health insurance as a foreigner. It was great for preventative visits to a dentist and periodic medical exams but absolute shit when I really needed it. I had to take my employer to court in order to pay medical expenses. I think that if they ever get socialised health cover then the lawyers will lose a lot of money. I am sure that is one reason they never will.

I spent some time in Israel after Alaska and even as a foreigner at the time I paid only a small fraction for medical expenses. When I went back to South Africa my medical expenses were reduced to almost nil. It would have been better had I been a citizen of Israel but it was still much much lower than Alaska.

North to the Future

During the 2008 United States presidential election people kept asking me what I think of Sarah Palin. I am not sure why. She became governor years after I left Alaska. She was mayor of Wasilla when I crashed in her backyard. I only met her once and I was flying high on medications at the time. It was nothing more than a photo op to her. It is not like we were best friends.

I have no particular insight into her abilities as a governor. She took office almost five years after I left the state. Frank Murkowski, the governor she replaced, took office after I left. Tony Knowles was governor when I lived there. That was an interesting guy. He was a Democrat governor in a largely Republican state. After he tried to run again in 2006 and lost to Sarah Palin he moved to Hawaii, a largely Democrat state with its first elected

Republican governor.

Is Sarah Palin experienced enough to be vice president? That is ironic when Barack Obama supporters ask. Does she have any foreign policy experience, they ask. Did Ronald Reagan, Jimmy Carter, Bill Clinton or George Bush have any? Maybe Bush is a bad example. Does Obama have any foreign policy experience? Why does Palin refuse to do interviews? Frankly I am glad that she does none. I see enough of these people already.

Would I vote for her? No. I would vote for one of the presidential candidates. I do not believe that the vice presidential candidate is that important. People say that John McCain is old so Sarah Palin could easily become president. That is as insulting as saying that Barack Obama is black so Joe Biden could easily become president. They are both true but why is it ok to say that an old guy in good health could drop dead at any time but it is bad to say that a black president might be assassinated in such a divisive country.

The thing about Sarah Palin that I think Democrats fail to understand is that she was selected to get the conservatives excited. And that is exactly what she is doing. Democrats say that she is there to take votes away from Hillary Clinton. Why would anybody who supports Clinton also support Palin? She is not there to get Clinton supporters. She is there because John McCain was never any conservative's favourite. Her job was to get them fired up and stir the pot. She has done that job very well.

After eight years of what can only conservatively be called a disastrous Republican presidential administration, the Democrats should win this election in a landslide. But all the so called experts are saying that it will be close. That is not because John McCain has everybody talking. If Barack Obama is half the saviour that his supporters think he is then McCain should be practically finished by now. You cannot dismiss Sarah Palin's influence.

Poor Joe Biden. Nobody talks about him.

There either is or used to be an American TV programme called *Sarah Palin's Alaska*. I know nothing of the programme's broadcast history. I do not believe it was ever shown here.

A friend sent me the episode where that show is visited by the mother with eight children show. Not because of the mother with eight children. I have never seen that programme either and I know nothing about it other than it is about a mother with eight children. It used to be a mother and father with eight children but I guess the father with eight children did what any father with eight children and cameras in his face all day would do and found himself some childless lady friends. Now it is just the mother with eight children.

I expected *Sarah Palin's Alaska* to be one long political sermon with a few shots of Alaska's incredible scenery in the background.

I was surprised to see more of Alaska. Though there still was not nearly enough. It is a pretty impressive part of the world and I think that as long as you are filming there you might as well show as much of it as you can. But in this particular case Palin and her family were playing host to the mother and her eight children. So there was more crossover promotion of the two programmes and less Alaska.

I was less impressed with Sarah Palin's acting skills than with the mother with eight children. The mother had a natural, albeit annoying, presence on camera. Everything Palin said seemed forced and stiff. It was like watching Paul McCartney act. This has nothing to do with her political opinions. Even though she gave the impression that she thinks she is superior to others and she spent too much time preaching her correct morality in an effort to enlighten the lesser people. Especially those in "the lower 48". Clearly those Americans are not real Americans.

My main complaint was that everything she said seemed scripted. I realise that it likely was and that these so called reality programmes have little to do with reality. Most of them are little more than long form game shows. But they should at least make it seem spontaneous.

The mother with eight children seemed genuine by contrast. When the two families went camping in the Alaskan wilderness the mother with eight children bitched and moaned every step of the trail. She complained that she did not like camping. Which begs the question of why she agreed to do it in the first place. She complained that she did not bring any insect repellent for her eight children. You would think somebody on the crew or one of the Palins would have some to share. She complained when it started to rain. Somebody should have pointed out to her beforehand that the Alaskan wilderness is wild. It will rain from time to time.

The mother with eight children seemed especially annoyed that she was cold. Apparently she never realised where Alaska is geographically. She complained that she did not have a proper kitchen to make lunch. She seems to have missed the camping concept.

Mostly she just complained. While her children seemed to have the time of their lives the mother stood under a tent, which she called her prison, the entire time complaining. But as annoying as all her whinging was at least it was genuine. She seemed to really hate where she was and what she was doing. Sarah Palin's use of "oh gosh" every five seconds seemed a bit much.

I lived in Alaska for a few years. I never heard an upset Alaskan say, "Gosh darn it, what the heck is this stuff?" Their vernacular was less American TV friendly. And I do not remember anybody constantly telling everybody the correct way to do things, as opposed to how "those people" do it in "the lower 48".

I understand the concept of state pride and

Alaska is a beautiful state of which to be proud. But if you are thinking about running for president some day then you might not want to insult most of the country's population at every opportunity. "The lower 48", according to Sarah Palin, must be full of raving idiots.

There was never any mention of Hawaii. Maybe Palin thinks they already know how to raise their children right. Unlike "those people".

An interesting sequence was where Palin and the mother with eight children went to a firing range to practise shooting at bear targets. Just in case. As if their only line of defence was Sarah Palin and the mother with eight children. The mother with eight children had never handled a firearm and made that fact perfectly clear. She genuinely seemed not to know what the instructor was talking about.

But much has been made of Palin's shooting at wolves from aircraft. Ignoring the fact that hunters generally consider this cowardly and point out that it is what poachers do, it takes a certain level of skill to hit a running animal from a moving aircraft. I would doubt that I could do it. When Palin was at the firing range she could not hit the side of a bullet with a barn.

Worse than her aim was that she did not know the difference between a cartridge in the magazine or in the chamber. This is a very important safety distinction that everybody should know before they even touch a firearm. She also seemed overly concerned about recoil.

This is something that an experienced hunter would not worry about. It would be like an Olympic swimmer asking if the water in the pool will be too cold.

Sarah Palin is either very inexperienced with firearms or she suddenly became a decent actor when the script called for her character to not know anything about firearms.

There is also supposed to be footage of her father loading a weapon for her, and her putting her finger in the trigger guard when he passes it to her. To be fair I have not seen this but if it is true then not only does she not know anything about firearms but she should never be allowed near any until she gets a few lessons. You never grab or hold a firearm with any fingers in the trigger guard. That is about as stupid as putting the muzzle into your mouth for fun. It is like grabbing a knife by the blade. Except that when you grab a firearm by the trigger guard you can kill other people.

There are entire websites dedicated to showing how Sarah Palin is not much of a hunter or fisherman. I do not care about any of that. I am sure they are mostly politically motivated anyway. Few people ever discuss Sarah Palin without calling her either the greatest person in the world or a raving idiot.

Her TV programme likely only showed the tourist side of Alaska rather than getting into the real Alaska because that is what TV programmes do. None of these travel programmes ever show you anything that is not in all the tourist books.

But I found Sarah Palin very condescending when she was preaching the proper way to live your life and raise your children. None of my mother's daughters got knocked up when they were teenagers. And my mother was never as bitchy about it. Anybody who wants to tell an entire country how they should live their lives should probably not have so many skeletons in their closet.

And then she handles a loaded firearm like some street punk. If you are going to portray yourself as a rugged outdoor type but you do not know anything about the outdoors then you might not want to have a TV crew follow you around.

And she and her father were condescending toward that mother with eight children after everybody left. That is not my definition of hospitality. That is certainly not how "those people" in "the lower 48" do it.

This is where American politics loses me. Do Americans not have enough real problems without making new things up? If Sarah Palin wants to pretend to be somebody whom she is clearly not then that is her prerogative. But telling others to do as she preaches is simply bad form.

Barack Obama's chief of staff called some of his Democratic colleagues "fucking retarded". Then Sarah Palin told Obama that he should fire Rahm Emanuel. Not in a phone call. Not in a scathing letter to any editor. She told her president to lose his chief of staff on Facebook. I cannot say if Barack Obama is on Sarah

Palin's buddy list but we should assume that he heard about it just the same.

Sarah Palin's moral outrage has nothing to do with "fucking". It would be hard to support people like George Bush, Dick Cheney, John McCain and then tell others not to use profanity. And obviously fucking is common in the Palin household.

We all know that Palin has a son with Down's syndrome. We know this because she tells us every chance she gets. If she does not get a chance then she will make one. She is a maverick. So naturally Sarah Palin is offended by a Democratic leader calling other Democrats fucking retarded. I guess because there is some kind of connection between the son of a private citizen in Alaska who works for Republicans, and Democratic lawmakers in Washington who upset the president's staff. I am not sure what that connection is.

I think she is outraged over the word retarded.

> "*Just as we'd be appalled if any public figure of Rahm's stature ever used the 'N word' or other such inappropriate language, Rahm's slur on all God's children with cognitive and developmental disabilities - and the people who love them - is unacceptable.*"

So when you say that your colleagues are fucking retarded because they do not vote your way, you are actually insulting children with developmental issues. And of course their parents. We cannot forget them. They are the real heroes.

Did Sarah Palin just call the Democrats retarded? That is very clever if that was her intent.

But I do not think it was. I think she was just being overly politically correct. When the Republicans became neohippies and started protesting, I guess they joined the PC police as well. It is a very confusing time in America.

Ignoring the fact that what Rahm Emanuel said had nothing to do with mental retardation, ignoring the fact that people with Down's syndrome are not retarded, ignoring the fact that he said it six months before Sarah Palin decided to be outraged by it, ignoring the fact that Republicans have always consistently opposed political correctness, ignoring the fact that Palin gives people like Rush Limbaugh a free pass whenever he calls anybody retarded, what really caught my attention was Palin's comparison of calling somebody retarded to calling them "the N word".

She is so politically correct that she will not even say the word "nigger". The word means nothing where I come from but I realise that it means something there. So I cannot blame her for not saying it. But she did use it. She used it as a political weapon.

If an American calls you retarded he is not saying you suffer from mental retardation. They used to tell each other to go fly a kite.

That does not mean that they literally want to fly kites. You would have to be retarded to think that.

But if an American calls a black person an "N word" it means so much more. There is a long and bitter history between whites and blacks that simply does not exist between the mentally challenged and the mentally retarded.

If Rahm Emanuel went up to a retarded person and called him fucking retarded that would be something else. It would be bizarre. And his career would be over. Then it would be a fair hypothetical comparison with him calling a black American a nigger.

By saying that the words "retarded" and "nigger" have the same connotation, Sarah Palin is taking something away from her future black constituents. Eventually the word "airhead" will be off limits. Somebody will say that calling anybody an airhead is as offensive to blondes and the people who love them as the word nigger is to blacks.

If you agree with Palin and think both words are unacceptable then ask yourself this question, if you are an American, which word would you least likely use in public? I have used both here repeatedly. On purpose. Reading which makes you most uncomfortable?

What is most disappointing to me is that I liked Sarah Palin when she first became known. I usually support all female candidates until I learn how crazy they are. I liked the idea of the United States having a female vice president and I really did not like the way her opponents attacked her accent and Alaska itself. They said the same things their foes said of Bill Clinton and Arkansas. History always repeats itself eventually but in American politics it repeats itself every four to eight years.

I also felt a personal connection to Palin when she entered that endless campaign. She was the mayor of Wasilla when I lived nearby and I even met her briefly whilst I was heavily medicated. She seemed like a nice person at the time.

Then she started talking. She disappointed me repeatedly until she resigned as governor after only two and a half years. Alaska deserved better.

FABRICATED CONTROVERSIES

It is difficult to discuss Israeli politics without mentioning the conflict with Arab states. It can certainly be done. Israel is a lively democracy with sometimes interesting elections and more than enough protests over VATs, pensions, conscription, and a wide variety of issues. But Arab states are often a focal point in elections, and ignoring the many wars and invasions would be intellectually dishonest.

I also have a lot of opinions on the subject, so why not.

Before I moved to Israel I subscribed to the international media narrative that the people of Palestine were being oppressed and that Israel was doing everything it could to prevent peace. Then I watched Israel give away more land, more convicted prisoners, more concessions, more appeasement. Israel was willing to give up half of its land. The only thing it asked in return was that Arab terrorists stop trying to murder Israelis, many of whom are also Arab.

The Arab sides rejected every offer of peace because not enough of their demands were met. They took more land, more convicted prisoners, more concessions, more appeasement every time they came to the negotiating table but they never gave anything in return. No Arab leader ever made any attempt to prevent their terrorists from murdering Jews, Muslims, Druze, Christians, anybody else.

I was always told by people with extreme views that Israel was the bad guy and Palestine was the poor downtrodden. I was told by people with more moderate views that both sides were equally at fault. Equal weight was always given to a modern liberal democracy and brutal dictatorships. Soldiers in a 21st century regulated army were equal to 8th century fanatics who strap on 20th century weapons in the name of their religion.

The international media will tell you that the crimes of Israel are building houses on land that has been part of Israel for 3082 of the last 3100 years and forcing foreigners to go through checkpoints in order to enter Israel. The settlements are debatable and there is room for negotiation but I have never lived in any country that let foreigners enter without showing some form of identification.

The international media will never tell you

that Israel provides most of the electricity, water, health care to Palestine free of charge, and gives billions of dollars in aid every year.

Much is made of Israel's blockade of Gaza but Egypt's and Palestine's blockade of Gaza is rarely mentioned, if ever. They will tell you that the people of Gaza live in a prison but they never mention that their terrorist dictators are keeping them prisoner. They will never report that millions of tonnes of food, water, medicine, building materials are routinely shipped into Gaza from Israel while weapons are shipped in from Egypt.

If Israel sends one soldier or launches one airstrike at any of its neighbours it will be highlighted on CNN and BBC. But those news organisations ignore the thousands upon thousands of rockets fired at Israel from its neighbours. They might mention a suicide bomber if he successfully kills a few Israelis, and somehow a person who straps on a bomb to murder children is equal to a soldier who defends his country. They will never mention the thousands of terrorists who are stopped at checkpoints and fail to murder anybody.

The governments in Israel change with practically every election while the dictators in Palestine keep themselves in office by any means necessary. The leaders of Israel are democratically elected and democratically retired. The leaders of most Arab states are brutal dictators who kill more of their own people than any Israeli air strike ever has.

Israelis of every religion and race are free to

complain openly about anything and everything. And they do. They disagree with each other on a wide variety of issues. But most will agree that they should all be free to live as Israelis.

People living in Arab states have limited freedoms, and most have no freedom of the press. People in Gaza are routinely executed for speaking out against their terrorist leaders.

There is no Arab unity when it comes to living. Arab groups want to kill each other as much as they want to kill Jews. Sometimes more so. Recent events in Syria, Egypt, Iraq, Lebanon, Libya, Yemen, Sudan, Tunisia have dramatically illustrated this. Fatah and Hamas have been waging a civil war since 2007. The fact that Arab terrorists kill more Arab Israelis than they kill Jewish Israelis is no surprise.

The people of Palestine are indeed being oppressed. But not by Israel. They are oppressed by their own leaders and the leaders of their allies who use them as pawns in their quest to destroy each other and the only democracy as far as the eye can see.

I was raised to try to look at the other person's point of view in a disagreement. I find it difficult to imagine life as a Palestinian. I would rebel against my dictators and likely be executed.

Even if I did not rebel I would do something that women are not allowed to do and find myself on the wrong side of a stoning or honour killing. I would never flourish under such oppression.

But that is assuming that I understood just how bleak my life was. Since I would have little access to information not provided by the rulers I might blindly follow the hate and violence that they preach.

If I grew up with textbooks that had no room for any positive or even neutral views of Israel or Jews I might only hold negative views. If I were told from childhood that Israel should not exist and that dying to kill it was glorious and heroic I might actually believe it. Sometimes when that is all you are ever told that is all you know.

I do not question why people who live in Judea and Samaria, Gaza, and other lands controlled by brutal dictators might zealously believe that their side is never wrong and Israel is never right. In some places even the mere suggestion that maybe their dictators are fallible can make one disappear. But I always question why anybody who lives in a place with free access to information would preach hate and violence against people they will never know.

Even the smallest amount of research shows that Israel is a melting pot of religions and races from all over the world with laws that include everybody.

The future state of Palestine will be one race and one religion with laws against diversity and expression. I can see the point of view of extremists who want to subjugate their fellow man but I would never want to live like that. I have a hard time seeing the point of view of the people who willingly want to destroy an open society in favour of sectarian autocracy.

A high school biology textbook from the Palestinian Authority used to state that the Jewish brain was half the size of the Muslim brain. Maybe that is my problem.

Israeli Apartheid

Few subjects irritate me as much as this one. Not so much because I disagree with the people who compare Israel with South Africa but because the level of ignorance, whether accidental or deliberate, is staggering.

I can handle antisemitism because it is simple racism. Racist people are often dangerous and sometimes violent but always easy to laugh at. If God gave the Jews one thing it is our intrinsic sense of humour. We can laugh at a racist person because we know a good joke when we see one. And they are usually not the sharpest spikes on the rail.

People who think that Israel is an apartheid regime are a different breed. Some of them are obviously motivated by antisemitism. But there are also intelligent people without any particular religious or racial axe to grind who truly believe one of the largest piles of horse shit I have ever heard. They read the opinion pages of their local newspaper, at least back when people used to read newspapers, and watch interviews on TV by people like Jimmy Carter.

I am not going to get into his performance as president but I will point out that all of his trips to Israel equal about one month in the country. Combined that is a pretty good vacation but it hardly makes him an expert. I have spent about a month in Japan. Does that qualify me to tell them who they are?

I think I am in a pretty good position to have an opinion on both Israel and apartheid. I lived under apartheid for fifteen years and have lived in Israel since 2005. I am certainly not the only one but we are a very small club.

It could be pointed out that I was considered white under apartheid and I am definitely considered Jewish in Israel, so I have always been in the ruling class, for lack of a better term. But if you think that I do not know what discrimination is then you are likely an idiot and should just stop reading this now.

Desmond Tutu knows about apartheid. He helped kill it. He and Nelson Mandela did more than anybody else to build a rainbow nation and keep the whites from being summarily kicked out of the country. Or worse. Unlike Mandela, Tutu has spoken out against the corrupt Jacob Zuma administration. He has spoken out for children and against violence. When it comes to African politics, Desmond Tutu knows what he is talking about.

But his experience with a lifetime of oppression seems to have given him the impression that whichever side of an argument has the least power is oppressed. That is not always true. Not everything happening here is the equivalent of what happened there. It is like comparing apples to asparagus.

Everybody has the right to blindly hate Jews or blindly worship Palestine to satisfy their prejudices or for whatever reason they want. But equating Israeli Jews with whites under apartheid or Palestine with blacks under apartheid is intellectually dishonest.

South Africa under apartheid was not a democracy by any stretch of the imagination. Blacks were not citizens of their own country. They could not vote in elections or hold any public office. Since they were not citizens of any country they could not get passports to go elsewhere. Not that many blacks had enough money to go anywhere. There was no legal black infrastructure and the only way to make any money was to work for whites. They could not use white hospitals, schools, parks, transportation.

Every Israeli citizen has the same rights and responsibilities as every other Israeli citizen, regardless of religion, race, gender, sexuality. Most Israeli leaders are Jewish but that is likely because most Israelis are Jewish. It is not a requirement. Israel is a liberal democracy with elected representatives from every religion, race, gender. There are laws against discrimination just like any other advanced democracy. Israelis of any race can leave the country any time and live somewhere else if they want.

The people of Palestine have limited rights, especially women, homosexuals, Christians.

Palestine is a dictatorship. Their president was never elected and his term ended in 2009, yet he continues to rule. Most Palestinians cannot legally leave the country, except to go into Israel. And if they go into neighbouring Arab states they are usually forced into refugee camps and never allowed to assimilate into that country.

Palestine's infrastructure should be the responsibility of the Palestinian government, though they get a great deal of assistance from Israel. That electricity, water, health care does not grow on date trees. Some people used to complain that Israeli funded hospitals in Palestine were occupation. But when Israel completely pulled out of Gaza those same people complained that Israel was hindering Palestinian access to health care.

People like Desmond Tutu have compared Israeli checkpoints with apartheid pass laws. But there is no similarity.

Under apartheid, blacks had to live where the government told them to live. This usually meant going into and through white areas to work. They had to show the police their identification and employment papers every time they went to work since they were foreigners in their own country.

Israeli checkpoints are where people enter and exit Israel from Palestine. To do so you have to show a passport or some form of identification just as you would to enter almost any country from another. It is not discrimination to ask foreigners to show some kind of ID before letting them in the country. If checkpoints are the same as apartheid pass laws then so is every passport control at every international airport in the world.

Palestinians do not have to work in Israel but many do because there are fewer jobs in Palestine. Rather than discriminating against Palestinians, I would say it is rather nice of Israel to let so many people in the country without passports. Though it is done because it is a good idea economically and not so much for any humanitarian reasons. Does your country let in foreigners without passports? If so, are you oppressing those people by making them show ID to enter?

Much has been made of checkpoints and the security fence. Some people like to call it a wall even though only ten percent is an actual wall. They like to compare it to the Berlin Wall, which was built to keep people in. The security fence was built to keep people out. A better comparison is the Great Wall of China, though Israel's is much uglier.

The biggest difference being that the Great Wall failed while Israel's fence has helped to reduce terrorist attacks by five thousand percent. People like to complain that Israel is keeping foreigners out but Palestinians can go to Jerusalem simply by showing some form of identification. Nobody complains that the Palestinian government will not let Israelis into Bethlehem.

Under apartheid, people were not supposed to interact with other ethnic groups, except in a white superior/black inferior situation. Apartheid means separate. Not separate but equal. Just separate. Blacks lived there, whites lived here. Friendship between the two was actually illegal, though difficult to enforce. Interracial or homosexual marriage was a fantasy.

In Israel you can live wherever you want, assuming you can afford to live in the neighbourhood. There are Jewish employees with Arab employers, and whoever your friends are is your own business. I can marry an Arab, European, Muslim, Christian, Palestinian, Mongolian, woman or man. Any single adult human basically.

Palestinian Muslim females can marry Palestinian Muslim males chosen by their families. Muslim males can have more than one Muslim wife while the wife can only have one husband. Muslims and Christians cannot marry each other. Christians are blocked access to some facilities and services and largely persecuted all across the board without media attention or international outrage.

There was no freedom of the press under apartheid. Newspapers were routinely ordered by the state to retract stories and were under constant threat of banning. To be banned under apartheid was basically to be put under house arrest. It was often used as the first step in quieting dissent.

Israeli media can say pretty much whatever they want, other than publish state secrets and hate speech. Some people have complained that recent governments have been more and more liberal in ignoring what may or may not be considered hate speech. The press are free to criticise anything having to do with the government, and routinely do. International reporters are usually given restricted access to combat operations, just as they are under American and British governments.

There is no freedom of the press in Palestine. Media outlets are tightly controlled and it is illegal to say anything against the Abbas government, just as it was against Arafat. Newspapers and TV are routinely anti Israel, mostly because reporters who write stories that are favourable to Israel are labelled collaborators and threatened, attacked and/or killed. International reporters have very limited access to combat operations and there is a history of intimidation and coercion from the dictatorship.

Apartheid whites never denied that blacks were there first. It has always been a mostly black continent. Most whites originally came from Holland and Britain. The earliest conflicts were more British and Dutch than black and white. Apartheid was a system where a very small minority controlled a much larger majority.

You can argue all day over who was in Israel and Palestine first. We know that Jews were here a few thousand years BCE and the tribes eventually became Saul's united Kingdom of Israel.

What we now call Lebanon, Syria, Jordan

were various Bedouin and Semitic tribes with a wide variety of different names. Whether those people evolved into what we now call Arabs is debatable and the answer depends largely on one's politics.

It was not until Islam came along that people decided Jews and Arabs all arrived on the scene at the same time. Or that Arabs came first, depending on your point of view. According to Islam, Ishmael was the first Arab Muslim and Isaac was the first Jew. Since Ishmael was born first, Arabs came first.

That is a bit of a stretch for a lot of reasons and I shall ignore how the Muslim story of Ishmael and Issac is different from the Jewish story. Even though the Muslim claim that they were here first is dependent on their religious history, it is very important that the Israeli/Palestinian issue is not viewed by the rest of the world in religious terms. If people think of it as Jews versus Muslims then there is no realistic way that Muslims were here before Jews. Despite the Ishmael and Issac claim, Jews were here thousands of years before Islam existed. Christians were here hundreds of years before Islam existed. Everybody was here before Muslims.

No matter who was where when, the modern state of Israel is here to stay. Arab extremists might as well accept it. We are not going anywhere.

The Philistines owned what is now a small part of western Israel? Congratulations. Israel used to own large chunks of what are now Syria and Jordan. England used to own the United States. Holland used to own Indonesia. Things change.

It might be worth noting that the Philistines died out a long time ago. The name sounds similar to Palestine but they are not the same people. The word Deutsch looks like Dutch but they are very much not the same language. It is probable that the Philistines were originally Greek. Does anybody advocate giving Gaza to Greece?

What will some day be the modern state of Palestine is also probably here to stay. It takes up almost half of what was Saul's Kingdom but Israelis might as well get used to it. When we give up more and more land for very temporary peace, that land is gone. Don't want to lose more land? Stop giving it away to people who are only going to use it as a missile base.

The conflict between blacks and whites under apartheid was a domestic racial issue with more than a hint of economic oppression. Blacks wanted equality while whites wanted absolute control. Most of the violence was committed by armed black militias and armed white police. The rest of the world pretty much stayed out of it. No other country ever invaded to help the blacks or the whites.

The conflict between Israel and Palestine is an international border dispute. Israelis want peace with its neighbours while Palestinian leaders want all of the land. Palestinian terrorist groups are supported by the governments of Palestine, Iran, Syria, and sometimes Lebanon. Israel has been invaded by all of its neighbours. Not for the sake of Palestinians, whom most Arab governments demonstrably do not care about, but to destroy Jews.

Apartheid governments did not deny the right of blacks to exist. They simply wanted them to exist in the corner out of sight. Israel does not deny anybody's right to exist. Palestinian leaders have always denied Israel's right to exist. Its leaders, fanatics, foreign leaders and their fanatics have been actively trying to eliminate Israel's existence for many years.

Israel is to apartheid what I am to an Olympic gymnast. Jews, Arabs, everybody else can and do work and play side by side in Israel. How much did blacks and whites integrate during apartheid? Jews are illegal in Palestine.

There are Arabs and Christians in Israel's Knesset. How many blacks were members of parliament during apartheid? How many Jews are in the Palestinian Authority?

Jews and Arabs can marry and live together openly in Israel. How many blacks married whites during apartheid? Bring your Jewish spouse into Palestine and see what happens.

According to the Talmud, the world stands on three things: justice, truth, peace. Apartheid had nothing to do with any of them. Israel's society is based on all of them. Palestine is an oppressive dictatorship.

There are only two reasons to claim that Israel is an apartheid state. One of them is ignorance or a blind trust in lazy journalism. The other has nothing to do with peace and love.

Take a Cruiser With All Hands

You say eviction, we say evacuation. You say occupation, we say sovereignty. Let's call the whole thing off.

Much to nobody's surprise Israel's High Court upheld the eviction/evacuation in August 2009 of two Palestinian families from Sheikh Jarrah to make way for a new apartment complex. But I guess some people were surprised since it got a lot of airtime. Legally the High Court did the only thing they could. Their job is not to set policy. They merely interpret the law. According to the law those Palestinians had to go.

Anybody who knows anything about prime minister Benjamin Netanyahu should not be at all surprised that he favours moving Palestinians out of Jerusalem. But this action began long before Netanyahu was prime minister. He could have stopped it but both British and American diplomats told him to. A word of friendly advice, if you are a foreigner and you tell Netanyahu not to do something in Israel then he will be more adamant about doing it. Try reverse psychology next time. It might not work but it is worth a go.

The British consulate said that these evictions will make it harder to divide

Jerusalem once Palestine finally gets the statehood that they have always rejected. I think they have missed the pass. Israel does not want to divide Jerusalem. No tiered politician, from the largest hawk to the sweetest dove, wants to divide Jerusalem. We did that in 1948 and it did not work out very well. For anybody.

The United Nations envoy to the Middle East said that evicting people was against the Geneva Conventions guidelines for occupied territory. Ignoring for a moment that the International Community did not complain in any way when Jews were evicted from Jerusalem after it was torn in two by an unprovoked military invasion, somebody needs to tell the United Nations that Israel does not consider any part of Israel occupied territory.

I would like Tel Aviv to be the capital just as much as any European. It would make my life easier on a number of levels. But sooner or later we are all going to have to face the fact that Jerusalem is Israel's capital. You cannot decide our capital any more than we can decide yours. And if we can then I say San Francisco is America's new capital. Just to force all those politicians to live there. Republicans will love the Castro.

And is evicting people from a building they do not own really against the Geneva Conventions? I was almost evicted once when I was at university. I suppose I should have contacted the nearest human rights advocate. I know there was one somewhere. Probably a

Jew.

And anybody whose job title is United Nations envoy to the Middle East should be sacked immediately. None of the parties involved care what the UN says. You might as well make Tony Blair a special peace envoy. That would be funny if it were not so appalling.

The American foreign minister at the time said the eviction was "unhelpful". Strong words indeed. I think she knows that screaming at Benjamin Netanyahu will only strengthen his resolve. She seems smarter than most of the politicians in her country or mine. Too bad her husband is a whore. That combined with the fact that she is a woman and she will never be president of the United States.

While I sympathise with the two families that have to move somewhere else, I can see why this happened legally and politically. And I do not know why there is such an outcry from the ever opinionated International Community. I do know why but if you take away the politically correct self righteousness then this is not the worst thing Israel has ever done. Not even close.

Security forces evicted or evacuated an entire Jewish settlement at Reches Sela on the same day as the High Court ruling without any outrage from the International Community. Why is there outrage over the Palestinian families who lost their homes but silence over the Jewish families who lost theirs? To paraphrase Shylock, if you send us out into the cold do we not chill?

What makes this whole affair incredibly stupid is the timing. The International Community do not approve of us just now. They are still upset over that Gaza incident. I think invading Gaza was justified, even if ineffective. But the International Community were terribly offended despite some of them conducting their own invasions at the time. If they publicly proclaim outrage over our invasion of an Arab neighbourhood then maybe Arabs will ignore their invasions of different Arab neighbourhoods. I hope they have a backdoor plan.

Israeli leaders should know by now that anything they do that might upset any Arabs is going to upset the International Community. This includes our existence, of course. And just about everything we do will upset the United Kingdom. We should not let the leaders of larger countries and their appointed minions tell us how to run our country when they visit us and some token Arab state for "negotiations". But would it kill us to maybe slow down the evictions and settlements until the sympathy pendulum swings a little our way?

Arabs are the most hated ethnic group to Americans and Europeans just now. They will move on to hate some other race sooner or later but for now they fear Arabs far more than they fear Jews. That really says something considering how long they have feared Jews.

If an American sees a man in a turban he thinks terrorist. If he sees a man in a kippah he thinks lawyer. Yet we keep coming across as the bad guy. The United States and United Kingdom, liberal democracies with a free press and basic human rights, favour totalitarian Arab dictatorships with state run media, laws against anybody different from themselves, executions of minors and homosexuals, over Israel, a liberal democracy with a free press and basic human rights. We are clearly doing something wrong.

Obviously "The West" favours Arab states because collectively there are far more corporate customers than Israel will ever have and most Arab states will not invest in any corporations that are also doing business in Israel. But when they claim moral outrage instead of economic expediency then one has to question their moral superiority.

Benjamin Netanyahu has spoken to the American congress a few times. It was a big media event the latest time. You probably saw it on the news even if you are not American or Israeli. It was on American news because somebody gave a big speech in Washington. It was all over the rest of the world because it happened in the United States. If Netanyahu gives a speech in New Delhi you will never hear about it unless you live in Israel or India. But anything happening in the United States is automatically important to the rest of the world. At least according to the people in charge of newspapers and TV news.

I am not a great fan of Netanyahu's. But I do think that he is doing a better job than Ehud

Olmert. Some people assume that makes me conservative. But I wanted Tzipi Livni to become prime minister. And she is more liberal than both of them. The main difference between Netanyahu and Olmert is not where they stand on the political spectrum. Netanyahu is a decent man, if more than a little arrogant. Olmert was a dick.

The speech itself was nothing groundbreaking. It is not going to make anybody who knows what is going on think about anything differently. But it was still a pretty good speech. And I think it would make a decent primer for anybody who does not know what is going on.

There were a few interesting points.

> *"Of the 300 million Arabs in the Middle East and North Africa, only Israel's Arab citizens enjoy real democratic rights. Of those 300 million Arabs, less than one half of one percent are truly free, and they're all citizens of Israel."*

This point pretty much says all you need to know about why Arab leaders have kept Palestinians in refugee camps for so long. Refugees anywhere else in the world are either integrated into that country or sent away. Palestinians in Lebanon, Syria, Saudi Arabia, Egypt are forced to stay in camps indefinitely. Only Jordan has ever let any of them become part of their society.

"There is something that makes the outrage even greater: The lack of outrage. In much of the international community, the calls for our destruction are met with utter silence. It is even worse because there are many who rush to condemn Israel for defending itself."

I have been saying this for years. The International Community are always silent whenever anybody does anything against Israel. But should Israel harm one hair on one terrorist's head there is moral outrage. It is a crime against humanity to harm a terrorist who actively targets children but it is fair and proper to support terrorists who target children. It is almost interesting if you can look at it objectively. In what other country in the world would this ever be the case?

"I recognize that in a genuine peace, we will be required to give up parts of the Jewish homeland. In Judea and Samaria, the Jewish people are not foreign occupiers. We are not the British in India. We are not the Belgians in the Congo. No distortion of history can deny the four thousand year old bond between the Jewish people and the Jewish land."

Any Jew or Israeli would hear this part and think, no kidding, Mr Obvious. Jews have been here forever. Judea and Samaria were part of Israel before they were taken by Jordan and then taken back by Israel. Everybody knows that.

But in the recent world of politically correct global politics this seems to be completely forgotten. Those who do not know history see Israel labelled as the occupier so often that they assume it must be true. They have no idea that Israel took this area back after Jordan's second invasion because the international media only mention that Israel took it and not that it was part of Israel. And you know what they say, those who do not learn the lessons of history talk about it all day online.

> *"Our conflict has never been about the establishment of a Palestinian state. It has always been about the existence of the Jewish state."*

This pretty much says all you need to know about the mindset of our neighbours. There could have been stable peace a dozen different times if Arab states would simply accept that Israel is here. Nobody is saying that they cannot continue to hate all Jews. All they are asked to do is accept that we exist.

When the British eventually let most of the land become a sovereign Arab state and a tiny piece of the land become a sovereign Jewish state, the Jews went to work building a modern democracy, and the Arabs went to work trying to wipe Israel off the map. The Arab state became Jordan but it was never enough. The Arab League wanted all or nothing. Jordan has since accepted the fact that it will never border the Mediterranean but the Arab League still pursues a policy of complete Arab domination.

> *"As for Jerusalem, only a democratic Israel has protected freedom of worship for all faiths in the city."*

The more you think about this the more amazing it is. In all of Jerusalem's 5000 year history, and all of the times it changed hands, only when it was under Israeli law could Jews, Christians, Muslims, Druze, anybody else freely do their thing. Only Israel has had Jerusalem as a democracy. Every other group that controlled the city was a dictatorship in one form or another.

To be fair, most of those religions were not around 5000 years ago but the point remains. There is no reason to assume that if Jerusalem were controlled by an Arab dictatorship that it would be a democratic city.

In the interest of balance against Netanyahu's speech calling for peace with Palestine I was going to discuss a speech by a Palestinian leader who called for peace with Israel. But there are none.

"American Secretary of State John Kerry, who came here very determined and operates based upon an unfathomable obsession and messianic fervor, cannot teach me anything about the Palestinians. I live and breathe the conflict with the Palestinians. I know what they think, what they want and what they really mean. The American security plan that was presented to us is not worth the paper it was written on. It contains no peace and no security. The only thing that might save us is if John Kerry wins the Nobel prize and leaves us be."

Defence Minister Moshe Ya'alon scratched some thin skin when he made these comments. As he has been doing for a long time. When will these sneaky Jews learn not to speak ill of their American saviours?

The funny part is how the American leaders are so terribly hurt and offended. Is this really the worst thing anybody has ever said about them? These people would not last a day in our shoes. This reminds me of the first time somebody called Barack Obama a liar during a congressional speech. Obama's people were twisting their panties over that one. I bet they look back on those days with longing.

John Kerry, for his part, has only given diplomatic responses. As far as I know. It is others who are trying to fuel this, not him. Like him or not, Moshe Ya'alon is a military expert in this field and he will tell you what he thinks of your agenda. Obama's team has no choice but to attack him.

Now many Americans, largely ignorant of their own foreign policies, will once again say that the United States should stop giving money to Israel. I think they would be very surprised if they knew how all that military aid actually worked. I think many of them would plotz if they realised how much research and technology Israel provides the United States as a result of that military aid.

Some Israelis will say that while Moshe Ya'alon makes an obvious point, we should be nicer to our closest ally. Especially when that ally is so sensitive.

Many Arabs will say this is proof that Jews are evil and should all be exterminated. There is nothing new there.

But what people should think about after this is all old news next week is that there will never be peace here as long as the United States tries to dictate that peace. There is nothing wrong with bringing in mediators to negotiate between Israel and terrorist leaders but those mediators should be somebody whom both sides trust, for lack of a better word, to some degree.

Nobody trusts the United States. They are in it for their own corporate interests. And for the Nobel Prize to a certain extent. They do not give a rat's tuchas about Israel's desire to not be murdered or about Arab terrorists' desire to murder Jews. Neither Jews nor Arabs are at the top of America's list of favourites. We are barely a notch above Africans as far as they are concerned.

I always wanted Thabo Mbeki to come here and do his thing. He was a skilled mediator. But then that corrupt asshole Jacob Zuma did his thing. Maybe it is unfair to blame Jacob Zuma for the troubles in Judea. But he is a corrupt asshole. Nobody can deny that with a straight face.

Moshe Ya'alon has never been my favourite person in the world. He was Chief of Staff when I was at Bahad 1. He said some things about female officers that can safely be described as ridiculously stupid. But his frustration at American presidents and secretaries of state who come here with academic theories about life in the Levant and tell us how we should exist is understandable.

Sooner or later the United States is going to have to realise that trying to force everybody to do it your way has failed miserably. Every continent in the world can attest to that.

Mia's Peace Plan

1. First and foremost, stop killing each other. This may seem like an obvious point but it has clearly been lost on all involved. And when I say stop killing each other I mean everybody stop killing anybody, not just whichever side

you do not like stop killing whichever side you like.

Israel has every right to defend its citizens and borders but month long offensives against entire Palestinian cities when one Israeli is injured or killed by Palestinian rockets has to end. The rationale has always been that if their attacks are met with a multiplied response then they will think twice about attacking again. That is clearly not working.

The people who do the initial attacking are usually not the people who have to deal with the response, and the countries that financially support Palestinian terrorists really do not care how many Palestinians are killed. The more the better for their agenda. Israel should instead target the people responsible whenever an attack occurs. We usually know who they are.

Failing that, Israel should announce its intention to respond to attacks against its citizens and soil in an orderly fashion. When anybody fires rockets into Israel from what we shall now call Palestine, Israel will first demand that the Palestinian Authority bring the people responsible to justice. When they do absolutely nothing then Israel will ask the United Nations to take appropriate action.

An act of war against Israel should be given equal treatment as an act of war against any other country. When the UN does nothing Israel will then be free to exercise any response option it sees fit and resolve the situation with all available resources. Those countries that favour Palestinian terrorism will be given time to convince the Palestinian Authority to bring the terrorists responsible to justice.

Should the International Community wish to respond then it will be given the opportunity to pressure the Palestinian Authority and United Nations to act. This is the appropriate time for moral outrage. If you did not complain to Palestine when it attacked Israel then do not complain to Israel when it responds.

If any territory is seized by Israel in any future retaliatory engagements it will be at the discretion of Israel. Anybody who does not want their land seized is free to take whatever actions are available to them to prevent terrorism in their community and use the election process to keep the countries that financially support terrorists out of their government. You cannot claim you want peace whilst idly watching your neighbours kill people.

2. Israel, Egypt, and the Palestinian Authority should immediately withdraw their blockade on Gaza, including the naval blockade. Any country that is attacked from this district is free to follow the steps outlined in Point 1. Any naval attacks carried out from Gaza against any country are subject to military response in accordance with international admiralty law.

When the blockade is lifted, Israel will no longer be obligated to provide food, fuel, electricity, materials, medical aid, humanitarian supplies to the people of Gaza.

Israel will continue to provide water for a set period of time, at which point the leadership of Gaza can negotiate future supplies.

Egypt and the United States will no longer be obligated to provide financial assistance to the people of Gaza. The leadership of Gaza will be free to negotiate the continuation of such supplies as it sees fit.

Israel will no longer have any obligation to allow anybody from Gaza to enter Israeli soil. Egypt and the Palestinian Authority can continue their policy of restricted access at their discretion.

The economic stability of Gaza will be the sole responsibility of its leadership and people of Gaza, pursuant to any negotiations and treaties it holds with other countries. The terrorist organisation that currently control this district will be held legally responsible for any materials and supplies that they prevent from reaching the intended destinations.

3. Stop building settlements. If Palestine is not part of Israel then Israelis have no right to build homes there. If Israelis have the right to build homes in Palestine then it is part of Israel and should be brought under Israeli control. Israel seized most of Judea and Samaria from Jordan in 1967, who seized it from Israel in 1948. If you think it is God's command that everybody build their house in the middle of Judea and Samaria then you should have done so years ago.

All settlements east of the barrier fence should be evacuated and all settlements west remain, as should Beit El.

Since Palestinian leaders will never agree to this, Israel and Palestine can settle on a population number and all settlements with a smaller population should be evacuated and all settlements with a larger population remain. In the guaranteed event that Israel and Palestine cannot agree on the population then representatives from three countries that really do not care either way should pick a number.

Returning the border to the 1967 armistice line is unrealistic, as is the 1949 line or the completely absurd 1947 line. A lot has changed since 1967. The barrier fence is a far better border since leaving large Israeli settlements within Palestine would be difficult to secure.

The 1967 line rewards Jordan for violently taking land that the International Community never protested. The British 1947 line only leaves both Israel and Palestine as islands of land weakly connected to each other.

Over two million people live in Judea and Samaria. Just over 300 000 of them are Israeli. Moving Israelis out will be logistically difficult and likely cripple the local economy but Israel will save money that would otherwise be spent protecting these towns and providing economic aid.

Palestine can deal with the economic issues as it sees fit. As a sovereign state it will be as responsible for its own economy as every other sovereign state. Israel should provide initial economic assistance to Palestine but it is under no obligation to do so once the IDF are out.

Israel should continue to provide water to Judea and Samaria until such time as the Palestinian Authority can somehow guarantee its own supply. Most aid to Palestine should stop but Israel should not let the people of Palestine die from lack of water.

Since history has shown that there is always an escalation of violence whenever Israeli settlements are evacuated, and removing Israeli security from Judea and Samaria is guaranteed to increase acts of terrorism against Israel, the Palestinian Authority will be responsible for security in the former settlements and Israel will be responsible for removing all materials and equipment that can be used against it. There should be nothing but empty land where any settlements once stood.

4. Palestine will grant all Palestinians and any Arabs, regardless of religion, who consider themselves Palestinian the right of return to Palestine at the discretion of Palestine's leadership. Palestinians will not have the right of return to Israel just as Israelis do not have the right of return to Palestine or any other Arab territory.

Many Palestinians left Israel sixty years ago and many Israelis left what we are now calling Palestine as well as other neighbouring Arab states. No Arab state has ever suggested that the Israelis should have the right of return. Flooding Israel with Arab refugees only serves a political agenda and does not contribute to peace in any way whatever. But if any Arab state is willing to let all of those Israelis and their descendants back in then maybe we can discuss the issue further.

If the Arab states that currently house many of these refugees would put aside their political agenda and allow them to integrate into those societies then it would not even be an issue. Where else in the world are refugees still living in camps sixty years later? Lebanon, Syria, Saudi Arabia, Egypt should finally allow these people the option to become citizens. Or at least contribute in some way to those states. Jordan did and they are the better for it.

5. Jerusalem is the capital of Israel. Deal with it. Jerusalem has always been the capital of modern Israel and was the capital of ancient Israel about 1500 years before Islam existed. It was never the capital of Palestine. There has never been a country called Palestine in the entire history of the world.

When you are building a new country you do not get to claim another country's capital as your own. South Sudan did not claim Khartoum as their capital. Macedonia did not get to claim Belgrade. If Quebec becomes an independent country they will not get to decide that Washington DC is their capital. It is never going to happen. Using this as a precondition to avoid discussing peace only serves more war.

Despite my perceived bias on this issue it is simply a logical choice. If you take a religious view then Jerusalem belongs to Israel. The city is important to Jews, Muslims, Christians but more important to Jews than anybody else.

It is Judaism's holiest city and Islam's third

holiest city. I do not know where Christianity ranks it but I have never heard of any Christian country that claimed it as their capital. And Judaism was around longer than the others. Islam is relatively new as far as religions go.

Jerusalem was under Jewish control for about 2000 years, Roman control for 500 years, Arab control for 400 years, Ottoman control for 400 years, Christian control for almost 100 years. The Christians were not very nice to Jews or Muslims and I think we have all decided they cannot have it back. The Romans were not very nice to anybody but their empire is long gone.

Jerusalem's current population is somewhere under one million. About seventy percent of those people are Israeli citizens. The other thirty percent are citizens of other countries, mostly in Europe, Russia, Jordan, United States, or hold Israeli ID cards but are not Israeli citizens, or claim only Palestine citizenship.

While the Muslim population is increasing and the Jewish population is decreasing, the number of Israelis remain stable relative to population growth. Moving all Israelis out of Jerusalem would be logistically absurd and would decimate the local economy. It just does not make any sense to move the overwhelming majority of people out of an established and fully developed city to make room for new people. It also completely contradicts the idea that Israeli settlements should be abandoned because those Jews are newer inhabitants.

Recent history has shown that when Jerusalem was divided it was difficult or impossible for Jews and Christians to enter important Jewish and Christian sites, many of which were repeatedly desecrated. As a united city, access has been unrestricted to everybody and important Muslim sites are under the jurisdiction of local Muslim leaders.

Dividing the city was detrimental to the local economy as movement of goods and people was heavily restricted. The economy has flourished as a united city and its citizens are free to travel.

6. Set a deadline for the formal creation of a sovereign Palestine and remove all Israeli military and security forces. At that point Palestine either has to step up to the plate or get off the field. If they refuse to have their own country yet again then make the territory part of Jordan, Syria, Lebanon or some kind of United Nations no man's land.

Once Palestine's leaders reject further proposals for a sovereign Palestine then they can no longer claim homeland privileges and must accept the rights and responsibilities of citizenship in whatever country Palestine is placed. If it is divided amongst several countries then its people will be given the opportunity to relocate to another area that is part of whichever of those countries they choose.

Alternately, a democratic election can be held at an announced date and whoever is elected will then become the leaders of what will then be called Palestine. Any country that wishes to recognise it may do so. Israel should be the first.

Those Palestinians who do not want to live in a sovereign Palestine will have the option to immigrate to any other country they wish, provided that other country accepts them. Any Arab country other than Jordan likely will not but everybody is welcome to try.

Should the leaders of Palestine finally accept a sovereign country then it is their responsibility to govern and control the people and territory without reliance on Israel for their survival or blaming Israel for all of their problems. Any acts of war committed by the people of Palestine or its leaders against any other sovereign country will be subject to the same consequences every other country in the world faces. See Point 1.

As a sovereign country Palestine will be free to negotiate any military and economic treaties with any country it sees fit, including those countries that have sworn to destroy Israel at all costs. Palestine should also be aware that as a sovereign country no other country is under any obligation to provide economic and humanitarian assistance. In other words, treaties with Iran and Syria might mean the loss of all that money, food, electricity from Israel and the United States. Maybe Iran will provide free health care to your people. Maybe not.

With the creation of a sovereign Palestine most of the Arab world will lose their only reason to wish death upon Israel and all Israelis. It is not like they want us all to die simply because we are Jewish, is it? This is the only logical reason why some of these countries have gone out of their way to keep Palestine as it is and refused to allow Palestinians within their borders any of the rights that every other immigrant would naturally receive.

To avoid any suppression of open hostility and bigotry, all Arab states that so choose will be released from any obligations to recognise Israel and treat Israelis as fellow human beings. Just because there is a Palestine does not mean that you have to stop hating. But you have to either let Palestine exist or stop trying to kill every Jew on the planet. You cannot have it both ways.

This plan would be summarily rejected by Palestinian dictators and every Arab state in the world for the following reasons:

A. All peace plans not submitted by Arab leaders have always been summarily rejected by Palestinian dictators and every Arab state in the world, except Jordan and Egypt.

B. It calls on Palestine's leaders to contain terrorist activities. This has always been rejected by Palestinian leaders as a non-negotiable condition in every peace conference. They have always refused to negotiate for peace if it means rejecting terrorism. Make of that what you will.

C. It calls on Israel to disengage from Palestine but does not require Israel to provide assistance to Palestine. This has always been rejected by Palestinian leaders as a non-negotiable condition in every peace conference. Palestinian leaders have always rejected the removal of Israeli money and aid.

D. It allows for some Israeli settlements to remain. This has always been rejected by Palestinian leaders as a non-negotiable condition in every peace conference.

E. It rejects Palestinian right of return to Israel. This has always been rejected by Palestinian leaders as a non-negotiable condition in every peace conference.

F. It allows Israel to retain control of Jerusalem. This has always been rejected by Palestinian leaders as a non-negotiable condition in every peace conference.

G. It sets a deadline for the creation of a sovereign Palestine. This has always been rejected by Palestinian leaders as a non-negotiable condition in every peace conference.

This plan would be summarily rejected by Israel for the following reasons:

A. It was written without any input by any elected Israeli officials. How can anybody use it to get reelected if they were not involved?

If that sounds unbalanced against Palestine then consider that Israel has routinely made concessions and compromised at its own expense without seeing any decrease in violence against Israel or acceptance of Israel's existence by its neighbours.

Israel has to release convicted murderers from prisons and give up land just to get Palestinian leaders to the table. Palestine's leaders have never begun a single negotiation without conditions. The Palestinian side has rejected every single Israeli proposal and every American and European proposal that required some compromise, and has never agreed to any concessions. At every peace summit Palestine's leaders are only willing to accept proposals that incorporate every one of their demands.

I do not understand why a country that does not officially exist gets to set all the rules. Where has that ever happened anywhere else in the world? The time has come to either take what they can get or declare an outright war against Israel. Either accept your country and take responsibility for it or just come out and say that you want nothing less than the complete destruction of Israel. Playing the victim loses something when you do everything you can to make sure that nothing ever changes. Making your adversary bend over backward simply to get you to talk only goes so far. Bending over backward eventually brings them back to the front again.

This peace plan is applicable in the Levant only. The rest of the world is on its own.

A Brief History of Two States

1917: The Balfour Declaration favoured creating a Jewish state in what would soon become the British Mandate of Palestine, what is now Israel, Jordan, Palestine. Everybody wanted the Ottoman Turks out. Arabs wanted all the Jews out as well.

1920: Jews were buying more and more land and prospering whilst Arab groups began protesting. The first riots began and Arabs started attacking Jewish towns. In March, Arab protesters killed eight Jews in Tel Hai. Arabs believed that the British favoured the Jews. Jews believed the British were not doing enough to police the Arabs. And the British greatly underestimated the entire situation.

In April 1920 a week long riot in Jerusalem was largely ignored by the British. Jewish leaders volunteered to defend Jewish residents but the British refused. Hundreds of Jews were evacuated anyway. This would later be "proof" that Jews left their homes voluntarily.

1921: When a Jewish communist group held a rally in Jaffa and a Jewish socialist group held a rally in Tel Aviv on the same day, British police called on local Arabs to help keep the peace. Once the Jewish groups started fighting each other the Arabs joined in and attacked houses and a hotel, killing dozens.

1929: Petty crimes and harassment against Jews in Hebron turned violent when hundreds of Jews marched to Hakotel Hama'aravi and sang songs. One murder quickly turned into 67. The entire Jewish population of Hebron was evacuated. This would later be "proof" that Jews left their homes voluntarily. Riots spread throughout Jerusalem, killing 133 Jews and about 100 Arabs. About 200 Arabs and 30 Jews were arrested.

1935: The first armed Palestinian terrorist

organisation was created. Their mission was to remove all Jews and British from the area. Their first attack killed two Palestinian police officers. The British retaliated and the group's leader was killed.

1936: The new terrorists killed two Jews. A new Jewish military group set up in response of the Hebron Massacre killed two Arabs who probably had nothing to do with the terrorists. The Arabs killed more Jews in retaliation and the Jews killed more Arabs. Thousands of Jewish farms were destroyed. This would later be "proof" that Jews left their homes voluntarily.

Arabs went on strike in April and stopped paying British taxes. Terrorist attacks against railways, oil pipelines, Jewish communities became all the rage. The British reacted violently, killing over one thousand Arabs, demolishing houses, imposing fines of over one million pounds collectively to mostly poor farmers.

Before the strike most Arabs thought the British were pro Jewish and anti Arab where in reality the British had bent over backward to satisfy Arab demands. After the strike and terrorist attacks the British became pro Jewish and anti Arab. Jews were allowed to create armed military groups and serve with British police, as Arabs had been doing for years.

In October the British ended the strike with help from neighbouring Arabs states.

1937: Arabs assassinated a British high commissioner in Nazareth. The British responded by restricting all movement and supplies in Arab neighbourhoods, making many Arab organisations illegal, and confiscating property.

The Peel Commission decided that the area should be divided into two separate states.

1938-1939: Terrorist attacks escalated, killing about 5000 people on all sides and destroying millions of pounds worth of British property and infrastructure.

1939: The British attempted the first Arab-Israeli peace talks. The Arab side refused to accept the existence of a Jewish state so the British held two separate talks. That failed miserably.

With war in Europe the British tried to win the Arabs onto their side. There was no reason to try to win over the Jews since they were not likely to support Germany. The result was the White Paper, which proposed creating a single state of mostly Arabs, and drastically limiting Jewish immigration.

This was seen on the Jewish side as a very bad move at a very bad time. Arab leaders rejected the White Paper because they felt that it did not limit Jewish immigration enough.

1946: The British gave about seventy percent of the Mandate of Palestine independence, thus creating a sovereign Palestinian Arab state. It called itself Jordan.

1947: The United Nations voted to kill the British Mandate entirely and divide what was left, after Jordan, in two. The proposal was to divide the remaining thirty percent of the

Mandate in half and create a Jewish state to the west and hand the eastern half over to Jordan. Every Arab member of the United Nations voted against it. Their counter proposal was to give all of the land to Jordan.

Random Arab attacks started killing random Jews. Jews retaliated and started killing Arabs. Military organisations that had been developed and encouraged under British rule got involved and the killing greatly escalated.

1948: The United States voted to put all of the former British Mandate that was not under Jordan control under UN control whilst the British decided to merge the Arab side with the new Jordan. The Arabs expanded their attacks and the Jews created an organised military.

When the British pulled out of the former Mandate, the UN invited Arab leaders to create another Arab state and Jewish leaders to create a Jewish state. In May, Israel declared its independence. The Arabs refused.

The Arab League decided instead to take all of the former Mandate by force and make it part of Jordan. Egypt, Iraq, Lebanon, Syria, Jordan all invaded Israel. The UN chose to sit back and wait to see what happened.

The Arab states sent 63 000 soldiers into Israel, which had an army of 29 677. By the end of the war 8000 Arab and 4000 Israeli soldiers were killed. Another 3000 Israeli civilians were killed.

1949: Israel signed separate cease fire agreements with each Arab state. Egypt captured Gaza, which had been part of Israel under the UN agreements. Jordan captured Judea and Samaria, which had been part of Israel since about 1000 BCE. No Arab leader ever made any attempt to make these areas into a Palestinian state.

Hundreds of thousands of Arabs fled their homes during the war and relocated to various Arab states. Many of these people and their descendants still live in refugee camps in Lebanon, Syria, Egypt.

Tens of thousands of Jews fled their homes and relocated to Israel where they were welcomed as full members of society.

1951-1956: Terrorists from neighbouring states attacked Israel. Israel retaliated.

1956: Egypt decided to make the Suez Canal part of Egypt. Britain, France, Israel invaded Egypt. As a result of the conflict Britain's international political policies were completely changed. France no longer trusted its allies and gave nuclear secrets to Israel. Maybe. That has neither been confirmed nor denied.

1964: Lebanon and Syria decided to divert water that flows from the Jordan River into Israel. Their goal was obviously to kill Jews but they permanently damaged entire ecosystems. Minor battles took place for the next two years.

1966: Israel raided a small city in Judea after multiple terrorist attacks. Jordan responded by sending troops in who were quickly pushed back. Jordan got mad at Egypt for not helping.

1967: Egypt sent troops to the Sinai/Israel border and closed international shipping traffic to Israel. Iraq and Jordan sent troops to Judea and Samaria. Syria increased its troops in Golan and continued its policy of isolated rocket attacks against Israel.

In June, Israel launched a massive air attack, completely destroying Egypt's air force in a single day. Egypt surrendered four days later and Israel captured Sinai and Gaza.

When Jordan was erroneously told that Egypt was winning in the south it invaded Israel from the east. Israel destroyed Jordan's small air force and captured Judea and Samaria in two days.

When Syria was told that Egypt had destroyed Israel it invaded through Golan. Israel destroyed most of Syria's air force and captured Golan in two days.

260 000 Israeli soldiers battled a combined force of 550 000 Arab soldiers. About 800 Israeli soldiers and 20 000 Arab soldiers were killed. Israel lost 46 aircraft. The combined Arab states lost about 460 aircraft.

The defence of Israel and destruction of three different states' air forces was so successful that much of the strategies used are still taught in military academies around the world. Not so much in Arab states.

1967-1970: Egypt tried to take back Sinai in several failed attacks. Egypt suffered heavy losses and only ceased hostilities when Gamal Nasser died.

1972: Arab terrorists kidnapped and murdered eleven Israeli Olympic athletes in Germany. Israel responded by targeting individuals directly and killing a few people who had nothing to do with anything.

1973: Egypt invaded Sinai, and Syria invaded Golan on Yom Kippur. Israeli intelligence knew about the attack but was told by the United States that if Israel struck first it would receive no assistance at all. So Israel let itself be attacked and the United States did absolutely nothing.

American leaders assumed that Israeli victory would be fast and easy, as it had been with every other Arab invasion. When the situation in Sinai got worse the United States learnt that Israel was considering using nuclear weapons. The United States then agreed to replace Israel's destroyed arms. This directly led to the military sales that continue today.

American involvement brought Soviet involvement as Russian weapons flooded into Egypt and Syria. Iraq and Jordan joined the war. Even Cuba sent some soldiers.

Just over two thousand Israeli soldiers were killed while Egypt and Syria lost sixteen thousand soldiers. Israel kept control of Sinai and Golan.

Israel, Jordan, Egypt, the United States attended a conference in Switzerland. Israel proposed that its Arab neighbours stop invading. Jordan and Egypt proposed that Israel give every inch of its land to them. No agreements were made.

1978: Arab terrorists went on a rampage and killed 37 Israelis and 1 American in northern Israel. Israel invaded southern Lebanon three days later and left when United Nations soldiers took over. Arab terrorists spent the next four years killing UN soldiers.

1978: Israel and Egypt signed the Camp David Accords which did not really do much except make the peace treaty possible.

1979: Israel and Egypt signed a peace treaty. Israel agreed to give Sinai back to Egypt and Egypt agreed to let Israel use the Suez Canal and other international waters. Egypt recognised Israel's existence and both sides established diplomatic relations.

For their efforts Menachem Begin and Anwar Sadat were given the Nobel Peace Prize and Egypt was suspended from the Arab League just before Sadat was assassinated by Arab terrorists.

1981-2000: Terrorists in Lebanon continued their policy of firing rockets into northern Israel. Israel bombed their headquarters in Beirut. Both sides fought each other intermittently for nineteen years.

1982: Israel launched a full invasion of Lebanon in June.

Israel left Sinai and Egypt took control.

1987-1993: Arab religious leaders launched the first intifada. Arab terrorists killed 164 Israelis. Israeli soldiers killed over 1000 Arabs. Arab terrorists killed another 1000 Arabs.

1990: Iraq invaded Kuwait. Iraq launched missiles into Israel in an effort to bring Israel into the war and push Arab states out. That plan failed miserably. Instead, several Arab states expelled thousands of Palestinian Arabs from refugee camps because the Palestinian Authority supported Iraq. The United States pushed Iraq out of Kuwait.

1991: Israel, Jordan, Syria, the Palestinian Authority met in Spain to make peace. Israeli negotiators proposed that Arab states stop attacking Israel. Arab negotiators proposed that Israel give all of its land to them. Nothing came of the conference.

1993: Israel and the Palestinian Authority signed the Oslo Accords, a framework for a lasting peace in the Middle East. American leaders announced a new age of friendship.

1994: Israel and Jordan signed a peace treaty. Both sides established diplomatic relations and agreed on a border between Israel and Palestine, which was then rejected by the Arab League. Israel agreed to supply Jordan with water.

2000: Israel and the Palestinian Authority met in America to make peace. Israel offered most of Judea and Samaria, even though it had been part of Israel for a few thousand years, and all of Gaza, which Israel never wanted in the first place. The Palestinian Authority refused.

Israel proposed keeping West Jerusalem and giving the Palestinian Authority control over East Jerusalem. The Palestinian Authority proposed taking all of Jerusalem and giving Israel authority but not sovereignty over West Jerusalem.

Israel proposed that Palestinian refugees return to Palestine. The Palestinian Authority proposed that they be allowed to live in Israel. Israel then proposed that Israeli refugees should be allowed to return to Judea and Samaria. The Palestinian Authority refused.

The Palestinian Authority proposed that all Israeli land be given to Palestine. Israel proposed that Palestine go fuck itself.

Both sides blamed the other for failure. Bill Clinton publicly blamed Yasser Arafat and said that Ehud Barak was open to painful concessions whilst Arafat was open to nothing but complete domination.

2000-2006: The second intifada killed just over 1000 Israelis. Israeli soldiers and Arab terrorists killed almost 5000 Arabs. Arab terrorists killed about 64 foreigners.

2002: The Arab League came up with their own peace plan. It suggested giving the Palestinian Authority all of its demands and giving Israel nothing except recognition from the states involved. Those at the summit also endorsed the second intifada. When Israel rejected the offer every Arab state announced that it was "proof" that Israel did not want peace.

2005: Israel left Gaza and handed control to the Palestinian Authority. All military personnel and equipment were withdrawn and civilians were removed. All Israeli houses and buildings were demolished. Terrorist attacks increased immediately and dramatically.

2006: Israel invaded Lebanon after twenty years of rocket attacks against northern Israel. 121 Israeli soldiers and 44 Israeli civilians were killed. Over 500 Arab terrorists and over 1000 Lebanese civilians were killed. Terrorists fired rockets into Israel just after the ceasefire, and fighting continues to this day.

Gilad Shalit was kidnapped in southern Israel and held hostage in violation of international law.

2007: Israel and Egypt agreed to blockade Gaza and prevent terrorist supplies from entering through Egypt.

Fatah politicians won local elections in Gaza but were displaced when Hamas violently declared itself the winner. Hamas quickly declared war on Israel and vowed to kill all Jews. Rocket attacks into Israel increased substantially. This was seen as "proof" that Israel did not want peace. The civil war between Fatah and Hamas continues to this day. Israel gave Mahmoud Abbas one hundred million US dollars in aid.

Israel and Syria began talking to each other until the United States demanded that they stop.

2008: After three years of rocket attacks from Gaza into Israel, Arab terrorists agreed not to fire any more rockets and Israel agreed not to retaliate. Four days later Arab terrorists resumed firing rockets into Israel. Israel invaded Gaza in December. 13 Israeli soldiers and 3 Israeli civilians were killed. About 1500 Arab terrorists and anywhere from 200 to 1000 civilians were killed.

2008: Israel and Syria began talking again in Turkey. This lasted a surprisingly long time but then Syria's leaders found other problems.

2010: Turkish boats with peace activists and a large cache of weapons were prevented from entering Gaza. Nine Turks were killed and the supplies were delivered to Gaza. Hamas leaders refused them.

2011: Gilad Shalit was released by Arab terrorists in exchange for the release of 1027 prisoners from Israeli jails, many of whom were mass murderers.

The Palestinian Authority attempted to gain United Nations membership but a vote was postponed indefinitely when the United States, United Kingdom, France announced that they would vote against it.

2012: Arab terrorists launched white phosphorus into Israel from Gaza. The United Nations issued no resolutions against Gaza.

Arab terrorists fired over 100 rockets toward Jerusalem and Tel Aviv from Gaza. Israel hit 1500 sites with air strikes. Israeli soldiers killed 170 Arabs, including 50 civilians. Arab terrorists killed 2 Israeli soldiers, 4 Israeli civilians, 68 Arab civilians, and executed 8 Arabs.

Why Xenophobia Is Stupid

Somebody once said that dogs are dogs all over the world. That is not really true. They are different everywhere you go.

Chinese dogs bark funny and are bullies to dogs in other yards. And there are just too many of them. But they make good kibble and they all know kung fu.

Japanese dogs bark funny and have tiny dog penises. But they are good with electronics and they all know karate.

German dogs bark loudly and hate all the other dogs. But they are good with electronics and love to chase cars.

Irish dogs lap up too much drink and love nothing more than fighting and drinking. But they make good hats.

American dogs are loud and complain too much whenever they visit another dog's yard. They are too lazy to step away from the TV but want to control the world.

American Indian dogs are drunks who will bite your head off if given half a chance. But they know how to run a casino.

Indian Indian dogs smell funny and are not satisfied with mating doggy style. But they are good for tech support if your collar goes offline.

Black dogs are lazy criminals and prone to fleas. Cross the street if you see one. But they are good at athletics and rhythmic barking.

White dogs are racist farmers and prone to ticks. They are all inbred. But they are good at middle management and eating fried foods.

Jewish dogs control the world's supply of bones and they all have large snouts. And they will eat your puppies and whatever crazy shit people come up with.

Muslim dogs will bite you. Count on it. They think that if they bite you they will be rewarded with 72 bitches in Valhowla.

Arab dogs control the world's supply of bones and they have thicker coats than other dogs. They all have large litters with multiple bitches.

Gay dogs love shopping and wearing girl collars. All of them will try to hump your leg. But they are good at fashion and can help you decorate your doghouse.

Lesbian dogs love welding and wearing boy collars. All of them hate male dogs. But they are fun to watch when they get oiled up and lick each other's tails.

DISPROPORTIONATE RESPONSE

I spend too much time online. I do not participate much but I do read a lot. Lately much of what I have been reading are opinions about Gaza. Mostly from people who only know what they see on their local news programmes. Rarely from people who have ever been there. I have been there so does that make my opinions more valid? No, but it has gone a long way toward shaping them.

Before living in Israel I shared some of the black and white views I often see online. Now I think it is all too complicated for easy campaign slogan answers. The problems between Israel and its Arab neighbours are not likely to be solved any time soon and even less likely to be solved by anybody's Facebook comment.

Since 1948 Arab terrorists have had two

mantras. One calls for the death of Israel. The other is that violence will stop just as soon as Israel ceases to exist. Or at least pulls out of any and all disputed territory. This is difficult since many Arab extremists consider all of Israel to be disputed territory. But in 2005 Israel pulled out of Gaza completely. There was no IDF presence and all settlements were destroyed. So did terrorism against Israel from Gaza end? Far from it. It escalated dramatically.

Fatah, a terrorist organisation that is now the ruling party of the Palestinian Authority, and Hamas, a terrorist organisation that would like to be the ruling party of whatever they consider theirs, fought each other for control of Gaza. What happened would have been considered a civil war in any other country on this planet. But since it happened in Gaza it was called a "democratic election" by the international press.

Hamas eventually won the bloody insurgency/election, killing many Fatah supporters on the way. Hamas, considered a terrorist organisation by the United States, European Union, Fatah, most Arab states, has always said that they will fight Israel until all Israelis are dead. By all Israelis they do not simply mean Jews. They are more than happy to kill Israeli Arabs, Christians, anybody else who does not follow them. So they were not too terribly impressed that Israel pulled out of Gaza.

I have read a lot about Israel's blockade

against Gaza. I think too many people are forgetting who is doing the blocking. Border crossings with Gaza are controlled by Israel, Egypt, the Palestinian Authority, depending on point of entry. All three entities instituted a blockade against Gaza once Hamas took over. Probably not because Hamas is a democratically elected body.

Israel wants to prevent Hamas terrorists from murdering Israelis. That would not be too much to ask in other parts of the world but it is considered disproportionate of Israel by some. The Palestinian Authority wants to prevent Hamas terrorists from killing Fatah terrorists. This is considered perfectly reasonable to the International Community. Except that the International Community never acknowledge that Fatah has a blockade against Gaza since that would interfere with their Evil Israel narrative. Egypt wants to prevent Hamas terrorists from gaining any influence in Egypt. None of the brutal dictators of Egypt want their people to suffer the brutal dictatorship of Hamas.

Since the blockade started, Israel has let in millions of tonnes in food, medicine, building supplies to Gaza. Israel has never prevented any Red Cross supplies from reaching Gaza and has only stopped one United Nations vessel. Israel supplies the majority of Gaza's electricity, food, water. Egypt has allowed crossings from Gaza into Egypt and supplied the area with nothing. The Palestinian Authority has done nothing other than enforce the blockade. Fatah is often the target of Hamas terrorism but most of their holy wrath is directed at Israel. It seems to me that killing the one country that is keeping you alive might not be the best strategy but then I do not know how to think like a terrorist organisation.

I think the theory is supposed to be that once Israel is finally killed then Arabs can move in to more beach front property and the area they call Palestine will be a bastion of peace and enlightenment. That theory is flawed for several reasons. Palestinian terrorists kill more Palestinians than anybody else. There is no reason they will stop killing each other without Israel around. In fact, without their common enemy, they will probably kill each other even more.

It is also worth noting that the economies of Gaza, Judea and Samaria would cease to exist without Israel. Some would say that other Arab states will help them once Israel is gone but history has shown that most Arab states do not give a rat's ass about Palestinians, except as a tool against Israel, and consider Palestinians inferior to themselves.

It might also be difficult to achieve that bastion of peace and enlightenment status when your form of government treats women like property, kills homosexuals, persecutes Christians, persecutes Muslims who do not follow your branch of Islam, and wants to exterminate all Jews from the face of the Earth. I could be wrong, and I have been wrong once or twice before, but this does not seem very enlightened to me.

After three years of rocket attacks from Gaza, Israel finally invaded. Normally I would say that invading another country or territory or whatever it is supposed to be is a bad idea but after three years of rocket attacks you have to do something. It is hard to negotiate diplomatically with terrorists who have vowed to kill you with their last breath. It is hard to talk to people who do not recognise your existence.

In any other part of the world a stable democracy would not be forced to negotiate with terrorists to keep from being murdered. Can you imagine the United States bending over backward to keep Puerto Rican terrorists from bombing Washington? Would the United States give Florida to Puerto Rico in a futile attempt at peace or would they invade the shit out of Puerto Rico?

There was a lot of outrage amongst the International Community over Israel violating international law by invading Gaza. Apparently you are not allowed to invade a place that fires rockets at you daily. Of course, this rule only applies to Israel. Any other country would be free to defend themselves.

I do not remember seeing any outrage over Hamas' persistent violation of international law by targeting civilians and bombing hospitals and schools. I am no expert on international law but it seems odd to me that it is illegal for Israel to invade a place that is attacking it but it is not illegal to fire rockets at

Israeli school and hospitals.

I have to give Hamas credit for doing so well in the public relations war. They bombed the Israeli power plant that supplies Gaza with electricity and told the International Community that Israel cut off the electricity. Naturally there was international outrage. Naturally it was not against Hamas. They use hospitals and schools as military headquarters while they fire rockets at Israeli hospitals and schools, and the International Community complain only about IDF retaliation. There is never any international outrage when an Israeli school is hit.

Hamas has killed hundreds of Palestinian civilians who may or may not support Israel and/or the Palestinian Authority and yet the International Community only express outrage over Palestinians killed by the IDF. Why is life only sacred when it is life taken at the hands of an Israeli? Why is Arab life so meaningless when it is taken by other Arabs? Some would say that I am only complaining because the International Community attack Israel. But they are not simply attacking Israel. They are completely ignoring all of the innocent Arabs killed by Palestinian terrorists. Why is there no international outrage over these murdered Arabs?

Israel is to blame for at least some, if not most, of the public relations failure. We use the word Palestine to refer to a territory that has not yet decided that it wants to be a country. Or at least the Arab League is not ready to let it be a country. Many Arabs call the entire area of land west of Jordan Palestine. This only confuses people looking in from the outside. It is not especially helpful to those of us looking in from the inside either.

When Israelis say Palestine we are generally talking about a piece of land that was once part of Israel, then taken by Jordan, taken back by Israel, now part of no country. When many Arabs say Palestine they are generally talking about Israel, Judea and Samaria, Gaza, sometimes parts of Jordan, depending on which Arab group is angry at another Arab group at any given point in time. I have no idea whom the United Nations is talking about when they say Palestine. It seems as though the UN is not particularly sure either. Their definitions change every time there is a Nobel Peace Prize ceremony.

Obviously I am biased. I am an Israeli citizen. I serve in the IDF. I want my side to win. Mostly because if we ever lose a war then we will all die. We do not have the luxury of losing a war on the other side of the world and carrying on as if nothing happened. But I do not think it is an issue of Jews versus Muslims or Israelis versus Arabs. It might be worth remembering that many Israelis are Muslim and/or Arab. Arab Israelis are killed by Palestinian terrorists just as easily as any other Israelis. If it were Jews versus Muslims then I doubt Palestinian terrorists would kill so many Palestinians. The issue is extremists versus moderates.

None of the Palestinians I know have any problems with Israel. They simply want their country to have a sovereign government recognised by the International Community. I think that is also what most Israelis want. From my point of view the biggest obstacle to this is terrorist activity against Israel.

The worst thing Israeli extremists want are more settlements in disputed territories. While Israeli settlements clearly do not help the issue, they also do not cause the deaths of innocent children with suicide bombers and rockets fired at school and hospitals. The worst thing Palestinian extremists want is the death of every last Israeli man, woman and child. I am biased but I think killing all Israelis is much worse than building a few houses in disputed territory. Both should probably stop but they are not equal actions by any sane definition.

Why did Israel invade Gaza?

The official answer is to stop the daily rocket attacks that have being going on for years. The unofficial answer is to dissolve Hamas once and for all. Defence minister Ehud Barak came out and said as much. Neither goal was achieved. Some have said it was a rehearsal for any potential invasion of Iran. I do not consider that an entirely crazy theory.

Why did Israel break the truce?

What truce? As soon as Hamas took control of Gaza they intensified attacks against Israel. Dramatically. Gaza was peaceful by comparison under Israeli control. Egypt negotiated a cease fire between Israel and

Hamas in June 2008. Four days later rockets were fired into Israel from Gaza. There was no condemnation of Hamas from the International Community. Throughout the cease fire Hamas continued to fire rockets into Israel. And Israel, Egypt, the Palestinian Authority continued their blockades of Gaza. Each side saying they would stop just as soon as the other does. Israel tried to broker a truce with Hamas but Hamas has always refused. They have vowed to fight until all Israelis are dead and buried. How do you reason with unreasonable people?

Wasn't it a disproportional response? Killing thousands in an organised invasion isn't the same as a few ineffective rockets.

Hamas rockets are not the most accurate and their training is far from the best but ineptitude does not give them the right to fire rockets every day for years into Israel. Rationalising attacks against Israel because it is stronger is unreasonable. What would your country do if a terrorist organisation operating next door was firing off rockets into your country every day year after year? Would it be acceptable if they were weak and you were strong? How long would you negotiate with a terrorist organisation that has vowed to fight until all of your people are dead?

Why doesn't Israel like peace?

Israel's leaders and the overwhelming majority of its citizens, Jewish, Muslim, Christian, Druze, miscellaneous, would love to live life in peace. We should remember that there is only one Jewish majority country on this planet surrounded by several Arab states, some of which deny Israel's right to exist, some of which deny that Israel exists, and some which have vowed to fight until Israel is completely destroyed. Israel has never made any such vows and accepts the existence of all Arab states.

Most Arab states have relaxed their rhetoric against Israel over the last few years but there are still some who do not even acknowledge our existence, yet they finance terrorist organisations whose sole purpose is to destroy Israel. Maps made in many Arab states call Israel Palestine and school children are taught that all of Israel is Palestine with the evil Jews as foreign occupiers. Maps made in Israel show both Israel and Palestine and Israeli school children are taught that Arabs exist. Palestinian school children are taught that Jews exist but that they are not Israeli, since there is no such place, and that we are evil monsters whom God wants destroyed for some reason.

This is not like the Cold War hysteria between the United States and Soviet Union where both countries could and did survive and thrive despite the existence of the other. There truly are some countries that want nothing more than to see Israel wiped off the map, whether it exists or not, and will happily kill its own children to make that happen. The International Community rarely, if ever, condemn these countries when they finance terrorists, strap bombs on children or attempt to invade Israel. But Israel is emphatically condemned when it builds houses in disputed territories and counters attacks against it. That is a disproportionate response.

The real question is why do the United Nations and a few Arab states not like peace. Or does their definition of peace require the death of Israel? A better question is how do you take the UN seriously when they do not condemn the use of children as suicide bombers against Israel. Do they hate Israel that much? Or do they simply hate Arab children?

What do you expect when you blockade Gaza?

I think people expected Hamas to run out of weapons. That was naïve. With all those tunnels into Egypt they are going to bring in more and more weapons. But if people think Israel has cut off Gaza's supply of food and water then they are even more naïve. Israel supplies food and water to Gaza and has let in countless shipments and millions of tonnes in aid since the blockade started. The blockade is meant as a stranglehold on the supply of weapons, not on civilian goods. Unfortunately its ineffectiveness has become a stranglehold on peace.

And even though the International Community never mention it whilst condemning Israel's blockade, Egypt and the Palestinian Authority also have blockades against Gaza. Neither of which send in any food, water, medicine, building materials, electricity. Only Israel's blockade, the only one that allows vital supplies into Gaza, is singled out for international outrage.

Why did Israel violate international law by killing civilians?

The IDF does more to avoid civilian casualties than probably any military in the world. If you listen to anti IDF propaganda then you would probably be surprised by how far Israeli soldiers go to avoid killing civilians. IDF soldiers are trained not to fire on children even if those children are pointing arms at the soldiers. It is better to take a bullet than to fire on a child. This is not something I read about in some online article or some guy's blog. This is what I experienced during my training.

How many armies do that? How many terrorists go out of their way to avoid killing civilians? I know that Hamas does not. Just the opposite. They are trained to fire on unarmed children. Terrorists do not follow any rules of international law. Hamas has been violating international law by targeting schools and hospitals for years. They specifically target civilians, especially children and the elderly, in violation of international law.

That does not give Israel any excuse to harm civilians but it does make me wonder where the international outrage is over the crimes committed by Hamas. They kill mostly civilians, most of whom are their own people, and a few soldiers. The IDF kills mostly terrorists and a few civilians.

Gaza is a very crowded place. If the IDF were really targeting civilians then there would be a lot more dead. It would be the catastrophic death zone that the international press wants it to be. Have you ever been to Gaza? It is not in a constant state of death and destruction. There are thriving businesses and beachside holiday resorts. It may not be the most popular tourist destination in the world but it is nothing like the post apocalyptic dystopia that the international press would have you believe. There are fresh produce markets every summer and spring, and lots of people playing volleyball on the beach in summer.

There are also failing businesses. Just as there are everywhere in the world. Sometimes when your business fails it is not the Jews' fault. I realise how much that goes against conventional wisdom but sometimes your failure is your fault.

The people of Gaza can buy a variety of international groceries as well as some very nice local bakery goods. Arab bakeries are outstanding. What they do not have is free speech. Anybody who speaks out against Hamas or in favour of Israel is subject to kidnapping, torture, rape, death. Hamas loves to rape women. And why not? They are only property. The International Community have no problem with that.

It would be easier to target civilians in Gaza and just wipe out everybody. Obviously the IDF is not doing that. I say obviously because it should be obvious to anybody with any common sense but from what I read about this situation it is also obvious that common sense is highly subjective.

One of the evils of war is that civilians will die. Strong countries like Israel and the United States would like to believe that their military attacks are surgical strikes that only hit the bad guys. But innocent civilians are always in danger when any military attacks anybody. That is true everywhere in the world. It does not make Israel right but it does not make us wrong either. A crucial difference between the IDF and Hamas, aside from one being the regulated army of a democracy and the other being a terrorist organisation, is that the IDF specifically target terrorists whilst Hamas specifically targets civilians, in direct violation of international law.

Hamas are the democratically elected leaders of Gaza. Deal with it.

Only if your idea of democratic elections involve torturing and murdering your opponents. Hamas "won" because they killed and frightened away enough of their rivals. Those democratic elections are best described as a coup. Almost every country outside of the Arab world considers Hamas a terrorist organisation. Even some Arab states do. The de facto leaders of the Palestinian Authority consider Hamas a terrorist organisation.

Most of Palestine has no democracy by any definition. Their dictators are not elected by the people. Their laws against women, homosexuals, Christians are barbaric by most definitions. Jews are not in that list because being Jewish is illegal in "democratic" Palestine. Yet Judea and Samaria is a political utopia compared to Gaza. Yosh leaders at least pretend to be democratic. Gaza leaders are nothing short of terrorists. They treat their own people far worse than Israel ever could. And if any of the people of Gaza speak out against them, they disappear. That is not my idea of democracy.

Why doesn't Israel just pull out of Palestine and leave them alone?

That is an easy one. Israel will leave when the Palestinian Authority disarms their terrorists. The Palestinian Authority will disarm their terrorists when Israel leaves.

Imagine Mexican terrorists sending thousands of rockets and suicide bombers into the United States and the International Community condemning the United States for any response against Mexico, and then telling the United States that they have to negotiate with Mexican terrorists by giving them California and Texas. What would the United States do?

Somewhere along the line somebody is going to have to compromise. History has shown that it will not be Arab terrorists. So far Israel has made many concessions, including more than a few that even the most rabid liberal considered going too far. Each time the response from Arab terrorists has been more violence. There has never been any violence from Israel as a result of Palestinian concessions. Partly because Palestinian leaders have never entered any negotiations with any concessions.

Israel does not want to control Palestine. Palestine has been the bane of Israel's existence since Jordan's second invasion. By being "the occupier" Israel is obligated to provide electricity, food, water, medicine, other supplies. Without Israel's economic assistance Palestine would have starved decades ago. Their Arab neighbours are not interested.

Palestine was offered sovereignty in 1947 but the Arab League refused. Israel practically begged Jordan to take over Judea and Samaria in 1968 but they refused. Israel offered to leave Gaza and almost all of Judea and Samaria in 2000 but the Palestinian Authority refused.

Arab states seem to think it is more advantageous for them if Palestine is a disputed territory. And it is. There is a reason all those Palestinian refugees in camps throughout the Arab world have never been integrated into those societies. Only Jordan has ever made any Palestinian refugees citizens of its country. Other states force Palestinians to live in camps indefinitely. Rather than condemn those Arab states, the International Community condemn Israel. Apparently Israel is so powerful that it can command how Arab states treat their own people. According to the United Nations at least.

It is not a control issue. When Israel gave Sinai back to Egypt they were happy and there was peace. When Israel gave part of Golan back to Syria they were not happy but there was peace. More or less. Every time Israel gives away more land to create Palestine for peace there is more violence. As soon as Israel pulled out of Gaza, Hamas took control from Fatah and terrorism escalated. If history is any indication, pulling out of Judea and Samaria would lead to a bloodbath. And a guaranteed condemnation from the United Nations.

Don't Palestinians deserve a homeland, too?
They do indeed. It is called Jordan. There is no mention of any Palestine or Palestinian people in the Jewish Tanakh, Christian Bible, Muslim Qur'an because no such country or people existed. There were Philistines but they were not today's Palestinians. Though some people hope you are ignorant enough of basic history to believe that they are. The Philistines were from Greece and not at all Arab. And they all died out a very long time ago. There were no Palestinians when the Persians, Romans, Egyptians, Ottoman, British invaded.

When the British finally left they handed over most of the land that they called Palestine to what is now called Jordan and a much smaller piece to Israel. Everybody who lived in the Levant, Jewish, Muslim, Christian, Arab, European, were called Palestinians by the British. The British never called the people in their colonies British.

Many Arabs were forced to leave Israel. People still talk about this today. This is proof of how evil Israel is, forcing these Arabs to leave a land they had lived in for many years. But these same people conveniently forget that many Jews were forced to leave what is now Jordan, Syria, Lebanon. These Jews had to leave a land they had lived in for many years. For some reason this is not proof of any evil.

Judea and Samaria were part of the small piece of land that the British handed over to Israel. Then Jordan, apparently unsatisfied with the largest piece of land, invaded and declared it part of Jordan. They were not the only Arab state to invade Israel but they were the only Arab state to capture a large part of Israel and claim it their own.

When Jordan and others invaded again two decades later, Israel took Judea and Samaria back from Jordan. But by then the Jews who had lived there for thousands of years were evicted and Arabs moved in. Fair enough. You conquer a land and you get to move in. At least that is how it has always worked in the entire history of the world up until some Jews were involved.

Suddenly the people in this small strip of Israel and/or Jordan were called Palestinians and the term no longer applied to everybody in the Levant. Not that anybody else wanted to be called Palestinian. This part of what used to be Jordan after it used to be Israel after it used to be part of the British Mandate after it used to be owned by everybody else in the world was now the ancient Palestinian homeland and all former uses of the word Palestine were ignored. Or used to make people who failed elementary history believe that Israel never existed before 1948.

Today a great many people want to give the descendants of the Arabs who were forced out of Israel the right to return to Israel as citizens. Absolutely none of these people want to give any of the descendants of the Jews forced out of Jordan or any other Arab state the right to return as Jordanian, Syrian, Lebanese citizens. The United Nations routinely condemn Israel for its refusal to let Arab descendants back in but has to date never condemned any Arab state for refusing to let Jewish descendants back in.

One could argue that I am biased. I am a Jewish Israeli. This is true. But the Jewish Israeli view is that Israel should control the land that was handed over to Israel by the British, and that Jordan and other Arab states should control the land that Britain handed over to Arab tribal leaders. One need not be biased to see this as a reasonable view. Some argue that Arabs have lived here for thousands of years. And they have. As have Jews.

The Palestinian view is that Arab states control the land where Arabs have lived for thousands of years as well as the land where Jews have lived for thousands of years. One side wants everybody to have peace in their neighbourhood. The other wants to drive the Jews to the sea. If you take your hatred of Jews out of the equation for the tiniest moment then it is not that difficult to see that this is unreasonable.

Nakba Day, as you probably know, is a national day of mourning amongst some Palestinians. It does not commemorate a day when millions of Palestinians were killed or when Arabs lost some war. It commemorates the independence of the modern state of Israel. They mourn the independence of another country. How is that for positive and peaceful.

On this particular Nakba Day some groups organised some "protests". Protests are all the rage in Arabia just now. Hopefully that will prove to be a good thing. But these particular protests were not for democracy or gender equality or better jobs. They were protesting the existence of Israel.

To Jordan and Egypt's credit, those countries stopped their citizens from violating their borders with Israel. Jordan and Egypt's security forces injured hundreds of people. I wonder if there will be any calls for international outrage. Probably not.

The outrage is reserved for the people injured by Israeli forces. As usual. Had Syria and Lebanon stopped their people as Jordan and Egypt stopped their own, they would never have been in any position to be injured by Israeli soldiers. Lebanon put up a token resistance. Syria did nothing. Some people are saying that members of Syria's government even organised the event. I cannot say if that is true but it would not surprise me at all. Syria is not exactly known for waving olive branches at Israel.

Some people are suggesting that these

protests were organised by the dictatorships in an effort to direct attention away from all of the democracy protests currently plaguing our undemocratic neighbours. Especially since this year just happens to be the most active and violent Nakba ever. Getting your people to hate somebody else has always been a good way to keep them from kicking you out of your palace. But regardless of motive an official Syrian policy of death and destruction to all Israelis is nothing new.

I have endless sympathy for the people who live in Judea and Samaria. They have been used as pawns by so many for so long. Hundreds of thousands of Arabs were displaced when the Ottomans and the British decided to carve up the land. So were hundreds of thousands of Jews. And I have never seen any Arab group anywhere advocate letting any of those Jews and their descendants back in.

But Jews have Israel. Do Arabs have any countries they can call their own? Obviously I am missing the point. It is not enough to have Jordan, Egypt, Syria, Lebanon, Saudi Arabia, Libya, Yemen, Iraq, Kuwait, Bahrain, Morocco, Qatar, Oman, Algeria, Tunisia, Somalia, Sudan, UAE, Judea and Samaria. They are simply incomplete without that tiny patch of land called Israel.

I think what bothers me the most is not the racist elements that want to destroy Israel. That is nothing new. There will always be racism as long as there are men. But now there is talk within Israel of limiting Nakba demonstrations amongst Israeli citizens. I do not like that at all. That is not how democracies operate. People should be free to protest whatever they want. It makes no difference that up until now this Nakba was a minor event and the opposite of noteworthy. We should not confuse armed hooligans sent from other countries to violate our borders with genuine protesters amongst our citizens. People trying to enter the country illegally to destroy should be stopped. People who live here who want to speak out should not. Israel does not need to fear protesters toppling governments as our neighbours do. That is what elections are for.

In June 2006 Sergeant Gilad Shalit was kidnapped by Palestinian terrorists who crossed under the Israeli border through a tunnel from Gaza. Palestinian leaders called Shalit a prisoner of war rather than a hostage despite the fact that the International Red Cross was never allowed to see him.

Not only does this tell us that Palestinian leaders consider themselves at war with Israel but they also violated international law and the Geneva Conventions by demanding a ransom for Shalit, repeatedly denied Red Cross meetings, denied any communication with his family, conducted torture against a prisoner of war. If he was a prisoner of war then Palestine committed war crimes. Yet I have never seen any moral outrage from the International Community.

Several world leaders and organisations called for Shalit's release, including the European Union, United Nations, Red Cross, Vatican, but I have not heard about any protests outside of Israel. The International Community will protest at the drop of a hat even the suspicion that somebody has violated international law and the Geneva Conventions. Unless it is done against Jews.

You might have heard about that Hamas cartoon. If it seems strange to think of a terrorist organisation making cartoons do not worry. This is not about chicks and bunnies. It is a cartoon about kidnapping and murder. But they do have a "popular" children's cartoon about a "jihad loving mouse". According to them. I will not even mention the irony of extremist Muslims making cartoons to attack other religions and express their political views. But something is definitely rotten in the state of terror.

One fine day in April 2010 an anonymous cartoon was posted on a Hamas website. Everybody has a website these days. The cartoon was a message to Gilad Shalit's father and really to all of us. It said that if Israel refused to trade Shalit for one thousand Palestinian prisoners then Shalit would come home in a coffin.

Gilad Shalit was kidnapped in June 2006 and was shown to be alive as of a video released in October 2009, though nobody knows when it was filmed. For his part Shalit's father remained dignified and refused to lower himself to their level.

This type of propaganda is nothing new for Hamas. The media that they control show anti Israeli and anti Jewish propaganda almost exclusively. But this cartoon received more attention because it was supposedly a personal appeal to Shalit's father and because of the timing.

A week prior a daughter of a top Hamas leader was taken to an Israeli hospital and flown to Jordan for additional treatment. At the expense of Israeli taxpayers. The Hamas leader was once in charge of the same group that posted the cartoon. He has yet to thank any Israelis for helping his daughter. In fact his last public statement with the word "Israel" also included "death to". You are welcome. I wonder if his daughter hates the infidels who saved her life.

Israel produces propaganda also. But it is usually more upbeat. Israeli propaganda is more along the lines of Israel being a beacon of light for Jews looking to escape oppression and bigotry. I have never seen anything with Jews decapitating anybody or calling for death to anybody who draws a cartoon about Moses. I suppose that is one of the differences between a stable democracy and a terrorist organisation.

It would be nice if the people within the international media who want to put Israel and terrorists on equal moral standing understood the difference between joining a developed army in a modern democracy and joining a group who hide in the shadows and strap on bombs. Israeli soldiers will use themselves as human shields to protect civilians. Terrorists use civilians as human shields. If you think both are equally honourable then you have some issue you might want to work on.

Another important difference between these "equals" is that terrorists can kidnap young men who serve their country and butcher them on camera whilst claiming that they are the victims. Where is the moral outrage from the International Community? If Israel posted videos of Israeli officials murdering Palestinians when their outrageous demands are not met there would be an enormous outcry from just about everybody. And rightly so. So where is the condemnation of Hamas?

And if these terrorists are proudly doing God's work then why do they always hide their faces? If I believe my cause is just I do not wear a ski mask.

After years of failed negotiations the Palestinians agreed to release Gilad Shalit in exchange for 1027 Palestinians held in Israeli jails. Palestinian terrorist groups call them prisoners of war. Israel calls them convicted criminals.

Gilad Shalit was kidnapped and held without trial whilst given substandard medical attention for the wounds he received when kidnapped. The 1027 Palestinians were arrested either while committing acts of terrorism or shortly afterward, given fair trials in accordance with Israeli law, which meets international standards, treated in accordance with international law. Prisoners in Israeli jails are given free medical care, free education, free communication with their families, free entertainment, unlimited Red Cross visits. Many have a much higher standard of living whilst in jail than they did in their own homes. They are also free to practise whatever religion they want. How did Shalit observe his faith all those years?

If Israel prevented a Palestinian murderer from observing his faith there would be international outrage and protests around the world. Where is the outrage for a 19-year-old who never killed anybody and was only minding his own business in his own country when he was kidnapped and held in violation of the Geneva Conventions for five years?

I can appreciate Israel's policy of bringing home every single soldier, dead or alive. It shows a moral strength that many countries simply do not want to have. Israel will bring its sons and daughters home no matter what. Palestine will let its people blow themselves up on foreign soil.

I am happy for Gilad Shalit and his family that he was finally released. If any of my family were kidnapped by these sociopaths I would want Israel to release every terrorist in every jail if that is what it took to bring them home.

But 1027 terrorists for one soldier is a heavy price to pay for having a soul. 279 of these terrorists were serving life sentences. That is the most severe punishment available under Israeli law. Unlike Palestine, Israel does not have capital punishment. Also unlike Palestine, Israel does not hand out life sentences like candy. Nobody in Israel is serving a life sentence for being homosexual or being a woman. Such a punishment requires a serious crime. You really have to earn it.

Israel agreed to release the cowards who kidnapped and murdered Ilan Saadon, Ilan Sasportas, Nachshon Wachsman, as well as the terrorist who bombed bus 405, the terrorist who murdered ten people at Wadi Harmiyeh, the terrorists who murdered fifteen people, including seven children, and injured 130 others when they bombed a pizzeria in Jerusalem.

These terrorists are not political prisoners. These are not conscientious objectors or people who failed to pay parking fines. These are cold blooded murderers responsible for the violent deaths of six hundred innocent men, women, children, including more than a few innocent Palestinian civilians. Palestinian terrorists kill more Palestinians than they kill Israelis. Why do the international media fail to mention that?

And now they are free to kill again. Gilad Shalit was 19 years old when he was kidnapped. He was 25 when he was released. When he finally went home he could go to school and get a job and live out his life as he would have had he never been kidnapped. Most of the 1027 terrorists will not live the rest of their lives peacefully. They will be welcomed back by rejoicing Palestinians before they return to killing more Palestinians in their quest to kill

Israel.

That is another thing that the international media fail to mention. When murderers are returned to Palestine they are given a hero's welcome. People literally dance in the street. They are actively praising a person who killed children.

Some will say that Israeli soldiers kill children. They conveniently ignore the difference between collateral damage, which is horrible, and purposely targeting civilians, which is specifically what terrorists do. They also ignore the fact that the dictatorship in Palestine actively encourages its people to praise and worship murderers whilst no Israeli soldier who has ever been arrested for any inappropriate action has ever brought about dancing and rejoicing. Israelis feel bad when their soldiers do anything untoward. Palestinians rejoice when their terrorists murder babies.

The Israeli government says that some of these murderers will not be allowed to return to their homes. Some will only be able to go to Judea and Samaria in ten to twenty five years. Some will never be allowed into the Yosh again. Some will be deported to Jordan. Read into that what you will.

Half will be sent to Gaza, regardless of where they came from. The reasoning is that if they are not in Judea and Samaria they cannot cause any problems. Gaza is a lawless backwater anyway so what is the harm? I think this is completely stupid. Sending convicted murderers into the mentoring arms of murderers is never a good idea. And who really believes that nobody will find a way around those restrictions?

"Prisoner releases only embolden terrorists by giving them the feeling that even if they are caught, their punishment will be brief. Worse, by leading terrorists to think such demands are likely to be met, they encourage precisely the terrorist blackmail they are supposed to defuse." Benjamin Netanyahu, 1995.

Terrorists in Palestine have already said that they plan to kidnap more Israelis in the near future. Nobody in the International Community have expressed any outrage over this.

Israel always refused to release murderers in exchange for kidnapped Israelis in the past. Now we are releasing mass murderers. In the so called negotiations between Israel and Palestine, Israel keeps giving away more and more concessions whilst Palestine has never agreed to a single meeting without preconditions.

Israel has the moral high ground, a much larger military, and the money that Palestine depends on for its survival. But if Palestine can keep taking while Israel keeps giving it should not be more than a few generations before they achieve their ultimate goal of Israel's complete destruction. And when that happens and they celebrate by firing guns in the streets and raping women I will bet that there will not be a single protest from the International Community. At most maybe the United Nations will issue a mild statement that maybe Israel should not have been wiped off the map.

Another way to see it, in December 2008 Israel invaded Gaza in response to repeated rocket attacks over a period of years. The invasion was limited partly because the IDF did not know where Gilad Shalit was being held. They did not want to risk injuring him in the attack.

Palestinian terrorists have always used other Palestinians as human shields but now they have lost their Israeli human shield. Mahmoud Abbas has practically begged Israel to tear Gaza apart. According to some of those wikileaks. It will be interesting to see what happens the next time Israel responds to constant rocket attacks from Gaza, which are completely illegal under international law but never protested.

Some politicians in Jordan are once again calling for the release of the man who killed seven young teenagers and wounded five of their classmates and a teacher in 1997.

A group of school children were on a trip to the Island of Peace, a park that was given to Jordan by Israel in one of many land extortions for peace. As with most land concessions, this one was quickly followed by violence. A Jordanian soldier stationed at the park fired on the girls when they arrived for a class trip.

To their credit, the people in charge of Jordan at the time arrested the man and sentenced him to twenty five years in prison, and King Hussein gave a sincere apology. Not surprisingly, the United Nations issued no resolutions condemning the murders. There was no international outrage and nobody protested at any embassies. These were only Jewish girls, after all.

The soldier who murdered the girls was never universally reviled in Jordan. Many still call him a hero. His own mother publicly praised his murder of teenage girls and said that her son "did a heroic deed and has pleased Allah and his own conscience. He lifts my head and the head of the entire Arab and Islamic nation." The Arab media mostly agreed with her.

Now that King Hussein is dead and political life in Jordan has changed, there are more frequent calls for the unconditional release of this murderer. Prominent leaders have tried to get him released since it happened, and came close in 2011. Now they are trying again, only with more public support than usual. With all of the revolutions and civil wars in Arab states, this is exactly the kind of thing that a government might cave in to just to appease the masses.

When an IDF soldier does something stupid like post a picture online of a child in sniper crosshairs, there is always international outrage. I do not agree that Israel should be destroyed and all Jews should die because of such a thing but I do agree that it is wrong to take such pictures, let alone post them online. The fact that this particular soldier did not actually take this particular picture is irrelevant. It was stupid.

But every single time an Israeli soldier does something stupid there is international outrage. I can see it being on the news because, let's face it, people love to hear about other people doing really stupid things. But calling for the deaths of eight million men, women and children because of it seems a bit much.

These soldiers are always disciplined and usually lose their jobs. Being dishonourably discharged from the IDF is a big deal around here. It is a lot harder to get a civilian job. Sometimes these soldiers go to jail, depending on the severity of the crime. Despite calls from Arab media that they be executed, that never happens. We do not do that here.

What strikes me as disappointing is that Israelis universally condemn soldiers doing stupid things whilst many Arabs openly praise anybody who murders Israeli children, whether Jewish or Arab. The balance is horribly off. Not only in the posting of inappropriate pictures versus the murder of children but in the reactions from the observers.

I was once told by an Arab Israeli that since we are the more civilised society it is up to us to be more outraged by the greater crimes whilst they, meaning the Arab states, can feign outrage over things that will never affect their lives. But I do not buy that. Arab states like Jordan are as advanced and developed as anybody else. They do not worship fire and fear full moons. They know the difference between reckless tweets and mass murder. Or at least they should.

I think the problem is simple bigotry. Taking a picture of Saddam without his shirt on is as bad as murdering Sara's entire family because Saddam is Arab and Sara and her family are Jews. It is acceptable to murder Jews because you think Israel stole your land. After all, if some farmers in Alaska built houses in Canada, it would be perfectly acceptable for Canadians to strap on bombs and blow up American babies. Right? Forget about who was where first. The penalty for perceived theft should be genocide. Who could disagree?

Now some people are calling Gilad Shalit a hero. I am not so sure about that. He was kidnapped and returned home five years later. His family had to wait five years, not knowing how he was being treated or if he was even alive. He had to live in captivity with terrorists who could kill him at any minute. He was held for ransom by representatives of people who call themselves a legitimate government yet break international law daily. And he survived.

But does that make him a hero? He did not really do anything.

I am not saying there is anything wrong with him. But I do not think being the victim of sociopaths with delusions of humanity makes you a hero.   Heroes have to do something. Ideally they do something heroic.

But calling Shalit a hero does not especially bother me.   What really does bother me is when cowards like Mahmoud Abbas call terrorists heroes.   I call Abbas a coward because he openly praises terrorists and publicly says that all of the Palestinian people are one nation in one struggle.   But behind closed doors he begs Israel to destroy the illegal government in Gaza, and he grovels to the Americans who call the people he calls heroes terrorists and who blockade and boycott the organisations that he says are his brothers.

He gladly accepts money from Israel and America and says that he will do everything he can to make Palestine a democracy even though he was never democratically elected and his term of office ended in 2009, yet he refuses to step down.   He has repeatedly threatened to resign if things did not go his way but is still in office.   He gives speeches at the United Nations saying that Palestinians should stop using violence against Israel but he has never done anything to actually stop any Palestinians from using violence against Israel. Then he throws parties for murderers who will willingly die to kill anybody who does not believe in their fanaticism.

Obviously I do not think that Abbas is a hero. His doctoral thesis alone qualifies him as an asshole. But even worse are the murderers, kidnappers, rapists, arsonists, thieves who are being hailed as heroes by people who would not ordinarily praise murderers, kidnappers, rapists, arsonists, thieves. If they murder a Palestinian child to buy drugs then they are bad. But if they murder a Palestinian child in an effort to kill Jews then they are heroes. This kind of thinking is inhuman, anti Muslim and should be anti Palestinian.

Most human beings are encouraged to get what they want through ethical means. Palestinian terrorists are actively encouraged to get what they want by blowing people up.

My boyfriend twisted his knee last month. It was a minor injury. The doctors patched it up, gave him some drugs, sent him on his way. It healed just in time to go out of town on a business trip.

I have been saving the world for democracy or committing genocide. Depending who you talk to. I think likely neither. Democracy does not live or die by my actions or even those of my country. It will survive long after the United Nations votes for us to be destroyed. And people who think defending ourselves from terrorists is genocide either do not know what the word means or do not know what is going on here. Even if we nuked Gaza it would not be genocide. There would still be plenty of Arabs and Jordanians in the world.

Genocide usually starts at home anyway. People always seem to kill their own first. We would have to kill Arab Israelis if we wanted to wipe out the entire race. That is never going to happen. Israelis are funny about not wanting to kill Israelis. The international media might think that all Israelis are Jews but most people know better.

At the other end of the extreme hyperbole spectrum, somebody called me a hero. I am not a hero in any way whatever and I do not like it when that word is thrown about casually. Heroes sacrifice their lives to save others. A few people died a long time ago to save my father's life. They were heroes.

I never do that. I fly places, pick up people, take them somewhere better. It is not particularly dangerous and the last thing I will ever do on the job is sacrifice myself. Not simply because that is the last thing anybody can do but because my job requires me to sacrifice other people before myself. It takes a pretty selfish person to do my job. If we get into a situation where I have to choose between the patient and myself, I have to choose myself. Not as a matter of self preservation but because that is an absolute requirement of my job.

The flight surgeon has the luxury of putting the patient first but he is no hero either. Doctors save lives, which is a very good thing, but not heroic. Cutting somebody open and putting them back together requires a great deal of training and skill but very little self sacrifice.

The soldiers we deal with are not necessarily heroes either. The current trend is to call all soldiers heroes but most just do a routine job. My boyfriend's job is anything but routine. If the day comes when he has to jump on the proverbial grenade then he will be a hero. I would rather that never happen. He would be called a hero but I would be too selfish to see it that way. If anybody told me he saved lives I would point out that he has also taken lives, so it all balances out. Some of the soldiers who actually sacrifice their own lives to save others have also killed others. There is nothing heroic about putting a bullet in somebody's brain.

What happens when a terrorist leader is killed? Blame Israel.

Dubai authorities are going out of their way to prove that Mossad killed some guy. I can see several problems with that.

You are supposed to investigate any crime without bias and let the evidence take you wherever it goes. When you have already decided who did it before you even know what happened then you are bound to make many mistakes. Ask Alfred Dreyfus about that.

The Mossad has a long history of targeted elimination. Some people might see that as a bad thing but it means they probably know what they are doing. This Dubai episode was handled poorly. Mossad agents would have done a better job. Unless they mucked it up on purpose to make people think Hamas did it. If that is the case then they failed miserably. It would also be a stupid move since Hamas is rarely blamed for all of the people they routinely murder.

And why are so many people upset that a terrorist leader was killed? I can understand that some countries are upset about all the fake passports. Nobody wants the world to know how easy it is to forge your passports. But who is upset over the death of a terrorist? Hamas is, even though it is possible that they killed him. They get upset over just about anything they can blame on Israel.

But here is the thing. Hamas is a terrorist organisation. They kill people all the time. They kill children and old people. They target schools and hospitals. And they do not just kill Jewish children. That is acceptable by international standards since Israel is the big bad bogeyman. But they also kill Palestinians. How do you think they got control of Gaza?

Opposing political parties in other countries often say hateful things about each other but Hamas and Fatah were literally at war. Not with tea parties and radio programmes. With guns and rockets. Hamas did not run a better campaign than Fatah. They killed enough Fatah supporters to stage a coup.

Now the International Community are expressing moral outrage over Tzipi Livni's comment that this particular death was a good thing. How can the International Community be morally outraged over the death of a terrorist? Why is the International Community always morally outraged over something? Why do we never hear about the International Community being pleasantly surprised over something?

The logic seems to be that since Livni is glad that this murderer is dead then Israel must have killed him. I can see problems with that, too.

Some British court in London issued an arrest warrant against Tzipi Livni. Apparently because she was acting prime minister or foreign minister during the invasion of Gaza. The warrant was quickly dropped. Another British court issued a warrant earlier against Ehud Barak since he was defence minister. That was dropped because he was in office at the time the warrant was issued and had diplomatic immunity.

Some people in Israel's government were upset by all this. The majority party are taking it personally even though Livni is leader of the opposition. We will bicker no end during an election but stand united when the pommies start a row.

I think it is funny. Obviously whoever is responsible for these warrants is sympathetic to the Palestine situation. Livni is the best friend Yosh Arabs have had in high office for a very long time. She is the highest ranking official who thinks that the two state solution can work. She was instrumental in Israel's withdrawal from Gaza in 2005.

Israel invaded Gaza after thousands of rockets were fired at Israeli civilians from Gaza. Britain invaded Iraq after the United States told them to. No Iraqi groups had ever shot anything at any British civilians. Have any British arrest warrants been issued for Tony Blair or Geoff Hoon? Remember that Hoon suggested using nuclear weapons in Iraq.

So invading and occupying a country on another continent that never attacked you is fine and fair but bombing an area occupied by a terrorist organisation that fires thousands of rockets at your schools and hospitals is a war crime as far as British courts are concerned. Or at least two courts. Never mind that British courts have no jurisdiction in Israel or Judea and Samaria. Or the Hague.

Tzipi Livni is as pro Palestine as they come and currently leader of the opposition to Netanyahu. He is not Palestine's best friend. Tony Blair favours Israel over Palestine any day. As soon as Blair left office he was appointed peace envoy to the Middle East by the world police. How is that for irony?

Tzipi Livni is the opposition leader. She does not run the government. She is not in charge of taking out terrorists. Not anymore at least. It has been pointed out that the International Community's moral outrage over her statement came conveniently close to Britain's attempt to arrest her for the Gaza invasion. I think that likely is a coincidence. The only reason to remove her from any position of power would be to destabilise any chance of Israel and Palestine finding peace. Who would want that besides everybody who profits from the status quo?

And she is only saying what everybody would say if Hamas were an Iranian or Libyan organisation. Hamas is largely funded by Iran but for the sake of discussion we shall say that they are not Iranian. Were the International Community morally outraged every time a Libyan terrorist was killed? So what is the difference? It happened in Dubai and that sort of thing hurts their resort image?

The difference is that Hamas terrorists do not generally kill Americans or Europeans. Unless they get caught in the crossfire. Hamas exists for the sole purpose of ridding the world of Israel. The International Community used to have a problem with people who wanted to wipe Israel off the map. Then something changed.

If you shoot rockets into Israel and the IDF shoot back, the International Community will cry disproportionate response. What does that even mean? Have you ever heard of any country that would not fight back if its neighbour fired rockets at it? I am not saying that Israel should use nuclear weapons after a single shot is fired at an Israeli but that has never happened. And Israel does not officially have nuclear weapons. How many bullets are you allowed to fire when you are under attack? What is the quota when fighting fanatical terrorists who will gladly kill their own children just to kill yours?

When the Mossad used to target individual terrorist leaders the International Community said that was a human rights violation. I have never heard anybody use the phrase human rights violation when Palestinian terrorists murder children. If Israel arrested all of its Arab citizens because they are as Arab as the Palestinian terrorists then that would be a clear human rights violation. But is arresting a murderer a violation of his human rights?

Most people would say no. So what if whilst trying to arrest him you happen to fire an AGM missile at his car? Israel does not have capital punishment. Imprisoned murderers are often traded for kidnapped Israeli soldiers, usually at a very disproportionate ratio. I am not sure why kidnapping Israeli soldiers is not a violation of their human rights. Sometimes it makes more sense to just kill Mussolini the first time instead of exile him on a mountain top.

How many options does Israel have? Targeting terrorist leaders is out. Bombing terrorist headquarters is out. Invading cities that house and train terrorists is out. And do not even think about building a security fence. That just upsets a lot of people. Security is bad in a world where terrorism is rationalised.

A simple solution might be to flood money and supplies into building schools and hospitals in Judea and Samaria and help them create a manageable infrastructure thereby convincing most Palestinians that Israel is not the enemy. But that is not going to happen. Israel already provides most of their food, water, medical supplies, electricity free of charge, and Palestinians still see Jews as the enemy.

But it is difficult to blame the average Palestinian. Their information and education are provided by their dictators. Palestinian school books say things about Jews that make Ann Coulter look like Dr Seuss. People who know nothing about the situation will say that if Israel simply pulled out of Judea and Samaria completely then there would be peace. These people need to look up a place called Gaza. And even if the average Palestinian on the street objectively understood what was going on it would never stop the fanatics from pledging eternal death and destruction. But they would have less support at home.

Take any story about the Israel/Palestine conflict where the International Community express moral outrage over whatever bad thing Israel did and replace Israel with America or any European country and replace Palestinian terrorist with guerilla or rebel fighter.

Are the International Community ever morally outraged when Spain kills a few Basque separatists? Imagine if Quebec launched rockets into the United States. Would the United States apologise for not speaking French and building the Erie Canal? Or would American Marines invade the hell out of Canada? Why is there more moral outrage over Israeli soldiers defending its borders at home than there is over American, British, French soldiers fighting half a world away from its borders?

In the propaganda war on the television and internet between the representative democracy Israel and the repressive totalitarian Hamas, I have heard too much about who is right and who is wrong, who did what bad things to whom. Everybody is convinced that they are right and, as usual, the people who suffer the most are the children. Not a single Israeli or

Palestinian child chose this. They do not care about what happened in 1967 or 1948 or 1500 years ago. The children of Israel and Palestine are being killed because their fathers and grandfathers cannot get over the past and live by the rules all children learn in the playground. Every other child is a potential friend if you share and play nice.

Siblings Hemda, Avraham and Ra'aya Schijveschuurder were 2, 4 and 14 years old when they were murdered with their parents Mordechai (43) and Tzira (41). Tamara Shimashvili was 8 years old when she and her mother Lily (33) were murdered. Yocheved Shoshan was 10 years old, Malka Roth was 15, Michal Raziel was 16, Tehila Maoz was 18. They were murdered along with Zvika Golombek (26), Frieda Mendelsohn (62), Brazilian Giora Balash (60), American Shoshana Greenbaum (31) by a few cowards who decided that the best way to get what they want was to blow up a pizzeria. 130 other innocent people were injured in the explosion.

Chanah Rogan (92), Alter Britvich (88) and his wife Frieda (86), Yulia Talmi (87), Lola Levkovitch and Eliahu Nakash (both 85), Miriam Gutenzgan (82), Ernest Weiss (79) and his wife Eva (75), Meir Yakobovitch (76) and his wife Anna (78), Perla Hermele (79), Michael Karim (78), Dvora Karim (73), Marianne Zaoui (77), David Anichovitch and Yehudit Korman (both 70), Shula Abramovitch (63), Furuk Na'imi (62), Ze'ev Vider (50), Sivan Vider (20), Andre and Idit Fried (both 47), Irit

Rashel (45), Ami Hamami (44), Shimon Ben-Aroya (42), Avraham Beckerman (25) were all murdered by some cowards who decided that the best way to get what they want was to bomb a Pesach seder filled with mostly older people. Sarah Levy-Hoffman (89) died 11 days after the bombing, Eliezer Korman (74) died one month after, Clara Rosenberger (77) died three months after. 140 other innocent, mostly older people were injured in the bombing.

Meir Haim (74), Viktor Shebayev (62), Moshe Aharfi (60), Amiram Zmora (55), Hannah Haimov (53), Mordechai Evioni (52), Boris Tepalshvili (51), Sapira Yulzari-Yaffe (46), Avi Kotzer (43), Lilya Zibstein (33), Ilanit Peled and Igor Zobokov (both 32), Andrei Friedman (30), Ramin Nasibov (25), Mazal Orkobi (20) were murdered along with Krassimir Angelov (32) of Bulgaria, Steven Cromwell (43) of Ghana, Ivan Gaptoniak (46) of Ukraine, Ion Nicolae (34) and Mihai Sabau (38) of Romania, Guo Ai Ping (47), Li Pei Zhong (41), Zhang Min Min (53) of China by some cowards who decided that the best way to get what they want was to blow up a bus station. 120 other innocent people were injured in the bombing.

Kamar Abu Hamed (12), Yuval Mendellevich (13), Abigail Litle (14), Tom Hershko (15) and his father Mordechai (41), Smadar Firstater and Daniel Haroush (both 16), Elizabeth Katzman, Asaf Zur, Tal Kehrmann (all 17), Anatoly Biryakov, Moran Shushan, Meital Katav (all 20), Be'eri Oved (21), Eliyahu Laham

(22), Maryam Atar (27), Mark Takash (54) were murdered by some cowards who decided that the best way to get what they want was to bomb a bus full of students going to school. 53 other innocent people, mostly children, were injured.

Admiral Ze'ev Almog (71) and his wife Ruth (70), their son Moshe (43) and grandsons Tomer (9) and Assaf (11), Bruria Zer-Aviv (59), her son Bezalel (30), his wife Keren (29) and their children Liran (4) and Noya (1), Lydia Zilberstein (56), Hana Francis (39), Irena Sofrin (38), Zvi Bahat (35), Mutanus Karkabi (31), Mark Biano (29) and his wife Naomi Biano (25), Osama Najar (28), Nir Regev (25), Sharbal Matar (23) were murdered by some cowards who decided that the best way to get what they want was to set off a roadside bomb in the middle of a busy street. George Matar (59) died two weeks later. Sixty other innocent people were injured in the explosion.

Segev Avihail and Neria Cohen (both 15), Yonatan Eldar and Avraham Moses (both 16), Yohai Lifshitz (17), Yehonadav Hirschfeld and Ro'i Roth (both 18), Doron Meherete (26) were murdered by some cowards who decided that the best way to get what they want was to shoot at students in a school library. 80 other innocent people, mostly teenagers, were injured.

Liran Nehmad was only 3 years old when she was murdered. Her sisters Shaul and Shiraz were 15 and 7. Their brother Avraham was also 7. They were murdered along with their parents Shlomo (40) and Gafnit Nehmad (32). Ya'akov Avraham was only 7 months old when he was murdered with his mother Tzofia Eliyahu (23). Oriah Ilan was 18 months old. Her brother Lidor was 12 years old. They were murdered along with Avi Hazan (37) by some cowards who decided that the best way to get what they want was to bomb a bar mitzvah simcha full of children. Fifty other innocent men, women and children were injured in the bombing.

The "heroes" who murdered the innocent human beings named above, as well as hundreds more, are now free to murder more people, Allah willing.

That "Allah willing" part should piss off a lot of people. It should especially piss off people who believe that God is about love, not about blowing up children for political reasons. But for some reason it never does.

I understand hating Jews. We do things slightly differently than you. When a heart is full of hate it is easy to hate people who are slightly different. But in their fanatical quest to murder all Jews these terrorists are murdering mostly Palestinians.

There are a lot of Arab names above. Where is the moral outrage from the International Community? They are busy protesting that Israel makes foreigners show identification before entering Israel.

THE COST OF FREEDOM

American president Bill Clinton hosted a Middle East peace summit at Camp David, Maryland in July 2000. Clinton's goal was to get Palestinian Authority chairman Yasser Arafat and Israel prime minister Ehud Barak to make nice and become best friends. Failing that, he was willing to settle for some kind of peace treaty.

According to Clinton, Barak was willing to make enormous compromises and give up very large sections of land to keep terrorists from killing more of his people. Rather than agreeing with anything or even submitting his own proposals, aside from the death of Israel and all its people, Arafat decided to end the summit and go home.

The world blamed the failed summit on whichever side they do not like. Bill Clinton, liberal pro Palestine Democrat, clearly placed the blame on Arafat.

Ariel Sharon visited Har Habayit in September 2000. This should not have been a problem as it is in Israel and is the single most sacred site in all of Judaism. A Jewish Israeli leader should be able to visit such a place.

But it is also where some Muslim leaders were nice enough to build a mosque on top of the remains of the Second Temple and make it impossible for the Third Temple to ever be built, which to Jews is the equivalent of forcing Christians to believe that Jesus was dead and buried and never came back to life.

Access to Judaism's most sacred site is restricted to Jews because Israel does not want to upset terrorists who want to kill us whether we go there or not.

Arab terrorists were outraged that a Jew would dare visit Judaism's most sacred site, and some of them declared war on Israel and Judaism. At least that is the official version. Several prominent terrorist leaders, including Hassan Yousef, Marwan Barghouti, Mahmoud al Zahar, have since said that the war against Judaism was planned well before Ariel Sharon went to Har Habayit and even before the summit in July.

1158 people, Jews, Arabs, Muslims, Christians, foreigners, were murdered in Israel by Arab terrorists between September 2000 and December 2013. This list does not include soldiers killed in action or accidental deaths in questionable situations. One could easily make the argument that far more Palestinians have been killed than Israelis. That is true. Arab terrorists kill more Palestinians than anybody else. But those numbers are impossible to verify, and information from the repressive Fatah and Hamas dictatorships is difficult to obtain.

2000 September 27: Sergeant David Biri (19) of Jerusalem, bombed near Netzarim.

2000 September 29: Police superintendent Yosef Tabeja (27) of Ramle, shot by his Palestinian counterpart on a joint patrol near Kalkilya.

2000 October 1: Police Corporal Madhat Yusuf (19) of Beit Jann, shot at Joseph's Tomb in Nablus.

2000 October 2: Wichlav Zalsevsky (24) of Ashdod, shot in Masha on the Trans-Samaria Highway. Sergeant Max Hazan (20) of Dimona, shot near Beit Sahur.

2000 October 8: Hillel Lieberman (36) of Elon Moreh, shot near Nablus.

2000 October 12: Corporal Yosef Avrahami and Sergeant Vadim Norzhich (33) lynched by a Palestinian mob at the police building in Ramallah.

2000 October 19: Rabbi Binyamin Herling (64) of Kedumim, shot at Mount Ebal near Nablus.

2000 October 28: Marik Gavrilov (25) of Bnei Aysh, immolated between the villages of Bitunia and Ramallah.

2000 October 30: Eish-Kodesh Gilmor (25) of Mevo Modi'in, shot at the National Insurance Institute's East Jerusalem branch. 1

other injured. Amos Machlouf (30) of Gilo, found dead in a ravine near Beit Jala.

2000 November 1: Lieutenant David-Hen Cohen (21) of Karmiel and Sergeant Shlomo Adshina (20) of Kibbutz Ze'elim, shot in the al Hader area. Major Amir Zohar (34) of Jerusalem, murdered in the Nahal Elisha settlement in the Jordan Valley.

2000 November 2: Hanan Levy (33) and Ayelet Shahar Levy (28) bombed near the Mahane Yehuda market in Jerusalem. 10 others injured.

2000 November 8: Noa Dahan (25) of Moshav Mivtahim, shot at the Rafah border crossing in Gaza.

2000 November 10: Sergeant Shahar Vekret (20) of Lod, shot by snipers near Rachel's Tomb in Bethlehem.

2000 November 11: Sergeant Avner Shalom (28) of Eilat, shot at the Gush Katif junction in Gaza.

2000 November 13: Sarah Leisha (42) of Neveh Tzuf, Corporal Amit Zanna (19) of Netanya, Corporal Elad Wallenstein (18) of Ashkelon, shot near Ofra. Gabi Zaghouri (36) of Netivot, shot near the Kissufim junction in Gaza.

2000 November 18: Sergeant Baruch Flum (21) of Tel Aviv and Sergeant Sharon Shitoubi (21) of Ramle, shot at the Kfar Darom greenhouses in Gaza.

2000 November 20: Miriam Amitai (35) and Gavriel Biton (34) both of Kfar Darom, bombed between Kfar Darom and Gush Katif. 9 others injured, including 5 children.

2000 November 21: Itamar Yefet (18) of Netzer Hazani, shot by sniper fire at the Gush Katif junction.

2000 November 22: Meir Bahrame (35) of Givat Olga and Shoshana Reis (21) of Hadera, bombed in Hadera. 60 others injured.

2000 November 23: Lieutenant Edward Matchnik (21) of Be'er Sheva, bombed at the DCO near Gush Katif in Gaza. Sergeant Samar Hussein (19) of Hurfeish, shot by snipers near the Erez crossing.

2000 November 24: Major Sharon Arameh (25) of Ashkelon, shot by sniper fire near Neve Dekalim in Gaza. Ariel Jeraffi (40) of Petah Tikva, shot near Otzarin in Palestine.

2000 December 8: Eliyahu ben Ami (41) of Otniel and Rina Didovsky (39) of Beit Hagai, shot near Kiryat Arba. Sergeant Tal Gordon (19), shot on the Jericho bypass road.

2000 December 21: Eliahu Cohen (29) of Modi'in, shot on a road between Givat Ze'ev and Beit Horon.

2000 December 28: Captain Gad Marasha (30) of Kiryat Arba and police Sergeant Major Yonatan Vermullen (29) of Ben-Shemen, killed whilst dismantling a bomb near the Sufa crossing in Gaza. 2 others injured.

2000 December 31: Binyamin Ze'ev Kahane and his wife Talia Kahane, shot by snipers on the Ramallah bypass road. 5 of their children (aged 2 months to 10 years) injured.

2001 January 5: Mordechai Cohen (34) of Hadera, found dead in the Caesarea industrial area.

2001 January 14: Ron Tzalah (32) of Kfar Yam in Gush Katif, shot near Kfar Yam.

2001 January 17: Ofir Rahum (16) of Ashkelon, shot 15 times near Ramallah.

2001 January 23: Etgar Zeituny (34) and Motti Dayan (27) of Tel Aviv, abducted in Tulkarem and murdered.

2001 January 25: Akiva Pashkos (45) of Jerusalem, shot near the Atarot industrial zone north of Jerusalem.

2001 January 29: Arye Hershkowitz (55) of Ofra, shot near the Rama junction north of Jerusalem.

2001 February 1: Doctor Shmuel Gillis (42) of Carmei Tzur, shot near the Arroub refugee camp on the Jerusalem-Hebron Highway. Lior Attiah (23) of Afula, shot near Jenin.

2001 February 4: Ishmael Abadyev (35) of Tirat Hacarmel, stabbed.

2001 February 5: Sergeant Rujayah Salameh (23), shot near Rafah.

2001 February 11: Tzachi Sasson (35) of Kibbutz Rosh Tzurim in Gush Etzion, shot near Tzurim.

2001 February 14: Simcha Shitrit (30) of Rishon Lezion, Sergeant David Iluz (21) and Sergeant Ofir Magidish (20) both of Kiryat Malachi, Sergeant Julie Weiner (21) of Jerusalem, Sergeant Rachel Levi (19), Sergeant Kochava Polanski (19), Corporal Alexander Manevich (18), Corporal Yasmin Karisi (18) all of Ashkelon, hit by a bus near Holon. 25 others injured.

2001 February 26: Mordechai Shefer (55) of Kfar Sava, murdered near Moshav Hagor.

2001 March 1: Claude Knap (29) of Tiberias, bombed in Wadi Ara. 9 others injured.

2001 March 4: Naftali Dean (85) of Tel Mond, Yevgenya Malchin (70) and Shlomit Ziv (58) both of Netanya, bombed in Netanya. 60 others injured.

2001 March 19: Baruch Cohen (59) of Efrat, shot near Gush Etzion.

2001 March 26: Shalhevet Pass (10 months), shot by snipers in Hebron.

2001 March 28: Eliran Rosenberg-Zayat (15) of Givat Shmuel and Naftali Lanzkorn (13) of Petah Tikva, bombed near the entrance to Kalkilya. 4 others injured.

2001 April 1: Dina Guetta (42) of Haifa, stabbed as part of an initiation rite on Ha'atzmaut Street in Haifa. Sergeant Ya'akov Krenschel (23) of Nahariya, shot near Nablus.

2001 April 2: Sergeant Danny Darai (20) of Arad, shot by snipers at Rachel's Tomb in Bethlehem.

2001 April 21: Stanislav Sandomirsky (38) of Beit Shemesh, mutilated and found in his car near Ramallah.

2001 April 22: Doctor Mario Goldin (53) of Kfar Sava, bombed in Kfar Sava. 60 others injured.

2001 April 28: Simcha Ron (60) of Nahariya, stabbed in Kfar Ba'aneh. Sergeant Shlomo Elmakias (20) of Netanya, shot on the Wadi Ara Highway in Galilee. 4 others injured.

2001 May 1: Assaf Hershkowitz (30) of Ofra,

shot between Ofra and Beit El.

2001 May 8: Arnaldo Agranionic (48), shot in Samaria.

2001 May 9: Yossi Ish-Ran (14) and Kobi Mandell (14) both of Tekoa, stoned to death in a cave about 200 metres from Tekoa.

2001 May 15: Idit Mizrahi (20) of Rimonim, shot as she drove with her father and brother on the Alon Highway to attend a family wedding.

2001 May 18: Tirza Polonsky (66) of Moshav Kfar Haim, Miriam Waxman (51) of Hadera, David Yarkoni (53), Yulia Tratiakova (21), Vladislav Sorokin (34) all of Netanya, bombed in Netanya. 100 others injured. Lieutenant Yair Nebenzahl (22) of Neve Tzuf, shot and his mother injured north of Jerusalem.

2001 May 23: Asher Iluz (33) of Modi'in, shot outside Ariel.

2001 May 25: Yosef Alfasi (50) of Rishon Lezion, immolated near Tulkarem.

2001 May 29: Sara Blaustein (53) and Esther Alvan (20) of Efrat, shot near Neve Daniel. Gilad Zar (41) of Itamar, shot between Kedumim and Yizhar.

2001 May 31: Zvi Shelef (63) of Mevo Dotan, shot north of Tulkarem.

2001 June 1: Ori Shahar (32), Jan Bloom (25), Katherine Kastaniyada-Talkir (15) all of Ramat Gan, Private Diez Normanov (21), Yelena Nelimov (18), Marina Berkovizki (17), Mariana Medvedenko (16), Yulia Nelimov (16), Liana Sakiyan (16) all of Tel Aviv, Roman Dezanshvili (21), Ilya Gutman (19), Irina

Nepomneschi (16), Yevgenia Dorfman (15) all of Bat Yam, Sergei Panchenko (20) and Aleksei Lupalu (16) both of Ukraine, Raisa Nimrovsky (15) and Maria Tagilchev (14) both of Netanya, Simona Rodin (18), Irena Usdachi (18), Anya Kazachkov (16), Yael-Yulia Sklianik (15) all of Holon, bombed outside a disco near Tel Aviv's Dolphinarium. 120 others injured.

2001 June 11: Yehuda Shoham (5 months) of Shilo, killed by a rock thrown at the family's car near Shilo in Samaria. Boris Korover (59) of Homesh, car attack.

2001 June 14: Lieutenant Colonel Yehuda Edri (45) of Ma'ale Adumim, shot by a Palestinian informant near Gush Etzion. 1 other injured.

2001 June 18: Doron Zisserman (38) of Einav, shot by sniper fire near Einav. Dan Yehuda (35) of Homesh, shot between Homesh and Shavei Shomron. 1 other injured.

2001 June 20: Ilya Krivitz (62) of Homesh, shot near Silat a Dahar.

2001 June 22: Sergeant Aviv Iszak (19) of Kfar Saba and Sergeant Ofir Kit (19) of Jerusalem, bombed near Dugit.

2001 June 28: Ekaterina Weintraub (27) of Ganim, shot on the Jenin bypass road. 1 other injured.

2001 July 2: Aharon Obadyan (41) of Zichron Ya'akov, shot near Baka a Sharkia. Yair Har Sinai (51) of Susiya, shot.

2001 July 4: Eliahu Na'aman (32) of Petah Tikva, shot near Tulkarem.

2001 July 9: Captain Shai Shalom Cohen

(22) of Pardes Hanna, bombed south of Hebron. 1 other injured.

2001 July 12: David Cohen (28) of Betar Illit, shot in Kiryat Arba.

2001 July 13: Yehezkel Mualem (49) of Kiryat Arba, shot whilst protesting the previous day's shooting.

2001 July 16: Sergeant Avi ben Harush (20) and Corporal Hanit Arami (19) both of Zichron Ya'akov, bombed in Binyamina. 11 others injured.

2001 July 24: Yuri Gushchin (18) of Jerusalem, stabbed and shot in Ramallah.

2001 July 26: Ronen Landau (17) of Givat Ze'ev, shot in front of his father whilst returning home from Jerusalem.

2001 August 5: Tehiya Bloomberg (40 years old and 5 months pregnant) of Karnei Shomron, shot between Alfei Menashe and Karnei Shomron. 3 others injured, including her husband Shimon and daughter Tzippi.

2001 August 6: Yitzhak Snir (51) of Ra'anana, shot in Amman.

2001 August 7: Zohar Shurgi (40) of Moshav Yafit, shot on the Trans-Samaria Highway. Wael Ghanem (32) of Taibeh, shot near Kalkilya.

2001 August 9: Aliza Malka (17) a student at Kibbutz Merav, shot at school. 3 teenage girls injured. Frieda Mendelsohn (62), Lily Shimashvili (33) and Tamara Shimashvili (8), Tehila Maoz (18), Michal Raziel (16), Malka Roth (15), Yocheved Shoshan (10) all of Jerusalem, Giora Balash (60) of Brazil,

Mordechai Schijveschuurder (43) and his wife Tzira Schijveschuurder (41) and their children Ra'aya (14), Avraham Yitzhak (4) and Hemda (2) of Neria, Shoshana Yehudit Greenbaum (31) of the United States, Zvika Golombek (26) of Karmiel, bombed at the Sbarro pizzeria in Jerusalem. 130 others injured. The terrorists responsible were released in 2011 in exchange for Gilad Shalit.

2001 August 25: Major Gil Oz (30) and Sergeant Kobi Nir (21) both of Kfar Sava, Sergeant Tzahi Grabli (19) of Holon, shot at the IDF base in Gush Katif. 7 soldiers wounded. Yaniv Ben-Shalom (27) and his wife Sharon Ben-Shalom (26) of Ofarim and her brother Doron Sviri (20) of Jerusalem, shot on the Jerusalem-Modi'in road. Their children (aged 1 and 2) were injured.

2001 August 26: Dov Rosman (58) of Netanya, shot near Zaita.

2001 August 27: Meir Lixenberg (38) of Itamar, shot between Har Bracha and Itamar.

2001 August 29: Oleg Sotnikov (35) of Ashdod, shot near Kutchin.

2001 August 30: Amos Tajouri (60) of Modi'in, shot in Na'alin.

2001 September 6: Lieutenant Erez Merhavi (23) of Moshav Tarum, shot near Kibbutz Bahan. 1 officer wounded.

2001 September 9: Ya'akov Hatzav (42) of Hamra and Sima Franko (24) of Beit She'an, shot near Adam Junction in the Jordan Valley. Doctor Yigal Goldstein (47) of Jerusalem, Morel Derfler (45) of Mevasseret Zion, and

Sergeant Daniel Yifrah (19) of Jerusalem, bombed near the Nahariya train station in northern Israel. 90 others injured.

2001 September 11: Sergeant Andrei Zledkin (26) of Karmiel and police Sergeant Tzachi David (19) of Tel Aviv, shot near Kibbutz Bachan.

2001 September 12: Ruth Shua'i (46) of Alfei Menashe, shot near Habla.

2001 September 15: Meir Weisshaus (23) of Jerusalem, shot on the Ramot-French Hill road in northern Jerusalem.

2001 September 20: Sarit Amrani (26) of Nokdim, shot in front of her 3 children near Tekoa. Her husband was injured.

2001 September 24: Salit Sheetrit (28) of Kibbutz Sde Eliyahu, shot near Shadmot Mehola.

2001 September 26: Zvia Pinhas (64) of Moshav Maor, stabbed in her home.

2001 October 2: Assaf Yitzhaki (20) of Lod and Corporal Liron Harpaz (19) of Alei Sinai, killed by artillery and grenades in Alei Sinai. 15 others injured.

2001 October 4: Haim ben Ezra (76) of Givat Hamoreh, Sergei Freidin (20) of Afula, Sergeant Tali ben Armon (19) of Pardesia, shot. 13 others injured.

2001 October 5: Hananya ben Avraham (46) of Elad, shot near Avnei Hefetz.

2001 October 7: Yair Mordechai (43) of Kibbutz Sheluhot, bombed near the kibbutz.

2001 October 17: Tourism Minister Rechavam Ze'evy (75), shot outside his room at the Jerusalem Hyatt Hotel.

2001 October 18: Lior Kaufman (30) of Ramat Sharon, shot near the Mar Saba monastery. 2 others injured.

2001 October 28: Lydia Marko (63) of Givat Ada, Ayala Levy (39) of Elyachin, Sima Menahem (30) of Zichron Ya'akov, Smadar Levy (23) of Hadera, shot in Hadera. 40 others injured. Sergeant Yaniv Levy (22) of Zichron Ya'akov, shot near Kibbutz Metzer.

2001 November 2: Sergeant Raz Mintz (19) of Kiryat Motzkin, shot near Ofra.

2001 November 4: Shoshana Ben-Ishai (16) of Betar Illit and Menashe Regev (14) of Jerusalem, shot in northern Jerusalem. 45 others injured.

2001 November 6: Captain Eyal Sela (39) of Moshav Nir Banim, shot on the southern Nablus bypass road.

2001 November 9: Hadas Abutbul (39) of Mevo Dotan, shot in Shaked.

2001 November 11: Aharon Ussishkin (50), shot at Moshav Kfar Hess.

2001 November 24: Sergeant Barak Madmon (26) of Holon, artillery fire in Gush Katif.

2001 November 27: Etty Fahima (45) of Netzer Hazani, grenade attack near Gush Katif. 3 others injured. Michal Mor (25) of Afula and Noam Gozovsky (23) of Moshav Ramat Zvi, shot in Afula. 10 others injured.

2001 November 29: Samuel Milshevsky (45) of Kfar Sava, Yehiav Elshad (28) of Tel Aviv, Inbal Weiss (22) of Zichron Ya'akov, bombed near Hadera. 9 others injured. Sergeant Yaron Pikholtz (20) of Ramat Gan, shot near Baka el Sharkiya. 1 soldier wounded.

2001 December 1: Michael Moshe Dahan (21), Guy Vaknin (19), Moshe Yedid-Levy (19), Sergeant Nir Haftzadi (19), Yosef El Ezra (18), Israel Ya'akov Danino (17), Ido Cohen (17), Assaf Avitan (15), Golan Turgeman (15), all of Jerusalem, Yuri Korganov (20) of Ma'alei Adumim, Adam Weinstein (14) of Givon Hahadasha, bombed on Ben Yehuda Street, Jerusalem. 180 others injured.

2001 December 2: Professor Baruch Singer (51) of Gedera, shot near Elei Sinai. Rassim Safulin (78), Cecilia Kozamin (76), Mark Khotimliansky (75), Leah Strick (73), Mikhail Zaraisky (71) Faina Zabiogailu (64), Samion Kalik (64), Yelena Lomakin (62), Ina Frenkel (60), Mara Fishman (51), Yitzhak Ringel (41), Ronen Kahalon (30), Tatiana Borovik (23) all of Haifa, Rosaria Reyes (42) of Philippines, Riki Hadad (30) of Yokne'am, bombed in Haifa. 40 others injured.

2001 December 12: Haim Chiprot (52, died 25 March 2002), Yirmiyahu Salem (48), Israel Sternberg (46), Esther Avraham (42), Moshe Gutman (40), Yair Amar (13) all of Emmanuel, Ya'akov Tzarfati (64) and Hananya Tzarfati (32) of Kfar Saba, David Tzarfati (38) of Ginot Shomron, police Warrant Officer Yoel Bienenfeld (35) of Moshav Tel Shahar, Avraham Nahman Nitzani (17) of Betar Illit, grenades, bomb and gunfire near Emmanuel. 30 others injured.

2001 December 17: Zion Ohana (45) of Adam, beaten to death in Jaba.

2001 December 25: Sergeant Michael Sitbon (23) of Beit Shemesh, shot near Beit She'an. 4 soldiers wounded.

2002 January 9: Major Ashraf Hawash (28) of Beit Zarzir, Sergeant Major Hana Abu-Ghanem (25) of Haifa, Sergeant Major Ibrahim Hamadieh (23) of Rehaniya, Sergeant Mofid Sawaid (25) of Abu Snan, grenades, explosives and gunfire near Kerem Shalom. 2 soldiers wounded.

2002 January 14: Sergeant Elad Abu-Gani (19) of Tiberias, shot near Kuchin. 1 officer wounded.

2002 January 15: Avraham Boaz (71) of the United States, kidnapped in Beit Jala, shot and found in a car in Beit Sahur. Yoela Chen (45) of Givat Ze'ev, shot near Givat Ze'ev. Her aunt was injured.

2002 January 16: Shahada Dadis (30) of Beit Hanina, shot south of Jenin.

2002 January 17: Anatoly Bakshayev (63) and Edward Bakshayev (48) of Or Akiva, Boris Melikhov (56) of Sderot, Dina Binayev (48) of Ashkelon, Aharon ben Yisrael-Ellis (32) of Ra'anana, Avi Yazdi (25) of Hadera, shot during a bat mitzvah simcha in Hadera. 35 others injured.

2002 January 22: Sarah Hamburger (79) and Svetlana Sandler (56) both of Jerusalem, shot in Jerusalem. 40 others injured.

2002 January 27: Pinhas Tokatli (81) of Jerusalem, bombed in Jerusalem by a female terrorist. 150 others injured.

2002 February 6: Miri Ohana (45) of Beit She'an and her daughter Yael (11) shot in their home. Sergeant Major Moshe Majos Meconen (33) of Beit She'an, shot in the ensuing gun battle.

2002 February 8: Moranne Amit (25) of Kibbutz Kfar Hanasi, stabbed by four Palestinians (aged 14 to 16) on the Sherover Promenade in Jerusalem.

2002 February 9: Atala Lipobsky (78) of Ma'ale Ephraim, shot in front of her son on the Trans-Samaria Highway.

2002 February 10: Lieutenant Keren Rothstein (20) of Ashkelon and Corporal Aya Malachi (18) of Moshav Ein Habesor, shot at the IDF Southern Command Base in Be'er Sheva. 4 others injured.

2002 February 15: Sergeant Lee Nahman Akunis (20) of Holon, shot north of Ramallah.

2002 February 16: Rachel Thaler (16, died 27 February), Nehemia Amar (15), Keren Shatsky (15), all of Ginot Shomron, bombed in Karnei Shomron. 30 others injured.

2002 February 18: Officer Ahmed Mazarib (32) of Beit Zarzir, bombed on the Ma'ale Adumim-Jerusalem road. Ahuva Amergi (30) of Ganei Tal, shot in Gush Katif. Major Mor Elraz (25) of Kiryat Ata and Sergeant Amir Mansouri (21) of Kiryat Arba, shot in the ensuing gun battle. 1 other injured.

2002 February 19: Lieutenant Moshe Eini (21) of Petah Tikva, Sergeant Tamir Atsmi (21) of Kiryat Ono, Sergeant Michael Oxsman (21) of Haifa, Sergeant Benny Kikis (20) of Karmiel, Sergeant Mark Podolsky (20) of Tel Aviv, Sergeant Erez Turgeman (20) of Jerusalem, shot near Ramallah. 1 soldier wounded.

2002 February 21: Minhal Dragma (22) of Baka al Garbiya, shot near Baka al Sharkiya.

2002 February 22: Valery Ahmir (59) of Beit Shemesh, shot on the Atarot-Givat Ze'ev road north of Jerusalem.

2002 February 25: Avraham Fish (65) and Aharon Gorov (46) both of Nokdim, shot near Bethlehem. Fish's daughter (9 months pregnant) was injured but delivered a baby girl. Officer Galit Arbiv (21) of Nesher, shot in northern Jerusalem. 8 others injured.

2002 February 27: Gad Rejwan (34) of Jerusalem, shot in the Atarot industrial area.

2002 February 28: Sergeant Haim Bachar (20) of Tel Aviv, shot in the Balata refugee camp near Nablus.

2002 March 1: Sergeant Ya'acov Avni (20) of Kiryat Ata, shot by snipers in the Jenin refugee camp.

2002 March 2: Police Chief Moshe Dayan (46) of Ma'aleh Adumim, shot near the Mar Saba monastery in the Judean Desert. Shlomo Nehmad (40) and his wife Gafnit Nehmad (32) and their daughters Shiraz (7) and Liran (3), Shaul Nehmad (15) and his brother Avraham Eliahu Nehmad (7, died 20 June), Lidor Ilan (12) and his sister Oriah (18 months) all of Rishon Lezion, Avi Hazan (37) of Moshav Adora, Tzofia Ya'arit Eliyahu (23) and her son Ya'akov Avraham (7 months) of Jerusalem, bombed in Beit Yisrael, Jerusalem at a bar mitzvah simcha. 50 others injured. The terrorist responsible was released in 2011 in exchange for Gilad Shalit.

2002 March 3: Didi Yitzhak (66) and Captain Ariel Hovav (25) of Eli, Lieutenant David Damelin (29) of Kibbutz Metzar, Sergeant Major Eran Gad (24) and Sergeant Rafael Levy (42) of Rishon Lezion, Sergeant Major Avraham Ezra (38) of Kiryat Bialik, Sergei Birmov (33) and Vadim Balagula (32) of Ariel, Sergeant Major Yochai Porat (26) of Kfar Sava, Sergeant Major Kfir Weiss (24) of Beit Shemesh, shot near Ofra. 6 others injured. Sergeant Steven Kenigsberg (19) of Hod Hasharon, shot near the Kissufim crossing. 4 soldiers wounded.

2002 March 5: Maharatu Tagana (85) of Upper Nazareth, bombed in Afula. Eli Dahan (53) of Lod, Yosef Habi (52) of Herzliya, Officer Salim Barakat (33) of Yarka, shot in Tel Aviv. 30 others injured. Devorah Friedman (45) of Efrat, shot on the Bethlehem bypass tunnel road. Her husband was injured.

2002 March 7: Asher Marcus (18), Eran Picard (18), Ariel Zana (18) all of Jerusalem, Arik Krogliak (18) of Beit El, Tal Kurtzweil (18) of Bnei Brak, shot in Atzmona. 23 others injured.

2002 March 8: Sergeant Edward Korol (20) of Ashdod, shot by snipers in Tulkarem.

2002 March 9: Israel Yihye (27) of Bnei Brak and Avia Malka (9 months) of South Africa, grenade and gunfire in Netanya. 50

others injured. Avraham Haim Rahamim (28) Livnat Dvash (28), Orit Ozerov (28), Limor Ben-Shoham (27), Tali Eliyahu (26), Dan Imani (23), all of Jerusalem, Natanel Kochavi (31) of Kiryat Ata, Baruch Lerner (29) of Eli, Danit Dagan (25) of Tel Aviv, Uri Felix (25) and Nir Borochov (22) of Givat Ze'ev, bombed in Rehavia, Jerusalem. 54 others injured.

2002 March 10: Sergeant Kobi Eichelboim (21), shot near Netzarim.

2002 March 12: Eyal Lieberman (42) of Tzoran, shot near Modi'in. 1 other injured. Lynne Livne (49) and her daughter Atara (15) of Kibbutz Hanita, Ofer Kanarick (44) of Moshav Betzet, Yehudit Cohen (33) of Shlomi, Alexei Kotman (29) of Kibbutz Beit Hashita, Lieutenant German Rozhkov (25) of Kiryat Shmona, shot between Shlomi and Kibbutz Metzuba. 7 others injured.

2002 March 13: Lieutenant Gil Badihi (21) of Nataf, shot in Ramallah.

2002 March 17: Noa Auerbach (18) of Kfar Sava, shot in Kfar Sava. 16 others injured.

2002 March 19: Lieutenant Tal Zemach (20) of Kibbutz Hulda, shot in the Jordan Valley. 3 soldiers wounded.

2002 March 20: Mogus Mahento (75) of Holon, Bella Schneider (53) and Warrant Officer Meir Fahima (40) of Hadera, Alon Goldenberg (28) of Tel Aviv, Sergeant Shimon Edri (20) and Sergeant Michael Altfiro (19) of Pardes Hanna, Corporal Aharon Revivo (19) of Afula, bombed at the Musmus junction on Highway 65 near Afula. 30 others injured.

2002 March 21: Yitzhak Cohen (48) of Modi'in, Gadi Shemesh (34) and Tzipi Shemesh (29) of Jerusalem, bombed in Jerusalem. 86 others injured.

2002 March 24: Avi Sabag (24) of Otniel, shot near Hebron. Esther Kleiman (23) of Neve Tzuf, shot near Ramallah.

2002 March 26: Major Cengiz Soytunc of Turkey and Catherine Berruex of Switzerland, members of the TIPH observer force in Hebron, shot near Halhul.

2002 March 27: Chanah Rogan (92), Alter Britvich (88) and his wife Frieda Britvich (86), Michael Karim (78), Marianne Myriam Lehmann Zaoui (77), Dvora Karim (73), David Anichovitch (70), Furuk Na'imi (62), Andre Fried (47), Idit Fried (47), Ami Hamami (44), Shimon ben Aroya (42) all of Netanya, Sarah Levy-Hoffman (89, died 7 April), Yulia Talmi (87), Eliahu Nakash (85) all of Tel Aviv, Lola Levkovitch (85) and Clara Rosenberger (77, died 25 June) of Jerusalem, Miriam Gutenzgan (82) of Ramat Gan, Perla Hermele (79) of Sweden, Ernest Weiss (79) and Eva Weiss (75) of Petah Tikva, Anna Yakobovitch (78, died 11 April), Meir Yakobovitch (76), Shula Abramovitch (63) all of Holon, Eliezer Korman (74, died 5 May) and Yehudit Korman (70) of Ramat Hasharon, Ze'ev Vider (50) of Moshav Bekaot, Irit Rashel (45) of Moshav Herev La'et, Sergeant Major Avraham Beckerman (25) of Ashdod, Sergeant Sivan Vider (20) of Bekaot, bombed in the Park Hotel, Netanya during Pesach seder. 140 others injured. The terrorist responsible was released in 2011 in exchange for Gilad Shalit.

2002 March 28: David Gavish (50), his wife Rachel Gavish (50) and their son Avraham Gavish (20), Rachel's father Yitzhak Kanner (83) all of Elon Moreh, shot in their home.

2002 March 29: Tuvia Wisner (79) of Petah Tikva and Michael Orlansky (70) of Tel Aviv, shot in Neztarim. Haim Smadar (55) and Rachel Levy (17) both of Jerusalem, bombed by a female terrorist in the Kiryat Yovel supermarket in Jerusalem. 28 others injured.

2002 March 30: Rachel Charhi (36) of Bat-Yam, bombed in Tel Aviv. 30 others injured. Police Sergeant Major Constantine Danilov (23) of Or Akiva, shot in Baka al Garbiyeh.

2002 March 31: Dov Chernobroda (67), Shimon Koren (55) and his sons Ran (18) and Gal (15), Aviel Ron (54) and his daughter Anat (21) and son Ofer (18), Ya'akov Shani (53), Moshe Levin (52), Daniel Carlos Wegman (50), Danielle Menchel (22), Adi Shiran (17) Orly Ofir (16), all of Haifa, Carlos Yerushalmi (52) of Karkur, Suheil Adawi (32) of Turan, bombed in Haifa. 40 others injured.

2002 April 1: Sergeant Major Ofir Roth (22) of Gan Yoshiya, shot by snipers near Har Homa, Jerusalem. Officer Tomer Mordechai (19) of Tel Aviv, bombed in Jerusalem.

2002 April 6: Sergeant Nisan Avraham (26) of Lod, shot near Rafiah Yam. 5 soldiers wounded.

2002 April 9: Major Oded Golomb (22) of Kibbutz Nir David, Captain Ya'akov Azoulai

(30) of Migdal Ha'emek, Lieutenant Dror Bar (28) of Kibbutz Einat, Lieutenant Eyal Yoel (28) of Kibbutz Ramat Rachel, Sergeant Avner Yaskov (34) of Be'er Sheva, Sergeant Tiran Arazi (33) of Hadera, Sergeant Yoram Levy (33) of Elad, Sergeant Ronen Alshochat (27) of Ramle, Sergeant Eyal Eliyahu Azouri (27) of Ramat Gan, Sergeant Shmuel Dani Mayzlish (27) of Moshav Hemed, Sergeant Menashe Hava (23) of Kfar Sava, Sergeant Amit Busidan (22) of Bat Yam, Sergeant Eyal Zimmerman (22) of Ra'anana, killed by explosives and gunfire in Jenin. 7 others injured. Major Assaf Assoulin (30) of Tel Aviv, shot in Nablus. Sergeant Gedaliah Mellick (21) of Jerusalem, bombed in Jenin. 12 soldiers wounded.

2002 April 10: Warrant Officer Shimshon Stelkol (33), Sergeant Major Shlomi ben Haim (27), Sergeant Michael Weissman (21), police Lance Corporal Keren Franco (18) all of Kiryat Yam, Avinoam Alfia (26) and Sergeant Major Nir Danieli (24) of Kiryat Ata, Sergeant Major Ze'ev Hanik (24) of Karmiel, police Lance Corporal Noa Shlomo (18) of Nahariya, bombed near Kibbutz Yagur. 22 others injured.

2002 April 12: Police Sergeant David Smirnoff (22) of Ashdod, shot near the Erez crossing. 8 others injured. Rivka Fink (75), Nissan Cohen (57), Suheila Hushi (48), Yelena Konrab (43) all of Jerusalem, Ling Chang Mai (34) and Yang Chai Siang (32) of China, bombed at Mahane Yehuda market in Jerusalem by a female terrorist. 104 others injured.

2002 April 20: Police Sergeant Uriel bar Maimon (21) of Ashkelon, shot near the Erez industrial park.

2002 April 22: Sergeant Major Nir Krichman (22) of Hadera, shot in Asira a Shamaliya.

2002 April 27: Ya'acov Katz (51) Katrina Greenberg (45) Arik Becker (22), Danielle Shefi (5) all of Adora, shot in their respective homes, most in their bedrooms. 7 others injured.

2002 May 7: Rafael Haim (64), Pnina Hikri (60), Nawa Hinawi (51), Shoshana Magmari (51) all of Tel Aviv, Edna Cohen (61) and Rassan Sharouk (60) both of Holon, Regina Malka Boslan (62) of Jaffa, Rahamim Kimchy (58), Israel Shikar (49), Nir Lovatin (31) all of Rishon Lezion, Yitzhak Bablar (57) and Esther Bablar (54) both of Bat Yam, Dalia Masa (56) of Nahalat Yehuda, Anat Teremforush (36) of Ashdod, Avi Bayaz (26) of Nes Ziona, bombed in Rishon Lezion. 55 others injured.

2002 May 12: Nisan Dolinger (43) of Pe'at Sadeh, shot in southern Gaza.

2002 May 19: Yosef Haviv (70), Victor Tatrinov (63), Arkady Vieselman (40) all of Netanya, bombed in Netanya. 59 others injured.

2002 May 22: Gary Tauzniaski (65) and Elmar Dezhabrielov (16) both of Rishon Lezion, bombed in Rishon Lezion. 40 others injured.

2002 May 27: Ruth Peled (56) of Herzliya and her granddaughter Sinai Keinan (14 months) of Petah Tikva, bombed in Petah Tikva. 37 others injured.

2002 May 28: Albert Maloul (50) of Jerusalem, shot on the Ramallah bypass road. His cousin was injured. Netanel Riachi (17) of Kochav Ya'akov, Avraham Siton (17) of Shilo, Gilad Stiglitz (14) of Yakir, shot whilst playing basketball at their school. 2 other students injured.

2002 June 5: Zion Agmon (50), Sergeant Dotan Reisel (22), Sergeant Eliran Buskila (21), Sergeant Ganadi Issakov (21), Sergeant Zvi Gelberd (20), Sergeant Violetta Hizgayev (20), Corporal Dennis Blumin (20), Corporal Liron Avitan (19), Corporal Vladimir Morari (19) all of Hadera, Shimon Timsit (35) of Tel Aviv, Eliyahu Timsit (32, body was identified in December) of Sderot, Sergeant David Stanislavksy (23) Sergeant Sariel Katz (21), Sergeant Yigal Nedipur (21), Corporal Avraham Barzilai (19) all of Netanya, Sergeant Sivan Wiener (19) of Holon, Adi Dahan (17) of Afula, car bomb collided with their bus at the Megiddo junction near Afula. 38 others injured.

2002 June 6: Erez Rund (18) of Ofra, shot near Ofra.

2002 June 8: Sergeant Major Shalom Mordechai (35) of Nahariya, Sergeant Eyal Sorek (23) and his wife Yael Sorek (24, 9 months pregnant) of Carmei Tzur, shot in the Gush Etzion bloc of Carmei Tzur. 5 others injured.

2002 June 11: Hadar Hershkowitz (14) of

Herzliya, bombed in Herzliya. 15 others injured.

2002 June 15: Lieutenant Anatoly Krasik (22) of Petah Tikva, Sergeant Haim Yehezkel Gutman (22) of Beit El, Sergeant Alexei Gladkov (20) of Be'er Sheva, shot near Alei Sinai and Dugit. 4 others injured.

2002 June 18: Mendel Bereson (72), Doctor Moshe Gottlieb (70), Raisa Dikstein (67), Helena Ivan (63), Baruch Gruani (60), Leah Baruch (59), Gila Nakav (55), Boaz Aluf (54), Rahamim Zidkiyahu (51) Yelena Plagov (42), Tatiana Braslavsky (41), Rafael Berger (28), Michal Biazi (24), Liat Yagen (24), Orit Hayla (21), Shiri Negari (21), Shani Avi-Zedek (15), Galila Bugala (11) all of Jerusalem, Iman Kabha (26) of Barta, bombed at the Patt Junction from Gilo. 74 others injured.

2002 June 19: Noa Alon (60) of Ofra, Tatiana Igelski (43) of Moldova, Michal Franklin (22) of Jerusalem, Hadassah Jungreis (20) of Migdal Haemek, Gila Sara Kessler (19) of Eli, Shmuel Yerushalmi (17) of Shilo, Gal Eisenman (5) of Ma'ale Adumim, bombed at French Hill, Jerusalem. 50 others injured.

2002 June 20: Rachel Shabo (40) and her sons Neria (16), Zvika (12), Avishai (5) and her neighbour who came to their aid Yosef Twito (31), shot when a terrorist entered their home in Itamar. 2 other children and 2 responding soldiers injured.

2002 July 16: Galila Ades (42), Ilana Siton (35), Gal Shilon (32) and his daughter Sarah Tiferet (8 months), her grandmother Zilpa

Kashi (65), Keren Kashani (29), Yocheved ben Hanan (21) Yonatan Gamliel (16) all of Emmanuel, bombed enroute to Emmanuel. 20 others injured, including Yehudit Weinberg, whose baby was born prematurely and died the next day.

2002 July 17: Lieutenant Elad Grenadier (21) of Haifa, shot whilst apprehending the July 16 terrorists in Emmanuel. 3 others injured. Xu Heng Yong (39) and Li Bin (33, died 24 July) both of China, Dmitri Pundikov (33, died 25 July) of Bat Yam, Adrian Andres (30) of Romania, Boris Shamis (25) of Tel Aviv, bombed in Tel Aviv. 40 others injured.

2002 July 25: Rabbi Elimelech Shapira (43) of Peduel, shot near Alei Zahav. 1 other injured.

2002 July 26: Rabbi Yosef Dikstein (45), his wife Hannah Dikstein (42) and their son Shuv'el Zion (9) of Psagot, Sergeant Elazar Lebovitch (21) of Hebron, shot near Hebron. 2 other children injured.

2002 July 30: Shlomo Odesser (60) and his brother Mordechai Odesser (52) both of Tapuach, shot in Jama'in.

2002 July 31: Daphna Spruch (61, died 10 August), Levina Shapira (53), Revital Barashi (30, died 13 August), David Diego Ladowski (29) all of Jerusalem, Dina Carter (37), Janis Ruth Coulter (36), Benjamin Blutstein (25), David Gritz (24) Marla Bennett (24) all of the United States, bombed at Hebrew University's Mount Scopus campus cafeteria. 85 others injured.

2002 August 1: Shani Ladani (27) of Moshav Olash, body found shot and bound near the Green Line.

2002 August 4: Rebecca Roga (40) and Adelina Kononen (37) of Philippines, Sergeant Major Roni Ghanem (28) of Maghar, Mordechai Yehuda Friedman (24) of Ramat Beit Shemesh, Marlene Menahem (22) of Moshav Safsufa, Sari Goldstein (21) of Karmiel, Sergeant Omri Goldin (20) of Mitzpe Aviv, Maysoun Amin Hassan (19) of Sajur, Sergeant Yifat Gavrieli (19) of Mitzpe Adi, bombed at the Meron junction between Haifa and Safed. 50 others injured. Nizal Awassat (52) of Jabel Mukaber and Yekutiel Amitai (34) of Jerusalem, shot near the Damascus Gate of the Old City, Jerusalem. 17 others injured.

2002 August 5: Avi Wolanski (29) and his wife Avital Wolanski (27) of Eli, shot on the Ramallah-Nablus road near Eli. Their child (3) was injured.

2002 August 10: Yafit Herenstein (31) of Moshav Mechora, shot outside her home. Her husband was injured.

2002 August 20: Sergeant Kevin Cohen (19) of Petah Tikva, shot by snipers near Khan Yunis.

2002 September 5: Lieutenant Malik Grifat (24) of Zarzir, shot near Nisanit. 1 soldier wounded.

2002 September 18: David Buhbut (67) of Ma'ale Adumim, burnt and shot body found near el Azzariya. Yosef Ajami (36) of Jerusalem, shot near Mevo Dotan. 1 other injured. Police Sergeant Moshe Hezkiyah (21) of Elyachin, bombed at the Umm al Fahm junction. 3 others injured.

2002 September 19: Solomon Hoenig (79) and Yaffa Shemtov (49) both of Tel Aviv, Rosanna Siso (63) of Gan Yavneh, Yossi Mamistavlov (39) of Or Yehuda, Ofer Zinger (29) of Moshav Pazael, Jonathan Jesner (19) of Scotland, bombed on a bus near the Great Synagogue in Tel Aviv. 70 others injured.

2002 September 23: Shlomo Yitzhak Shapira (48) of Jerusalem, shot near the Cave of the Patriarchs in Hebron. 3 of his children injured.

2002 September 30: Sergeant Ari Weiss (21) of Ra'anana, shot in the Nablus casbah. 1 soldier wounded.

2002 October 8: Oded Wolk (51) of Modi'in, shot south of Hebron. 3 others injured.

2002 October 10: Sa'ada Aharon (71) of Ramat Gan, bombed on a bus from Bar Ilan University on the Geha Highway. 30 others injured.

2002 October 21: Iris Lavi (68) of Netanya, Ofra Burger (56) of Hod Hasharon, Indelou Ashati (54) of Hadera, Corporal Ilona Hanukayev (20) of Hadera, Sergeant Major Eliezer Moskovitch (40) of Petah Tikva, Sergei Shavchuk (35) of Afula, Anat Shimshon (33) of Ra'anana, Suad Jaber (23) of Taibe, Sergeant Aiman Sharuf (20) of Ussfiyeh, Sergeant Liat ben Ami (20) of Haifa, Sergeant Nir Nahum (20) of Karmiel, Sergeant Esther Pesachov (19) of Givat Olga, Corporal Sharon Tubol (19) of

Arad, Osnat Abramov (16) of Holon, bombed on a bus along Wadi Ara toward Hadera. 50 others injured.

2002 October 27: Major Tamir Masad (41) of Ben Shemen, Lieutenant Matan Zagron (22) of Itamar, Sergeant Major Amihud Hasid (32) of Tapuah, bombed at the entrance to Ariel whilst trying to prevent a terrorist from detonating the bomb. 20 others injured.

2002 October 29: Orna Eshel (53), Linoy Saroussi (14), Hadas Turgeman (14) all of Hermesh, shot in northern Samaria. 2 others injured.

2002 November 4: Julio Pedro Magram (51) of Kfar Sava and Gastón Perpiñal (15) of Ra'anana, bombed at a shopping mall in Kfar Sava. 70 others injured.

2002 November 6: Amos Sa'ada (52) of Rafiah Yam and Assaf Tzfira (18) of B'dolah, shot at Pe'at Sadeh.

2002 November 10: Yitzhak Dori (44), Revital Ohayon (34) and her sons Matan (5) and Noam (4) all of Kibbutz Metzer, Tirza Damari (42) of Elyachin, shot at the kibbutz.

2002 November 15: Yitzhak Buanish (46), Alexander Dohan (33), Alexander Zwitman (26) all of Kiryat Arba, Colonel Dror Weinberg (38) of Jerusalem, Superintendent Samih Sweidan (31) of Arab al Aramsha, Lieutenant Dan Cohen (22) of Jerusalem, Sergeant Yeshayahu Davidov (20) of Netanya, Sergeant Igor Drobitsky (20) of Nahariya, Sergeant Tomer Nov (19) of Ashdod, Sergeant Gad Rahamim (19) of Kiryat Malachi, Sergeant

Netanel Machluf (19) of Hadera, Corporal David Marcus (20) of Ma'aleh Adumim, grenades and gunfire as worshipers walked home from Sabbath prayers at the Cave of the Patriarchs in Hebron. Most of the officers were ambushed as they pursued the terrorists. 15 others injured.

2002 November 18: Esther Galia (48) of Kochav Hashahar, shot near Rimonim.

2002 November 21: Kira Perlman (67) and her grandson Ilan (8), Sima Novak (56), Marina Bazarski (46), Ella Sharshevsky (44) and her son Michael (16), Hadassah Ben-David (32), Dikla Zino (22) Yafit Ravivo (14), Hodaya Asraf (13) all of Jerusalem, Mircea Varga (25) of Romania, bombed on a bus in the Kiryat Menahem neighbourhood of Jerusalem. 50 others injured.

2002 November 28: Haim Amar (56), Ehud Avitan (54), David Peretz (48) Mordechai Avraham (44), Ya'acov Lary (35) all of Beit She'an, Shaul Zilberstein (36) of Upper Nazareth, grenades and gunfire at a polling station in Beit She'an during the Likud primary. 40 others injured.

2002 December 20: Rabbi Yitzhak Arama (40) of Netzer Hazani, shot on the Kissufim corridor road whilst driving with his wife and six children to attend a wedding Sabbath celebration in Afula.

2002 December 27: Sergeant Noam Apter (23) of Shilo, Private Yehuda Bamberger (20) of Karnei Shomron, Zvi Zieman (18) of Reut, Gavriel Hoter (17) of Alonei Habashan, shot whilst serving Shabbat meal to 100 students in Otniel. 10 others injured.

2003 January 2: Massoud Makhluf Alon (72) of Menahemiya, his burnt body was found in his car in the northern Jordan Valley.

2003 January 5: Meir Haim (74), Ilanit Peled (32) Sergeant Mazal Orkobi (20) all of Azor, Viktor Shebayev (62), Amiram Zmora (55) Mordechai Evioni (52) all of Holon, Moshe Aharfi (60), Hannah Haimov (53), Andrei Friedman (30), Ramin Nasibov (25) all of Tel Aviv, Zhang Min Min (53), Guo Ai Ping (47), Li Pei Zhong (41) all of China, Boris Tepalshvili (51) of Yehud, Sapira Shoshana Yulzari-Yaffe (46), Avi Kotzer (43), Igor Zobokov (32) all of Bat Yam, Ivan Gaptoniak (46) of Ukraine, Steven Arthur Cromwell (43) of Ghana, Mihai Sabau (38) and Ion Nicolae (34) of Romania, Lilya Zibstein (33) of Haifa, Krassimir Mitkov Angelov (32) of Bulgaria, bombed near the old Central Bus Station in Tel Aviv. 120 others injured. One of the terrorists responsible was released in 2011 in exchange for Gilad Shalit.

2003 January 12: Eli Biton (48) of Moshav Gadish, shot near his home. 4 others injured. Sergeant Mikhail Kazakov (34) of Jerusalem, shot near the Negev town of Nitzana.

2003 January 17: Netanel Ozeri (34) of Kiryat Arba, shot in his home. 3 others injured, including his daughter (5).

2003 February 6: Lieutenant Amir ben Aryeh (21) of Maccabim and Sergeant Idan Suzin (20) of Kiryat Tivon, shot near Nablus. 2 soldiers wounded.

2003 February 11: Major Shahar Shmul (24) of Jerusalem, shot by snipers near the Church of the Nativity in Bethlehem whilst checking a suspicious vehicle.

2003 March 5: Mark Takash (54), Mordechai Hershko (41), Maryam Atar (27), Sergeant Eliyahu Laham (22), Meital Katav (20), Anatoly Biryakov (20), Moran Shushan (20) Elizabeth Katzman (17), Tal Kehrmann (17), Asaf Zur (17), Smadar Firstater (16), Tom Hershko (15), Abigail Litle (14), Yuval Mendellevich (13) all of Haifa, Sergeant Be'eri Oved (21) of Rosh Pina, Daniel Haroush (16) of Safed, Kamar Abu Hamed (12) of Daliyat al Karmel, bombed on a bus in the Karmel section of Haifa enroute to Haifa University. 53 others injured. The terrorist responsible was released in 2011 in exchange for Gilad Shalit.

2003 March 7: Rabbi Eli Horowitz (52) and his wife Dina Horowitz (50) of Kiryat Arba, shot in their home. 5 others injured.

2003 March 10: Sergeant Tomer Ron (20) of Moshav Moledet, shot between the Cave of the Patriarchs and Kiryat Arba. 4 soldiers wounded.

2003 March 12: Sergeant Assaf Moshe Fuchs (21) of Kibbutz Gvat, shot in Saida. 1 soldier wounded.

2003 March 18: Sergeant Major Ami Cohen (27) of Netanya, shot south of Bethlehem. 1 soldier wounded.

2003 March 19: Zion Boshirian (51) of Mevo Dotan, shot whilst driving between Mevo Dotan and Shaked.

2003 April 10: Sergeant Ofer Sharabi (21) of Givat Shmuel and Sergeant Yigal Lifshitz (20) of Rishon Lezion, shot near Bekaot. 9 others injured.

2003 April 15: Zachar Rahamin Hanukayev (39) of Sderot, Ahmed Salah Kara (20) of Shuafat, shot at the Karni industrial zone crossing. 4 others injured. Lieutenant Daniel Mandel (24) of Alon Shvut, shot in Nablus. 1 soldier wounded.

2003 April 20: Corporal Lior Ziv (19) of Holon, shot whilst photographing a Hamas smuggling tunnel in Rafah. 3 others injured.

2003 April 24: Alexander Kostyuk (23) of Bat Yam, bombed outside the train station in Kfar Sava. 13 others injured.

2003 April 30: Yanai Weiss (46) of Holon, Dominique Caroline Hass (29) and Ran Baron (23) both of Tel Aviv, bombed at a beachfront pub in Tel Aviv by 2 British Palestinian terrorists. 60 others injured.

2003 May 5: Gideon Lichterman (27) of Ahiya, shot near Shvut Rachel. 2 others injured, including his daughter Moriah (6).

2003 May 11: Zion David (53) of Givat Ze'ev, shot near Ofra.

2003 May 17: Gadi Levy (37) and his wife Dina Levy (31) of Kiryat Arba, bombed in Hebron.

2003 May 18: Shimon Ustinsky (68), Yitzhak Moyal (64), Nelly Perov (55), Olga Brenner (52), Marina Tsahivershvili (44), Roni Yisraeli (34) all of Pisgat Ze'ev, Ghalab Tawil (42) of Shuafat, bombed on a bus near French

Hill, Jerusalem. 20 others injured. A second bomber detonated his bomb without casualties when intercepted by police.

2003 May 19: Hassan Ismail Tawatha (41) of Jisr a Zarqa, Avi Zerihan (36) of Beit Shean, Kiryl Shremko (22) of Afula, bombed at the Amakim Mall in Afula. 70 others injured.

2003 June 5: David Shambik (26) and Moran Menachem (17) both of Jerusalem, found beaten and stabbed near Hadassah Ein Karem Hospital in Jerusalem.

2003 June 8: Sergeant Matan Gadri (21) of Moshav Moledet, shot whilst pursuing two gunmen who earlier had wounded a police officer at the Tomb of the Patriarchs in Hebron.

2003 June 11: Alexander Kazaris (77), Bertin Tita (75), Miriam Levy (74) Elsa Cohen (70), Malka Sultan (67), Yaffa Mualem (65), Bianca Rivka Shichrur (62), Anna Orgal (55), Eugenia Berman (50), Alan Beer (46), Zvi Cohen (39) all of Jerusalem, Haile Abraha Hawki (56, identified 24 June) of Eritrea, Zippora Pesahovitch (54) of Zur Hadassah, Roi Eliraz (22) of Mevaseret Zion, Yaniv Obayed (22) of Herzliya, Bat-El Ohana (21) of Kiryat Ata, Sergeant Tamar Ben-Eliahu (20) of Moshav Paran, bombed on a bus on Jaffa Road, Jerusalem. 100 others injured.

2003 June 12: Avner Maimon (51) of Netanya, shot in his car near Yabed.

2003 June 13: Sergeant Mordechai Sayada (22) of Tirat Carmel, shot in Jenin.

2003 June 17: Noam Leibowitz (7) of Yemin Orde, shot near the Kibbutz Eyal junction. 3

relatives injured.

2003 June 19: Avner Mordechai (58) of Moshav Sde Trumot, bombed in his market south of Beit Shean.

2003 June 20: Zvi Goldstein (47) of Eli, shot in his car near Ofra. His wife and parents, Eugene and Lorraine Goldstein of the United States were injured.

2003 June 26: Amos Mantin (31) of Hadera, shot in Baka al Garbiyeh.

2003 June 27: Sergeant Major Erez Ashkenazi (21) of Kibbutz Reshafim, shot in Gaza.

2003 June 30: Krastyu Radkov (46) of Bulgaria, shot on the Yabed bypass road in northern Samaria.

2003 July 7: Mazal Afari (65) of Moshav Kfar Yavetz, bombed in her home. 3 of her grandchildren were injured.

2003 July 15: Amir Simhon (24) of Bat Yam, stabbed in Tel Aviv.

2003 July 21: Corporal Oleg Shaichat (20) of Upper Nazareth, shot on his way home.

2003 August 12: Yehezkel Yekutieli (43) of Rosh Ha'ayin, bombed in a local market. Uli Nisanevitch (22, died 28 August) of Nofim and Erez Hershkovitz (18) of Eilon Moreh, bombed at a bus stop outside Ariel 20 minutes after the Rosh Ha'ayin attack. 3 others injured.

2003 August 19: Fruma Rahel Weitz (73) Liba Schwartz (54), Ya'akov Binder (50), Feiga Dushinski (50), Shmuel Wilner (50), Rabbi Eliezer Weisfish (42), Menachem Leibel (24), Lilach Kardi (22), Binyamin Bergman (15),

Avraham Bar-Or (12), Shmuel Zargari (11 months) all of Jerusalem, Hanoch Segal (65), Tova Lev (37, died 12 September), Miriam Eisenstein (20), Chava Nechama Rechnitzer (19), Elisheva Meshulami (16) all of Bnei Brak, Mordechai Reinitz (49), Mordechai Laufer (27, died 5 September), Issachar Reinitz (9) all of Netanya, Goldie Taubenfeld (43) and Shmuel Taubenfeld (3 months) of the United States, Maria Antonia Reslas (39) of Philippines, Tehilla Nathanson (3) of Zichron Ya'acov, bombed on a bus in Shmuel Hanavi, Jerusalem. 130 others injured.

2003 August 29: Shalom Har-Melekh (25) of Homesh, shot whilst driving near Ramallah. His wife Limor Har-Melekh (7 months pregnant) was injured and gave birth to a baby girl.

2003 September 4: Sergeant Gabriel Uziel (20) of Givat Ze'ev, shot in Jenin.

2003 September 5: Petty Officer Ra'anan Komemi (23) of Moshav Aminadav, shot in Nablus just after killing a senior Hamas bombmaker. 4 soldiers wounded.

2003 September 9: Captain Yael Kfir (21) of Ashkelon, Warrant Officer Haim Alfasi (39) of Haifa, Warrant Officer Ya'akov ben Shabbat (39) of Pardes Hanna, Sergeant Yonatan Peleg (19) of Moshav Yanuv, Sergeant Efrat Schwartzman (19) of Moshav Ganei Yehuda, Sergeant Liron Siboni (19, died 19 November) of Ramat Gan, Corporal Prosper Twito (20) of Upper Nazareth, Corporal Felix Nikolaichuk (20) of Bat Yam, Corporal Mazi Grego (19) of

Holon, bombed outside Assaf Harofeh Hospital in Tzrifin. 30 others injured. Yehiel Tubol (52), Doctor David Appelbaum (51) and his daughter Nava Appelbaum (20), Gila Moshe (40), Alon Mizrahi (22) all of Jerusalem, David Shimon Avizadris (51) of Mevaseret Zion, Shafik Kerem (27) of Beit Hanina, bombed in Jerusalem. 50 others injured.

2003 September 26: Eyal Yeberbaum (27) and Shaked Avraham (7 months) both of Negohot, shot in their home during Rosh Hashanah.

2003 October 4: Admiral Ze'ev Almog (71) and his wife Ruth Almog (70), their son Moshe Almog (43) and grandsons Assaf (11) and Tomer (9), George Matar (59, died 15 October), Lydia Zilberstein (56) Zvi Bahat (35), Mutanus Karkabi (31), Mark Biano (29) and his wife Naomi Biano (25), Osama Najar (28) all of Haifa, Bruria Zer-Aviv (59) and her son Bezalel Zer-Aviv (30), his wife Keren Zer-Aviv (29) and their children Liran (4) and Noya (1) all of Kibbutz Yagur, Hana Francis (39) and Sharbal Matar (23) both of Fassouta, Irena Sofrin (38) of Kiryat Bialik, Nir Regev (25) of Nahariya, bombed by a female terrorist in Haifa. 60 others injured. The terrorist responsible was released in 2011 in exchange for Gilad Shalit.

2003 October 15: John Eric Branchizio (37) of Texas, Mark T Parson (31) of New York, John Martin Linde, Jr (30) of Missouri, American diplomatic escorts attempting to bring Palestinian students to the United States, bombed at the Beit Hanoun junction in Gaza. 1

other injured.

2003 October 24: Sergeant Alon Avrahami (21) of Or Yehuda, Sergeant Adi Osman (19) of Kfar Sava, Sergeant Sarit Schneor Sr. (19) of Shoham, shot in Netzarim.

2003 November 18: Sergeant Major Shlomi Belsky (23) of Haifa, Sergeant Shaul Lahav (20) of Kibbutz Shomrat, shot at a checkpoint on the tunnel bypass road between Jerusalem and Gush Etzion.

2003 November 19: Patricia Ter'n Navarrete (33) of Ecuador, shot at the Israel-Jordan border crossing terminal north of Eilat. 4 others injured.

2003 November 22: Ilya Reiger (58) of Jerusalem and Samer Fathi Afan (25) of Uzeir, shot along the security fence near Abu Dis.

2003 December 22: Captain Hagai Bibi (24) of Ma'aleh Adumim and Captain Leonardo Weissman (23) of Afula, grenade and gunfire on the Kissufim-Gush Katif road in Gaza.

2003 December 25: Sergeant Noam Leibowitz (22) of Elkana, Adva Fisher (20), Corporal Angelina Shcherov (19), Corporal Rotem Weinberger (19) all of Kfar Sava, bombed at a bus stop near Petah Tikva. 20 others injured.

2004 January 13: Ro'i Arbel (29) of Talmon, shot near his home in Samaria. 3 others injured.

2004 January 14: Gal Shapira (29) of Ashkelon, Sergeant Vladimir Trostinsky (22) of Rehovot, Sergeant Tzur Or (20) of Rishon Lezion, Corporal Andrei Kegeles (19) of

Nahariya, bombed by a female terrorist at the Erez Crossing in Gaza. 10 others injured.

2004 January 29: Natalia Gamril (53), Eli Zfira (48) Viorel Octavian Florescu (42), Rose Boneh (39), Hava Hannah Bonder (38), Baruch Hondiashvili (38), Avraham Balhasan (28), Dana Itach (24) all of Jerusalem, Yechezkel Isser Goldberg (41) of Betar Illit, Mehbere Kifile (35) of Ethiopia, Anat Darom (23) of Netanya, bombed on a bus at the corner of Gaza and Arlozorov streets in Jerusalem. 50 others injured.

2004 February 22: Yaffa Ben-Shimol (57), Israel Ilan Avisidris (41), Yuval Ozana (32), Sergeant Netanel Havshush (20), Lior Azulai (18), Benaya Yehonatan Zuckerman (18) all of Jerusalem, Yehuda Haim (48) of Givat Ze'ev, Rahamim Doga (38) of Mevasseret Zion, bombed on a bus near the Liberty Bell Park in Jerusalem. 60 others injured, including 11 children.

2004 February 26: Sergeant Major Amir Zimmerman (25) of Kfar Monash, shot near the Erez Crossing between Gaza and Israel. 2 soldiers wounded.

2004 February 27: Eitan Kukoi (30) and his wife Rima Novikov Kukoi (25), shot on the Lahav-Ashkelon road along the Green Line.

2004 March 14: Danny Assulin (51), Gil Abutbul (38), Avraham Avraham (34), Zion Dahan (30), Mazal Marciano (30), Maurice Tubul (30) all of Ashdod, Avi Suissa (56) of Kiryat Malakhi, Pinhas Avraham Zilberman (45) of Tel Aviv, Ophir Damari (31) and Moshe

Hendler (29) both of Rehovot, bombed at Ashdod Port. 16 others injured.

2004 March 19: George Khoury (20) of Beit Hanina, son of Elias Khoury, shot whilst jogging in French Hill, Jerusalem. The terrorist group responsible declared him a martyr for their cause after they learnt that he was an Arab Christian. Khoury's grandfather was murdered by Arab terrorists 30 years earlier.

2004 April 3: Ya'akov Zagha (40) of Avnei Hefetz, shot outside his home. His daughter Hani (14) was injured.

2004 April 17: Police Corporal Kfir Ohayon (20) of Eilat, bombed at the Erez Crossing. 3 others injured.

2004 April 25: Police Corporal Yaniv Mashiah (20) of Jaffa, shot near Hebron. 3 others injured.

2004 May 2: Tali Hatuel (34) and her daughters Hila (11), Hadar (9), Roni (7) and Merav (2) of Katif, shot at Gush Katif. 3 others injured.

2004 May 14: Sergeant Rotem Adam (21) of Rishon Lezion, Sergeant Alexei Hayat (21) of Be'er Sheva, shot by snipers in the Rafah refugee camp. 2 soldiers wounded.

2004 May 29: Major Shachar Ben-Yishai (25) of Menahemia, shot near Nablus.

2004 June 21: Weerachai Wongput (37) of Thailand, hit by mortar shrapnel in Kfar Darom from terrorists unsuccessfully attempting to divert attention from a settlement attack.

2004 June 27: Sergeant Roi Nissim (20) of Rishon Lezion, bombed from an underground tunnel in Gaza. 5 soldiers wounded.

2004 June 28: Mordechai Yosepov (49) and Afik Zahavi (4) killed by rocket shrapnel at a nursery school in Sderot.

2004 June 29: Moshe Yohai (63) of Ashdod, shot in the Palestinian Authority controlled village of Beit Rima.

2004 July 4: Victor Kreiderman (49) of Mevo Dotan, shot whilst driving near Yabad. His wife Emma was injured.

2004 July 6: Captain Moran Vardi (25) of Binyamina, shot whilst arresting terrorists in Nablus. 3 others injured.

2004 July 11: Sergeant Ma'ayan Na'im (19) of Bat Yam, bombed at a bus stop in Tel Aviv. 33 others injured.

2004 August 13: Shlomo Miller (50) of Itamar, shot near his home.

2004 August 31: Tamara Dibrashvilli (70), Shoshana Amos (64), Eliyahu Uzan (58), Maria Sokolov (57), Raisa Forer (55), Nargiz Ostrovsky (54), Roman Sokolovsky (53), Vitaly Brodsky (52), Denise Hadad (50), Tatiana Kortchenko (49), Larisa Gomanenko (48), Rosita Lehman (45), Tiroayent Takala (33), Emmanuel Yosef (28) Karine Malka (23), Aviel Atash (3) all of Be'er Sheva, bombed on 2 buses near Be'er Sheva City Hall. 100 others injured.

2004 September 22: Lance Corporal Mamoya Tahio (20) of Rehovot and police Corporal Menashe Komemi (19) of Moshav Aminadav, bombed at French Hill, Jerusalem.

17 others injured.

2004 September 23: Captain Tal Bardugo (21) and Sergeant Nir Sami (21) both of Jerusalem, Sergeant Israel Lutati (20) of Neve Dekalim, grenade and gunfire near Morag. 1 soldier and 1 journalist wounded.

2004 September 24: Tiferet Tratner (24) of Neveh Dekalim, mortar shrapnel in her home.

2004 September 29: Yuval Abebeh (4) and Dorit Benisian (2) both of Sderot, rocket attack whilst playing. 20 others injured.

2004 September 30: Shlomit Batito (36) of Nissanit, shot whilst jogging near his home, medical Sergeant Victor Ariel (20) of Kadima, grenade as he tried to aid Batito. Sergeant Gilad Fisher (22) of Mitzpeh Hoshaya, shot near Beit Hanoun. 2 soldiers wounded.

2004 October 6: Pratheep Nanongkham (24) of Thailand, shot in Kfar Darom.

2004 October 7: Tzila Niv (43), her sons Gilad (11) and Lior (3) of Rakefet, Hafez al Hafi (39) of Lod, Oleg Paizakov (32), his wife Ludmilla Paizakov (30) of Bat Yam, Assaf Greenwald (27) of Ramat Gan, Rotem Moriah (27) of Tel Aviv, Khalil Zeitounya (10) of Jaffa, bombed at the Taba Hilton in Sinai. Roy Avisaf (28) of Kfar Sava, Michal Alexander (27) of Ganei Tikva, Einat Naor (27) of Kibbutz Zikim, bombed at Ras a Satan in Sinai. 122 others injured.

2004 October 19: Sergeant Yair Nisim Turgemann (22) of Kiryat Arba, shot near Mevo Dotan.

2004 October 21: Sergeant Major Moshe

Almaliach (35) of Dimona, bombed during an engineering project on Philadelphi road in Gaza.

2004 October 28: Sergeant Michael Chizhik (21) of Tiberias, mortar shells at Morag. 6 soldiers wounded.

2004 November 1: Shmuel Levy (65) of Jaffa, Leah Levine (64) of Givatayim, Tatiana Ackerman (32) of Tel Aviv, bombed at the Carmel Market in Tel Aviv. 30 others injured.

2004 December 7: Sergeant Nadav Kudinski (20) of Kiryat Gat and his bomb sniffing dog, bombed at the Karni Crossing in Gaza. 4 soldiers wounded whilst evacuating Kudinski and Diablo.

2004 December 12: Sergeant Hussein Abu Leil (23) of Ein Mahal, Sergeant Tarek al Ziadne (20) of Rahat Bedouin village, Sergeant Araf Azbarga (19) of Kseifeh, Sergeant Sa'id Jahaja (19) of Arara, Corporal Adham Shehada (19) of Turan, bombed from a tunnel at the Rafah crossing. 5 others wounded.

2004 December 14: Jitladda Taparsa (19) of Thailand, mortar shells at Ganei Tal in the Gush Katif. 2 other foreign nationals injured.

2004 December 21: Ariella Fahima (39) of Moshav Nehusha, stabbed at her house.

2004 December 22: Salem al Kimlat (28) of Rahat Bedouin village, shot near Hebron.

2005 January 2: Vladimir Rubin (66) of Kiryat Gat, shot at Bet Guvrin National Park. Nissim Arbiv (25, died 11 January) of Nissanit, mortar shell in the Erez Industrial Zone. 2 others injured.

2005 January 7: Lieutenant Ariel Buda (21, died 15 October) of Tel Aviv, Sergeant Yosef Atia (21) of Petah Tikva, shot whilst driving on the Trans-Samaria Highway. 3 others injured.

2005 January 12: Gideon Rivlin (50) of Ganei Tal, bombed near Morag. 3 soldiers wounded.

2005 January 13: Ivan Shmilov (53), Herzl Shlomo (51), Dror Gizri (30) all of Sderot, Ibrahim Kahili (46) of Umm al Ghanem, Munam Abu Sabia (33) of Daburiyeh, Ofer Tiri (23) of Ashkelon, shot and bombed at Karni Crossing. 5 others injured.

2005 January 15: Ayala-Haya Abukasis (17) of Sderot, rocket shrapnel whilst protecting her younger brother near their home. Her brother was injured.

2005 January 18: Oded Sharon (36) of Gan Yavne, bombed at the Gush Katif junction in Gaza. 8 others injured.

2005 February 25: Yitzhak Buzaglo (40) of Mishmar Hayarden, Aryeh Nagar (37) of Kfar Sava, Ronen Reuvenov (30) of Tel Aviv. Yael Orbach (28) of Rehovot, Odelia Hubara (26) of Jerusalem, bombed in Tel Aviv. 50 others injured.

2005 May 2: Sergeant Dan Talasnikov (21) of Nir Galim, shot in Saida whilst arresting the terrorists responsible for the 25 February bombing. 1 soldier wounded.

2005 June 7: Salah Ayash Imran (57) and Muhammed Mahmoud Jaroun, both of Palestine, Bi Shu De (46) of China, rocket fire in Ganei Tal, Gaza. 5 others injured.

2005 June 19: Sergeant Major Avi Karouchi (25) of Be'er Sheva, missile and gunfire on the Philadelphi route along the Israel-Egypt border. 2 soldiers wounded.

2005 June 20: Yevgeny Reider (28) of Hermesh, shot in Baka a Sharkiya. 1 other injured.

2005 June 24: Avihai Levy (17) of Beit Hagai and Aviad Mansour (16) of Otniel, shot near Beit Hagai. 3 others injured.

2005 July 12: Anya Lifshitz (50), Julia Voloshin (31), Corporal Moshe Maor Jan (21) all of Netanya, Rachel Ben-Abu (16) and Nofar Horowitz (16) both of Tel Aviv, bombed outside Hasharon Mall in Netanya. 90 others injured.

2005 July 14: Dana Galkowicz (22) of Kibbutz Bror Hayil, rocket fire at Netiv Ha'asara.

2005 July 23: Dov Kol (58) and Rachel Kol (53) of Jerusalem, shot near the Kissufim crossing in Gaza. 3 others injured.

2005 August 24: Shmuel Mett (21) of the United Kingdom, stabbed near the Jaffa Gate in the Old City, Jerusalem. 2 others injured.

2005 September 21: Sasson Nuriel (55) of Jerusalem, kidnapped and shot in the industrial zone of Bitunya.

2005 October 16: Kineret Mandel (23) and her cousin Matat Adler (21) both of Carmel, Oz ben Meir (15) of Maon, shot at the Gush Etzion junction. 4 others injured.

2005 October 23: Katy David (27) of Kfar Yona, beaten and stabbed near Hadera. The murderers were not part of any terrorist organisation but proudly confessed that they murdered her "because she was a Jew."

2005 October 26: Michael Kaufman (68), Ya'acov Rahmani (68), Genia Poleis (66), Pirhiya Machlouf (53) all of Hadera, Sabiha Nissim (66) of Moshav Ahituv, Jamil Qa'adan (48) of Baka al Gharbiya, bombed in Hadera. 55 others injured.

2005 November 2: Sergeant Yonatan Evron (20) of Rishon Lezion, shot near Jenin.

2005 December 5: Alexandra Garmitzky (65), Daniel Golani (45) Haim Amram (26), all of Nahariya, Elia Rosen (38) of Bat Hefer, Keinan Tsuami (20) of Petah Tikva, bombed at the Sharon shopping mall in Netanya. 50 others injured.

2005 December 8: Sergeant Nir Kahane (20) of Kiryat Tivon, stabbed at the Kalandiya checkpoint.

2005 December 16: Yosef Shok (35) of Beit Hagai, shot whilst driving home in the southern Hebron hills. 2 others injured.

2005 December 29: Lieutenant Ori Binamo (21) of Nesher, bombed near Tulkarm. 10 others injured, mostly Palestinians.

2006 February 5: Kinneret Ben Shalom Hajbi (58) of Petah Tikva, stabbed in a taxi enroute to Tel Aviv. 5 other passengers injured.

2006 March 1: Eldar Abir (48) of Migdalim, shot near Migdalim.

2006 March 30: Rafi Halevy (63) and his wife Helena Halevy (58) of Kedumim, Re'ut Feldman (20) of Herzliya, Shaked Lasker (16) of Kedumim, bombed near Kedumim.

2006 April 17: Marcel Cohen (73) of France, Victor Erez (60) of Givatayim, Piroşca Boda (50) and Rozalia Beseneyi (48) of Romania, Binyamin Haputa (47) of Lod, Philip Balhasan (45) of Ashdod, Lily Yunes (42) of Oranit, Ariel Darhi (31) of Bat Yam, David Shaulov (29) of Holon, Lior Anidzar (26, died 13 May) of Tel Aviv, Daniel Wultz (16, died 14 May) of the United States, bombed near the old central bus station in Tel Aviv during the Pesach celebration. 60 others injured.

2006 June 11: Marwan Abed Shweika (35) of Abu Tor, Jerusalem, shot whilst driving north of Jerusalem. 2 others injured.

2006 June 25: Lieutenant Hanan Barak (20) of Arad and Sergeant Pavel Slutzker (20) of Dimona, shot between the Kerem Shalom and Sufa crossings. 4 soldiers wounded, 1 kidnapped. Eliyahu Pinhas Asheri (18) of Itamar, kidnapped and shot between Betar Illit and Neveh Tzuf.

2006 July 12: Sergeant Ehud Goldwasser (30) of Nahariya and Sergeant Eldad Regev (26) of Kiryat Motzkin, kidnapped between Za'it and Shtula along the Israel-Lebanon border. Their bodies were returned to Israel 16 July 2008.

2006 July 17: Sergeant Osher Damari (20) of Netanya, bombed in Nablus. 6 soldiers wounded.

2006 July 27: Doctor Daniel Yaakobi (59) of Yakir, immolated in his car near Qalqilya.

2006 August 10: Angelo Frammartino (24)

of Italy, stabbed whilst walking with friends in east Jerusalem.

2006 August 19: Sergeant Ro'i Farjoun (21) of Yehud, shot at the Bekaot chekpoint in the Jordan Valley.

2006 November 1: Sergeant Kiril Golenshein (21) of Moshav Keshet, shot by snipers in Beit Hanoun whilst pursuing terrorists.

2006 November 15: Fatima Slutsker (57) of Sderot, rocket fire in Sderot. 1 other injured.

2006 November 21: Ya'akov Ya'akobov (43) of Sderot, rocket fire in Sderot.

2007 January 29: Emi Haim Elmaliah (32), Michael ben Sa'adon (27), Israel Zamalloa (26) all of Eilat, bombed in a bakery in Eilat.

2007 February 25: Erez Levanon (42) of Bat Ayin, stabbed near Beit Omar.

2007 May 21: Shirel Friedman (32) of Sderot, rocket fire in Sderot.

2007 May 27: Oshri Oz (36) of Hod Hasharon, rocket fire in Sderot.

2007 July 12: Sergeant Arbel Reich (21) of Yuvalim, grenade and gunfire in the Bureij refugee camp, Gaza.

2007 September 18: Sergeant Ben-Zion Haneman (21) of Moshav Nov, shot in the Ein Beit Ilmeh refugee camp, Nablus.

2007 October 17: Sergeant Ben Kubani (20) of Hadera, shot near Khan Younis, Gaza.

2007 October 29: Sergeant Major Ehud Efrati (34) of Beit Yehoshua, shot near the Sufa crossing, Gaza.

2007 November 19: Ido Zoldan (29) of Shavei Shomron, shot near Kedumim,

Samarian Hills.

2007 December 28: Sergeant David Rubin (21) and Corporal Ahikam Amihai (20) both of Kiryat Arba, shot whilst hiking in the Hebron area. The terrorists responsible turned themselves in to Palestinian General Intelligence to avoid being apprehended by IDF.

2008 January 15: Carlos Andrés Mosquera Chávez (21) of Ecuador, shot by a sniper in the fields of Kibbutz Ein Hashlosha.

2008 January 24: Corporal Rami Zuari (20) of Be'er Sheva, shot near Shuafat.

2008 February 4: Lyubov Razdolskaya (73) of Dimona, bombed in Dimona. 38 others injured.

2008 February 27: Roni Yihye (47) of Moshav Bitcha, rocket fire in Sderot.

2008 March 1: Sergeant Doron Asulin (20) of Be'er Sheva and Sergeant Eran Dan-Gur (20) of Jerusalem, mortar, grenade and gunfire in northern Gaza.

2008 March 6: Sergeant Liran Banai (20) of Ashkelon, bombed near Kissufim. 1 other injured. Doron Meherete (26) of Ashdod, Yehonadav Haim Hirschfeld (18) of Kokhav Hashahar, Ro'i Roth (18) of Elkana, Yohai Lifshitz (17) and Neria Cohen (15) of Jerusalem, Yonatan Yitzhak Eldar (16) of Shilo, Avraham David Moses (16) of Efrat, Segev Peniel Avihail (15) of Neve Daniel, shot in the Mercaz Harav Yeshiva library in Jerusalem. 80 others injured, mostly teenagers. One of the terrorists responsible was released in 2011 in exchange for Gilad Shalit.

2008 April 9: Oleg Lipson (37) and Lev Cherniak (53) both of Be'er Sheva, mortar fire in Nahal Oz. Sergeant Sayef Bisan (21) of the Druze village of Jat, shot in southern Gaza. 2 soldiers wounded.

2008 April 16: Sergeant David Papian (21) of Tel Aviv, Sergeant Menhash al Banyat (20) of the Bedouin community of Kseife, Sergeant Matan Ovdati (19) of Moshav Patish, shot in Nahal Oz. 3 soldiers wounded.

2008 April 25: Shimon Mizrahi (53) of Bat Hefer and Eli Wasserman (51) of Alfei Menashe, shot in the Nitzanei Shalom industrial park.

2008 May 9: Jimmy Kadoshim (48) of Kibbutz Kfar Aza, mortar fire whilst tending his garden.

2008 May 12: Shuli Katz (70) of Kibbutz Gevaram, mortar fire at Moshav Yesha.

2008 June 5: Amnon Rosenberg (51) of Kibbutz Nirim, mortar fire in Kibbutz Nir Oz. 4 others injured.

2008 July 2: Jean Relevy (68), Elizabeth Goren-Friedman (54), Batsheva Unterman (33) all of Jerusalem, bulldozer attack between the Central Bus Station and the Mahane Yehuda market in Jerusalem. 50 others injured.

2008 July 11: Corporal David Shriki (died 23 July) of Rishon Lezion, shot near the Lion's Gate in the Old City, Jerusalem. 1 soldier wounded.

2008 October 23: Avraham Ozeri (86) of Gilo, stabbed near his home.

2008 December 27: Beber Vaknin (58) of Netivot, rocket fire in Netivot.

2008 December 29: Irit She'etrit (39) of Ashdod, rocket fire in Ashdod. Hani al Mahdi (27) of Aroar, rocket fire in Ashkelon. 16 others injured.

2009 January 27: Bedouin IDF soldier (name withheld at family's request) of Rahat Bedouin village, explosives at Kissufim Crossing. 3 soldiers wounded.

2009 March 15: Warrant Officer Yehezkel Ramzarkar (50) of Ma'ale Ephraim, Warrant Officer David Rabinowitz (42) of Ariel, shot near Massua.

2009 April 2: Shlomo Nativ (13) of Bat Ayin, axe attack near his home.

2009 May 9: Gregory Rabinowitz (56) of Ashdod, kidnapped and strangled near Gan Yavne.

2009 December 24: Rabbi Meir Avshalom Chai (45) of Shavei Shomron, drive by shooting near his home.

2010 February 10: Sergeant Ihab Khatib (28) of Kfar Maghar, stabbed at the Tapuach junction by a senior Palestinian police officer.

2010 March 18: Manee Singmueangphon (34) of Thailand, rocket fire in Netiv Ha'asara.

2010 March 26: Major Eliraz Peretz (32) of Eli and Sergeant Ilan Sviatkovsky (21) of Rishon Lezion, exchange of fire with terrorists who were planting explosives along the security fence in southern Gaza.

2010 June 14: Sergeant Major Yehoshua Sofer (39) of Be'er Sheva, shot at al Fawar

Junction south of Hebron. 3 others wounded.

2010 August 31: Yitzhak Ames (47), his wife Talya Ames (45) who was 9 months pregnant with her seventh child, Kochava Even Chaim (37), Avishai Shindler (24) all of Beit Hagai, shot whilst driving on Route 60 near Kiryat Arba. Amongst the first responders on the scene was Kochava Even Chaim's husband.

2010 December 18: Kristine Luken (46) of the United States, stabbed whilst hiking west of Jerusalem.

2011 March 11: Udi Fogel (36), Ruth Fogel (35) and their children Yoav (11), Elad (4), Hadas (3 months), stabbed in their home in Itamar, northern Samaria.

2011 March 23: Mary Jean Gardner (55) of the United Kingdom, bombed near Jerusalem Convention Centre. 50 others injured.

2011 April 7: Daniel Viflic (16, died 17 April) of Bet Shemesh, missile fire at a school bus near Kibbutz Sa'ad in the Negev.

2011 April 24: Ben-Yosef Livnat (24) of Jerusalem, shot by a Palestinian policeman at Joseph's Tomb in Nablus.

2011 August 18: Yosef Levy (57) of Holon, Shula Karlinsky (54), her sister Flora Gez (52), their husbands Dov Karlinsky (58) and Moshe Gez (53) all of Kfar Sava, bus driver Yitzhak Sela (56) of Be'er Sheva, bombed and shot on a bus to Eilat by terrorists entering Israel through Egypt. 31 others injured.

2011 August 20: Yossi Shushan (38) of Ofakim, Gazan rocket fire in Be'er Sheva.

2011 August 22: Eliyahu Naim (79, died 4

September) of Ashkelon, Gazan rocket fire in Ashkelon.

2011 September 23: Asher Palmer (25) of Kiryat Arba and his son Yonatan (1), stone attack in their car near Hebron.

2011 October 29: Moshe Ami (56) of Ashkelon, Gazan rocket fire in Ashkelon.

2012 June 1: Sergeant Netanel Moshiashvili (21) of Ashkelon, shot by terrorists from Gaza attempting to kidnap IDF soldiers.

2012 June 18: Said Fashapshe (35) of Haifa, explosives from Gaza in Philadelphi.

2012 September 21: Corporal Netanel Yahalomi (20) of Nof Ayalon, shot by terrorists at Har Harif entering from Egypt.

2012 November 15: Aharon Smadja (49), Mirah Scharf (25), Itzik Amsalem (24), Gazan rocket fire hit their apartment building in Kiryat Malachi.

2012 November 20: Alayaan Salem al Nabari (33) of Rejwan Beduin village, Corporal Yosef Fartuk (18) of Emmanuel, Gazan rocket fire in Eshkol.

2012 November 21: Lieutenant Boris Yarmulnik (28, died 22 November) of Netanya, Gazan rocket fire in Netanya.

2013 April 30: Evyatar Borovsky (31) of Yitzhar, stabbed at Tapuah junction.

2013 September 20: Sergeant Tomer Hazan (20) of Bat Yam, lured by a Palestinian coworker in Siniria and thrown down a well.

2013 September 22: Sergeant Major Gabriel Kobi (20) of Tirat Carmel, shot near Cave of Patriarchs in Hebron.

2013 October 11: Colonel (ret) Seraya Ofer (61) beaten to death with axes outside his home in Brosh Habika.

2013 November 13: Private Eden Atias (19) of Nazareth Illit, stabbed at Afula Central Bus Station.

2013 December 24: Salah Shukri Abu Latyef (22) of Rahat Bedouin village, shot by sniper fire near Gaza border fence.

ADRIFT IN TRANSLATION

How many members of a certain demographic group does it take to perform a specified task?

A finite number. One to perform the task and the remainder to act in a manner stereotypical of the group in question.

Commands Met

I have never been the best Jew in the world. There are 613 mitzvot. Most were invalidated when the temple was destroyed. Some only apply to men. Some only in Israel. And there has always been a debate about which laws fit which category. I cannot really keep track. I like the idea of keeping mitzvah but it is not always practical.

We are always told to obey the laws of

whatever country we are in when they contradict halakha but in Israel the line gets blurred. You would think Israeli lawmakers would always ensure that their laws follow halakha but you would be wrong. I generally err on the side that is more likely to put me in prison. In an extreme case I might break a civil law to follow moral principle but I mostly live in a more mundane world.

I have always preferred aseret had'varim, the laws God gave Moses at Sinai. What Charlton Heston called the ten commandments. They are mostly pretty straightforward and can apply to everybody everywhere. There is a reason every major religion in the world uses them as their moral foundation. Even I can follow most of them.

I am the Lord your God.

No argument from me. I questioned everything when I was a child. I went through a rebellious phase when I was a teenager and dramatically announced that I was an atheist.

I did not pray when I was the closest I have ever been to death. I did not think about God helping me or abandoning me. I would rather rely on myself or others to help me out instead of sit back and let God do all the work. But at every point in my life I have never doubted my fundamental belief in God's existence.

No other gods before God or worshipping idols.

Check. I have looked into Buddhism but I never worshipped the Buddha. I took off my shoes in the temples and showed respect for the culture but I have never put anybody or anything above God. I will show respect for the idols of whatever temple I am in, Buddhist, Hindu, Christian, but I do not worship them any more than I would worship nice architecture. The Hagia Sophia is very impressive but I am not going to pray to it.

No wrongful use of God's name.

I have broken this one plenty of times. I have used God's name in vain. I have blamed God for things I did not like. I have never sworn an insincere oath in God's name but I have used God's name in profanity. Many times. I try not to but sometimes it is goddamn hard.

Keep Shabbat holy.

Not so much. I violate both the observance and remembrance of Shabbat all the time. I engage in many of the prohibited melachot whilst observing others by default. Some of those activities are things I never do anyway, like all of the prohibitions regarding cultivation and livestock. I live nowhere close to any farms. But I mostly violate the remembrance portion.

I do not always have Sabbath meals. This was hard to obey when I lived in China and Alaska but even in Israel I am remiss. And there is really no excuse. I can go to my grandmother's house, my mother's house, sisters, friends. Sometimes I have other things to do.

I do not always recite kiddush and havdalah. I do not avoid talking about money, business, unpleasantries. I do not always go to shul. My rabbi can tell you just how often I am not there. I do not always read the Talmud or discuss the Torah. It is far less than always.

But I almost always commemorate Yom Kippur, Rosh Hashanah, Pesach, Purim, Yom Hashoah. There has been a debate for the last few thousand years about whether Yom Kippur or Shabbat is more important. I am firmly in the Yom Kippur camp.

My continual violation of this commandment is essentially the main reason I am not such a great Jew.

Honour your father and mother.

Mostly. I had a rebellious period with my mother but I think God understands the mother-daughter dynamic. Especially when one of them is a teenager. I was always better at honouring my father.

This commandment mostly stems from the ancient practice of killing your parents to get their land and abusing them when they are older. I would never consider doing either. I do not always do what my mother wants but I have always respected her. There will never be a time when she is not welcome in my home.

No murdering.

Check. Some religions interpret this one as not killing but in Hebrew it is murder. That makes it much easier. I do not want to kill either but you can get absurd and say that we are forbidden from killing insects or bacteria. Murder is pretty human specific. And not something I plan on doing any time soon.

No adultery.

The traditional definition is sex between a man and a married woman who is not his wife. Since I have never been married there is no way I can break this one. When I get married we shall have to wait and see.

Do not steal.

In Hebrew this one is about kidnapping. I have never kidnapped anybody. I never plan to kidnap anybody. Even in English it is an easy one to follow. Simply do not take anything or anybody that is not yours.

Do not bear false witness against your neighbour.

Check. I have never lied in a court of law about my neighbours or anything. I had to sue my employers when I lived in a country where people have to pay large sums for medical treatment but I never said anything that was not true.

Do not covet your neighbour's wife or property.

Check. My neighbour's wife is attractive but I can keep my distance. As for property I have never been the type of person who gets jealous because somebody has better toys. People tell me that I do not have enough worldly goods. I think I have too much.

The Lord Jehovah has given unto you these fifteen...Oy. Ten. Ten commandments for all to obey.

Medium of Peace

The international media have been talking about Muslims a lot lately. Specifically the bad things they do. We never hear about the good things. Probably because that is not good for ratings.

There is a small group in England who want Islam to take over the country and make Buckingham Palace a giant mosque. That is funny for too many reasons. There is a small group in Germany who periodically announce that they are going to bomb a factory or railway station. Nothing ever happens. There is a small group in America who praise Osama bin Laden and think that New York deserved it. They have chutzpah for saying so in public but little else on their side.

I do not think that these people deserve the attention they are getting. They are not credible threats. Queen Elizabeth will not be converting to Islam in the near future. German trains will remain as efficient as ever. If New York explodes it will be because of Wall Street, not wasat. The only reason these tiny groups are getting any attention at all is because they are making all their noise in "The West". Meaning the proper Christian countries. You never hear about tiny fringe groups threatening to bomb shops in Indonesia unless you live in or near Indonesia.

This current anti Muslim media blitz started when an American military officer shot some people at his base. Everything I have ever read about it mentions that he is Muslim. There are articles about his family saying that he is not a terrorist after the American military investigated the possibility.

Americans like to shoot each other. They mostly do it in schools but where they work is another common location. This particular American shot people where he worked. I do not remember reading about the religions of others who have done the same. And when they are white I never hear about investigations into possible terrorist affiliations. Usually they just tell us that the shooter was overstressed about something and finally snapped. But the media feel compelled to tell us what religion this shooter practises.

We have genuine cause to be concerned about terrorists where I live. But when somebody commits a crime they are not automatically labelled a terrorist until proven such. It is generally the opposite. The media seem surprised if an Arab stabs somebody and he turns out to be a terrorist. Most crimes here have nothing to do with terrorism. Just like in the Christian West.

So why does it matter if a criminal is Muslim and not Christian or Jewish? Fear. Christians do not fear other Christians. They do not fear Jews as much as they used to, even though some think that we are responsible for all the world's problems. But many fear Muslims, even the billion or so who never chanted "death to America" and never held a firearm. That fear probably stems from ignorance, both willful and circumstantial.

Most people in The West have an intimate knowledge of Christianity. If they are not Christian themselves they more than likely know people who are. Lots of people. They have probably met a Jew once or twice. Even if not then they have seen our big hats and diamond cutting skills in movies. Woody Allen, Mel Brooks, Jerry Seinfeld are all Jewish. Nothing to fear there.

But what of Muslims? They are not funny. They do not celebrate Christmas like normal people. They wear robes in the daytime. And they do not even eat bacon. How can you not fear people who are so different?

Sooner or later that irrational fear of Muslims will translate as irrational fear from Muslims.

I have no idea when Easter is celebrated throughout the world. I know it has something to do with Spring and falls at different times each year. But I know that it must be Easter time.

A group of Arabs in Dearborn, Michigan protested a local Presbyterian church's Easter egg hunt, dubbed an "eggstravaganza".

I know how Arabs in the United States feel. More or less. I grew up in South Africa. Not exactly a bastion of Judaism. Most of the people around me were Christians. Mostly because I was not allowed to spend any serious amount of time with any black Africans and their less than Christian religions. Actually, I have no idea how Arabs in the United States feel. They can hang out with whomever they want.

I was surrounded by Christians through no fault of my own. People in the United States can surround themselves with pretty much anything.

I never understood the Easter egg concept. Rabbits laying coloured chicken eggs symbolise Jesus rising from the dead somehow. But I was never offended by Christians having an Easter egg hunt. The children seem to enjoy it and it hurts absolutely nobody. Unless you are vegan it should not be a problem.

The issue in this fabricated controversy is supposed to be that pamphlets for this egg hunt were handed out at a local school. The United States has a separation of church and state. Supposedly. That means that the state is not allowed to tell people how to worship. Supposedly.

I can get behind that. I do not want any government anywhere in the world telling me how to pray. Whether I voted for you or not it is absolutely none of your business. But in this instance no American government agency was handing out pamphlets or advertising this event. The local church did that and, this part might be important, the egg hunt was open to anybody and everybody, regardless of religious persuasion. Muslim children were just as welcome to dig around for chicken eggs as anybody else.

The school was not at all involved. As far as

I know. Pamphlets were handed out at the school because this is a neighbourhood event for children. Schools are a good place to find flocks of children in their natural habitat. The school did not force anybody to worship anything in any way. It did not force anybody to attend the egg hunt. Blaming the school for this is like blaming the road when your car runs out of fuel. And once you take the school out of it there is no church and state issue.

Far more troubling than the Easter egg hunt is that many Christians eat ham for dinner on a day set aside to honour Jesus. Did Jesus eat pork? Even more disturbing is that this event was called an eggstravaganza. That alone deserves an honour killing.

Communism is all but dead. North Korea and Cuba will never invade you. The Japanese and German menace was taken care of years ago. The colonies are gone. Uprisings are not much of an issue anymore. The indigenous people of your country are probably dead or marginalised. There is no more slavery. The European monarchs are mostly impotent. What is there left to fear besides people who are not like you?

<u>Always From Now Until Then</u>

So a pope walks into a bar.

I do not pretend to understand Catholicism but I really do not understand the furor over Pope Benedict's resignation. Is it because it has not been done in hundreds of years? Things change. You might as well get used to it. Those who cannot adapt are doomed to perish. I realise that an organisation like the Catholic church is inherently resistant to change but life is still going to move forward regardless.

It might be worth remembering that hundreds of years ago people did not live nearly as long as they do now. As humans get older we are going to have to get used to them living far beyond their most active years. Pope John Paul was kept alive far longer than nature intended. Did he do the best job he possibly could have in the last few years? I cannot say but my guess is not a snowball's chance in hell. But there was no way anybody was ever going to let him resign, even if he wanted to.

This current pope is doing the right thing. I do not know the man, and I am certainly not his doctor, but if he says he is too old and weak to do the job then I am inclined to believe him. I do not see the benefit in forcing him to continue doing a job that he thinks he cannot adequately do.

I have been told by more than a few Catholics that they do not worship their popes. I hope that is true since that would violate the first two commandments. I shall ignore the whole Jesus issue for the sake of discussion. But the way I see some Catholics act around images of their popes makes me wonder.

If you do not worship these men then what difference does it make if they resign rather than stay in the job for life? I see the benefit in not having people resign helter skelter but anybody who hits 80, 90, 100 has earned the right to take a break. If you want them to stay in office longer then pick younger people. Being the pope is a job, no matter how important a job you might think it is. Everybody should have the right to retire from their job. Even the queen of England can retire. Though nobody wants her to because then her son would be king.

Now there is talk of getting an American pope. Why would anybody want that? Do Americans not have enough influence in the world? Are they underrepresented? I would be surprised if anybody other than an old white European male gets the job. Do not hold your breath for a black pope. But at least that is physically possible. There is probably not going to be a female pope any time soon.

For the old pope's part, he promised "unconditional obedience" to the new pope. I think his point was that he does not want his people divided between him and the new guy. But I really do not think anybody should be unconditionally obedient to any person. Especially a person whom you do not worship.

Just after I wrote this, Pope Benedict retired and they chose a new pope. My prediction that it would be a white European was just as accurate as most of my election predictions. Specifically, I was completely wrong. As was my prediction that Sinéad O'Connor would be exonerated once people started openly discussing the issue that made her a pariah

For as long as I can remember, people have been talking about Catholic priests molesting children. I have always heard jokes about it. Though I cannot see what is funny. I guess sometimes you have to laugh to keep from screaming.

Now it is no longer the world's worst kept secret. Everybody knows it has happened and is probably still happening. The issues now seem to be how to make excuses for it, how to rationalise it, how to get people to stop talking about it. I have not heard much about how to stop it.

I am not going to try and say this is all about Catholics. It could theoretically happen within any religion. But can you imagine if these were imams instead of priests? Islam would be outlawed all over Europe.

I think any adult doing anything illegal, immoral, indecent, creepy with any child is just about the worst possible thing anybody can do. It does not matter if you are in a position of authority or not. A garbage collector molesting a child is just as evil as a teacher molesting a child. It does not help when the attacker is a trusted authority figure but the sin is as horrible either way.

I have read a lot of the Catholic church's spin and deflection. One spokesperson for an American organisation affiliated with the Vatican went to great lengths to define the differences between a paedophile and a garden variety rapist. He gave a lot of statistics and research article information showing that most of the priests in question are not technically paedophiles.

That is nice but saying that these priests should all be removed from their posts and brought to their local police would have gone a lot further with me. I can understand why they feel they need to cover themselves but I think they would make most of us feel much better if they would spend less time saying they are not all bad and more time getting the few who are bad to justice.

And that is what really upsets most people. The sins against these children, teenagers, young adults is bad enough but the fact that too many of the priests were protected from prosecution, and church leaders went out of their way to claim nothing bad ever happened is what gained international media attention.

I have no doubt that the highest ranking Catholic leaders are an arrogant bunch. When you are in charge of the most powerful religion in the world and hold sway over a billion people with little accountability in this life you are bound to grow a thick head. But covering up the rape and molestation of who knows how many children for who knows how many centuries is not the same as murdering people who refuse to convert.

Killing people is easy to rationalise. Especially people who are different. Humans have a great talent for this. The history of our species is all about killing each other. But attacking children, your own children, is not something most people can accept. This is the kind of thing that can really turn people off. Without all those people you lose all that power and influence. Not to mention all that money.

Instead of asking the victims to forgive their attackers and asking the attackers to rub beads and burn candles, I will admit that I am no expert on Catholic rituals, I think the pope should fire all of those priests and give them a narrow deadline to turn themselves over to the police. After which time his people should turn them over.

Then they should do absolutely everything in their considerable power to make sure it stops happening and never happens again. Do not point to studies that say the percentage of abusive priests is equal to or lesser than the percentage of civilian abusers. One priest who attacks one child is too many. And everybody knows it.

Fix the problems. I do not know exactly what they are but I assume some of these people found themselves in positions of power and slowly got it in their heads that it would be ok to do what they did. Thorough psychological evaluations of anybody who will be in any position of authority over children might be a good idea.

Some people are saying that forced celibacy is to blame. I think if you are raping children then you are not celibate. Priests who are truly celibate are not the people you have to worry about. But it might be time to abandon that archaic practice anyway. I cannot see why priests should not be able to marry. It might not stop anybody from abusing children but it seems like letting priests be human is a good idea.

Let all of your priests and the world know that this kind of crime will never be tolerated. A priest who lectures his sheep about sin and who himself commits the ultimate sin is a hypocrite of the worst colour. A church that preaches against sin and then ignores or hides the ultimate sin is organised crime. Attacking children does not just go against church dogma. It is against the law. All religions think they are God's favourite. All religious leaders hold themselves to a higher authority. But anybody who wants to claim they are holier than the rest of us should not act like the mafia. Michael Corleone might shoot you over a plate of veal but he would never harm a child.

I have not read the United Nation's report about the Catholic priest sex issue and have no intention of doing so. The UN is intellectually dishonest and their reports and condemnations are a joke more often than not. The UN telling countries how to live is as impotent as people arguing politics online. But I am surprised that they found the time to criticise somebody besides Israel. It is not as though Israel and the Vatican have historically been best friends.

I realise that "Vatican" and "Holy See" are not interchangeable but I call it the Vatican anyway. Deal with it.

From what I gather the United Nations is opposed to priests raping children. Mazel tov.

I know of no person or organisation that supports priests raping children. Even a few popes have spoken out against it. I have never come across anybody in favour of it. Though to be fair I rarely associate with sociopaths.

How long did it take the United Nations to arrive at this groundbreaking decision? Why did this report come out now and not twenty or one hundred years ago?

Apparently the UN thinks that the Vatican is legally responsible for the actions of priests all over the world. My first thought was that yes, of course they are. There is a hierarchy in the Catholic church with Vatican leaders and the pope at the top of the ladder. But is that true? Is a priest living in Indonesia bound by Vatican law or Indonesian law? Obviously he should follow his church's rules, which likely do not include raping children, but if he ignores the laws of where he lives in favour of the laws of his religion then he can find himself in an uncomfortable position. Raping children is often acceptable in places like Saudi Arabia. Does that mean a priest in Saudi Arabia is free to practise local customs?

Obviously I know the answer to that last question but I sincerely have no idea about the others. My religion has no such international hierarchy. Rabbanim are hired and fired by the community and answer to their shul, not to any committee in Israel or anywhere else. A rabbi in Saudi Arabia could theoretically eat at KFC every day and tattoo a giant swastika on his forehead. That is if being Jewish in Saudi

Arabia was not punishable by death.

How does the Catholic church deal with local laws that contradict their own rules? Staying with Saudi Arabia as an example, since it is a such a fun loving country, how do priests ignore their mission to proselytise in a country that will happily kill them for proselytising? I would assume that Vatican leaders have already thought about such issues but has the UN? If the UN is saying that all priests are under the direct supervision of the Vatican then have they considered the international differences in cultures and customs? Somehow I think the Vatican has whilst the UN, ironically, has not.

The UN report demands that the Vatican do things their way. This is common practice for the UN. It is their version of the American policy of spreading democracy to weaker countries whether they want it or not. I even think the UN is genuinely surprised when countries choose not to do things their way.

The one part of the report that I read calls on the Vatican to change its teachings to bring them closer to the 20th century. While I do agree that some Catholic rules are painfully out of date, as are some rules of Judaism and Islam, I find it laughably appalling that the UN is telling any church how to be a church. I thought the UN was supposed to favour freedom of religion. Does that only apply to religious teachings of which they approve? Is it not exceptionally dangerous for the UN to be the arbiters of religious dogma?

If the United Nations decided that all Jews should pray a certain way, which they more or less already do from time to time, then there would be a large collection of middle fingers rising in the air.

Some people say keep your religion out of my bedroom. I agree with that. I would also add to keep the UN out of religion.

Thou Shalt Not Proselytise

Go to any online discussion of religion and you will find atheists and the faithless on one side and Christians on the other. Maybe you will see a Muslim as well. Maybe, just maybe, a Buddhist. Or at least an American who read a few books and chants a mantra and calls himself a Buddhist. If there are any Jews in there they rarely announce the fact. And since most of the faithful talk about Jesus we can assume that they are Christians.

In my experience the least tolerant are the atheists. They will often accuse anybody with a different point of view of "bible thumping" even when such people never quote their particular bible or push any belief. The atheists always seem much angrier than anybody else. Online at least. People often behave very differently offline.

Even the most fire and brimstone Christians cannot match the hateful online rhetoric of some atheists. I do not need anybody telling me that Jesus died for my sins and I do not believe he did. But the people who say so usually also tell you to have a nice day and are much friendlier than the atheists who blame anybody with faith for all that is wrong with the world. If religious people are so judgemental and want everybody to believe what they believe, and the atheists are supposed to be the opposite, then should they be more open minded toward different beliefs?

Buddhists have the right idea. They are supposed to live and let live and show respect for everybody's beliefs. Even if those beliefs completely contradict their own. Maybe that is why you never see many Buddhists in these discussions. You cannot rant and rave at everybody and talk down to them if you are a good Buddhist. I would be very surprised if any online bullies are Buddhist.

The faithless will say that all wars are fought for religion. But most wars are about land, power, politics, vengeance. History books are full of wars between Christians versus Christians, Muslims versus Muslims, Hindu versus Hindu, tribe versus tribe. Kings and emperors went to war to build their political base at home and to feed on the spoils of war. Tribes went to war over disputes over land and personal grudges. Modern wars are fought over natural resources and national pride. Racism and ego cause more wars than religion.

The faithless will point to many religious wars in Europe. But these were mostly Catholic versus Protestant. They are all Christians. They believe in the same God and the same Jesus. They just have a different way of showing it.

Whenever Europeans went to Africa, Asia, the Americas, Australia and slaughtered most of the indigenous people it was not a religious crusade. If you want somebody's land and are willing to kill for it, and they want to keep it and are willing to die for it, there will be blood.

But what about the Crusades? Surely those were holy wars. They were Catholic versus Muslim. A mission to bring Jerusalem under Christian control. They were sanctioned by the pope. One of the central benefactors was the Holy Roman Empire.

But the Catholic crusaders also fought indigenous groups outside of Jerusalem and many Greek and Russian Christians. One of the Crusades was against Constantinople, which was under Christian control at the time. Taking Jersusalem was always more about power and glory than religion. Religion was just an excuse for violent men to find their fame and fortune.

If you are a French Catholic you can worship Jesus at your local cathedral whether Jerusalem is controlled by Catholics, Muslims, Jews, nomads. Getting the pope to bless your invasion was not an especially difficult task in the 12th century. Europeans were mad about invading each other and the popes had their share of political enemies to vanquish.

I have seen a lot of people say that the Crusades were holy wars because the Holy Roman Empire was involved. They get caught up in the name. But the Holy Roman Empire was not holy or Roman or an empire.

When Christian America went to war with Shinto-Buddhist Japan it had nothing to do with religion. Japan did not attack Pearl Harbor because it was full of Christians. They did not attack Russia and China earlier because they were Christians and Buddhists.

A good point can be made about the Shoah. Mostly Christian Germans and Austrians killed millions of Jews. But they also killed a lot of Christians. And pretty much anybody they did not like. Jews were targeted not because they were a different religion but because they were a different race. German leaders of the day were interested in racial supremacy, not religious supremacy.

More people have been killed in the name of Jesus than in anybody else's name, including Mohammed, Buddha and Bill Gates. So does that make Christianity violent and bloodthirsty? And if Christians are so violent then all religions must be since every online religious discussion I have ever seen equates religion with Christianity. And in the age of political correctness you have to be inclusive.

But Jesus never once told his followers to torture and murder people. As far as I know. There is nothing in the books of Christianity, Islam, Judaism that command people to murder. In fact all of them say that murder is very bad. There is an entire commandment against it. All of them say that wars will inevitably happen but you should show mercy and compassion for the enemy.

The atheists and faithless in Cyberia discussions are always either people raised that way or former Christians. I have met only a few former Muslims in my life and every one of them still believes in God. They have simply rejected most of the tenets of Islam. I have never met a former Buddhist. Discounting people who took it up as a hobby and lost interest. Buddhism is not really a belief system anyway so there is not much to reject.

There are lots of former Jews. Jews who have rejected Judaism probably come in second only to Christians who have rejected Christianity. But almost every atheist who was not raised that way in every religious discussion I have ever seen was a former Christian. They did not like something about their former faith and decided that God does not exist. Or that he does exist but organised religion has perverted its original purpose. Since their particular sect of Christianity did not work out for them they have gone ahead and rejected all religion. That is their right but I cannot help but wonder why anybody would assume that every sect of every religion in the world is the same.

People often use the pope as an example. The pope did not stop the sex abuse so all religions are abusive. The pope did something bad when he was younger so all religions are corrupt. That does not make any sense to me. Even if the pope goes on a shooting spree in the Vatican that does not mean that Christianity is inherently violent. He may be their leader but he is not all of them. I have never met any popes but I assume that they would all admit they are not God. And even if Christianity is inherently violent that does not mean that every other religion in the world is.

But because so many of the atheists are former Christians they see everything from a Christian perspective. So these discussions inevitably revolve around Christianity. But most people in the world are not Christians and never were. The way that you were raised and the beliefs that you were taught do not necessarily have anything to do with what the rest of us were taught. Thinking that the entire world follows your rules does not make it true.

I think it also has a lot to do with proselytisation. Christians are commanded to proselytise. A good Christian is supposed to convert as many people as possible. I suppose the more souls you have saved the better your seat on the bus to Heaven. Muslims are discouraged from proselytising but told to welcome converts as if they were born into Islam. Jews are supposed to discourage others from converting at all.

So I guess it makes sense that former Christians would be just as eager to recruit people to their new faithlessness as they were to their old faith. People tend to do what they know even when rejecting everything they used to believe. Former Jews seem to have the same attitude as observant Jews. You do what you want. I am going to have a knish.

My younger sister reads my rantings probably more than anybody. She has pointed out that I seem to get more conservative when it comes to Palestine and Islam, and religion in general, whilst my general attitude is as liberal as ever. I have read some of what I wrote in the past and I can see what she means.

But I do not generally write about the most mundane aspects of daily life. There is nothing interesting about doing the laundry. Yet I do it all the time. I trimmed my fingernails recently but I am not going to wax philosophically about it. My attack against atheists is an attack against religious intolerance. If you claim no religion and you are intolerant of people who do then you are just as bad as people who claim one religion and are intolerant of others. Otherwise I have no issue with atheists. It is nothing off me what people want to believe. As long as they do not try to convert me. Atheism may not be organised but it is very much a belief.

The Hamas cartoon was such an abnormal thing. If it were an everyday event and everybody did it then I would have never mentioned it. But I would be sad to live in such a callous world.

The Catholic child abuse was both a current event and ongoing abomination. It has been going on forever but it has been given more media attention lately. What I said about it may seem anti Catholic but it is really anti child abuse. How can anybody be pro child abuse? There might be a way to talk about it without mentioning that these priests and the leaders who protected them are Catholic but I do not know how to do that.

My peace plan is very liberal to Palestine. They would say it is not because they do not get all of their demands. But some of their demands are unrealistic and everybody knows it. Real peace requires real compromise. Compromise works best when it is not one sided.

It has always been easy for me to get on with just about anybody. I grew up in a predominantly Christian country with a large population of indigenous religions. I have lived peacefully amongst Buddhists, Jews, Muslims, Druze, Communists, Arabs, Zulu, Xhosa, Afrikaner, Han, Hispanics, Mojave and other American Indians, Dena'ina, Eskimos and other Alaskan Natives, Africans, Asians, Americans, Europeans, intellectuals, illiterates, liberals, conservatives, young, old, rich, poor, homosexuals, heterosexuals, snobs, rednecks, men, women.

The people I never seem to deal well with are the my way or the highway types. Believe what they believe, like what they like, think what they think or else. I would rather talk all day with somebody who disagrees with everything I say than spend five minutes with that type.

Outside of Cyberia I have always had good relationships with Muslims. Islam and Judaism are really very similar. We share beliefs in God, prayer, trying to lead a good life.

Our cultures are very similar. Islam's early prophets were all Jews, and Moses is the most important behind Mohammed. Jews are righteous people according to the Qur'an. A true Muslim should never hate Jews for being Jewish. Judaism sees Muslims as B'nei Noach. They have all the rights and responsibilities as any Jew. I have never met a Jew who hates Muslims or any Muslim who hates Jews. Then again, I spend little time with terrorists and have never lived in a place where children are indoctrinated by despots.

The differences are mostly political. Christian persecution of Jews started as a power struggle for dominance in the Roman Empire and evolved into institutional bigotry. The execution of Jesus was simply the first of many excuses for violence against Jews. In contrast, Arab persecution of Jews was always more complicated and never had a single event to latch unto. The conflict in Palestine is the current excuse but it all began long before 1967. It is more of a family feud than a religious conflict.

The only predominantly Jewish country in the world has a secular prime minister. They have always been Jewish but it is not a requirement. Most predominantly Muslim countries have secular leaders. They are usually Muslim but it is theoretically possible that somebody else could get installed. Most Arab states have hereditary leaders who happen to be Muslim. They inherit their jobs because of their families, not their religion.

Religious leaders and political leaders rarely mix, even in predominantly religious countries.

Catholics have a pope. If he tells them all to wear blue shirts you will hear about it. You will probably even see a few people wearing blue shirts.

Jews have not had any central leader since the temple was destroyed. There are community leaders all over the place and influential organisations. Israel's chief rabbinate is generally regarded as the highest governing body, though many people in other countries disagree. If they tell everybody to wear blue shirts you might hear about it. I am not sure how many people would actually do it. Probably very few. Most would likely debate the theological implications of the colour blue.

Muslims have different leaders in different countries, and different leaders within each sect in a single country. Iran has their ayatollah but he is mostly a political leader. He does not hold much sway outside of Iran. If he told everybody to wear blue shirts you would probably never hear about it and it is even less likely you would see anybody do it.

It takes many years of study to become a rabbi. The most respected rabbis have been studying all their lives. A rabbi of eighty years will tell you that he is still learning.

I assume it takes some effort to become a Christian priest. The ministers I have known personally all had advanced university degrees, usually doctorates in theology or divinity. Some universities actually have doctors of divinity.

Technically anybody can lead a Muslim prayer service. It takes more study to get certain titles within certain denominations but the power and influence of those titles seem to vary.

It is easy to side with Palestine. They are smaller and weaker. Israel could level their buildings and kill everybody if it wanted to. Israel builds settlements in Palestine and puts up a large fence to keep Palestinians out. Israel controls the electricity, borders, water supply. Israel is supported by the United States, which has a history of replacing existing leaders with its own allies and selling weapons to Israel that are used against Palestine. Never mind the fact that the United States supports Palestine financially and sells weapons to several Arab states.

Favouring the underdog and opposing the big bully makes it easier to ignore the fact that Israel is the only democracy in the region. Its neighbours are dictatorships and monarchies. Israeli women have had the right to vote since the modern state was founded. Israel has had a female prime minister. Egypt allows women to vote but it is a one party system with only one candidate running at a time. Jordan allows women to vote but it is a monarchy and kings are not elected. No Arab state has ever had a female head of government or head of state.

Homosexuals in Israel have the same rights as heterosexuals. Homosexuality is illegal in all of Israel's neighbours except Jordan but gay

Jordanians cannot marry or serve in military and government posts. Honour killings of homosexuals usually receive lesser punishments than killing heterosexuals. Homosexuals in Saudi Arabia face the death penalty simply for having sex. Homosexuals in Palestine can be imprisoned for ten years.

This is not a difference between Jew and Muslim. This is Israeli and Arab. Many Israelis are not Jewish at all. Some Arabs are not Muslim. The Qur'an is far more liberal socially than the Torah or Christian Bible. Arabs are more like Americans in their fundamentalist attitude toward homosexuality. Israelis are more like many socialist Europeans.

I have always defended Palestine's right to exist. Technically there is no country in the world called Palestine but I call it Palestine because that is what it should be and that is what I hope it will be one day. I hesitated coming to Israel because I always had issues with its treatment of Palestinians. I shall always favour the underdog and oppose the mighty oppressor.

But the more I learnt about the situation the harder it was to feel sorry for Palestine. If Israel has Palestine under its boot then why has Israel repeatedly offered to spend a great deal of money and energy to help create a sovereign state of Palestine, and why have Palestinian leaders always rejected it? If I am being oppressed and my oppressors offer me my freedom time and again I am not going to say no.

I still have sympathy for the people of Palestine but I think their leaders are doing more harm than good. Israeli leaders have not always been the best and brightest but their job is to protect Israelis, not Palestinians. And no matter what your opinion is of Palestine and oppression you cannot deny that some of the more extremist elements amongst the Palestinians are a serious threat to Israel's citizens, regardless of religion or race.

It is not Muslim against Jew. If it were there would not be terrorism in Iraq, India, Pakistan, Afghanistan, Sudan, Yemen, the Philippines. These are not hotbeds of Judaism.

Jews and Muslims are told to respect each other in their books. Muslims are not mentioned specifically in Jewish scripture, mostly because they did not yet exist, but there are laws about how to treat all believers in God. The Qur'an states that the Tanakh is the original Word of God. According to Tanakh the mitzvot of Judaism are a covenant between God and Israel, establishing the state of Israel and its laws. So any Muslim who wants to destroy Israel is trying to destroy a covenant with God. Any Muslim who tries to claim that Israel did not exist before 1948 is contradicting God. Obviously no Muslim wants to do that.

It is not even Arab against Israeli. If it were there would not be over a million Arabs living peacefully in Israel. And Jordan and Egypt would not have formal relations with Israel.

Israel and Saudi Arabia together convinced

the United States to defend Kuwait against Iraq long before the United States was hellbent on invading. Either Jews and Muslims convinced Christians to protect a Muslim country from other Muslims or a democracy and a dictatorship convinced another democracy to protect an economic ally from a dicatatorship that wanted to damage trade relations. Which is more likely?

Somebody recently asked me how I can feel safe amongst Muslims when they are terrorists. That is stupid for several reasons. Muslims are not terrorists. There are about a billion of them. If there were a billion terrorists who hated your country and mine and were perfectly happy to kill themselves in order to kill us then I do not think we would be here any more.

The Qur'an says that murder is an insult to God. Even during war it has rules about how to treat people and they are mostly liberal. Saying that Islam supports terrorism is like saying that Christianity supports child abuse. Some terrorists claim to be Muslim just as some child molesters claim to be Christian. None of these people are faithfully following the rules of their religion. But you cannot tell that to people living in ignorance and fear.

The Torah and Christian Bible are sometimes vague and can be interpreted different ways. And many people have. The Qur'an is straightforward. You are supposed to read it in Arabic so that nothing gets twisted in translation.

The hate and violence you see in viral e-mails and blogs is sometimes very bad English translations and usually just something somebody made up. You will not find that business about 72 virgins anywhere in the Qur'an. It is from a bad translation of a medieval writer's essays that describes a total of 72 maidens in Heaven. It also says that they are 27 metres tall, 3 metres wide, and transparent. And they are not your reward for blowing yourself up. They are supposed to be the hosts of Heaven. Give some of those English translations to somebody who can read Arabic and they will be surprised.

I think most people are generally peaceful no matter what religion they believe in. Even people who do not believe in anything. But there are terrorists in the world. According to your TV they are mostly Muslims. Your TV is wrong. Murder goes against Islam. Suicide goes against Islam. Harming children goes against Islam. If you strap on a bomb and blow up yourself and a bus full of children then you are not Muslim. What you are doing goes against everything Muslims believe.

When I lived in California there was a big gang problem. Gangs were shooting each other and innocent bystanders. Some people call them terrorists. Most of the gang members call themselves Christian. Is Christianity a religion of murderers who shoot babies on the streets? Did Jesus tell his followers to bust a cap in anybody that disses you? What is the difference between a Syrian who says God is great when he shoots you and an American who holds a crucifix when he shoots you?

The obvious argument is that terrorists who claim to act for God are more accepted in their communities, and that living in more liberal societies is radicalising some younger uneducated Muslims. But Los Angeles gang members who claim to love God are just as accepted in their communities, and it can easily be said that living in poverty and social inequality has radicalised them.

One of the biggest differences is that when a gang member shoots somebody in a drive by it might get mentioned on the nightly news. When a terrorist shoots somebody in a holy war it is front page news.

The situation in Palestine today is about land, not religion. Their argument is that we stole their land, even though Israelis were here thousands of years ago. If it were about religion there would be absolutely no way any Muslim could say they were around before Jews.

Mia's Annual Christmas Message

Happy Christmas.

Notice how I said Happy Christmas and not Happy Holidays. That is because Christmas is really the only holiday that a lot of people are celebrating at the end of December. Kwanzaa is a fake festival created in the 1960s by an American. It is supposed to be African but nobody in Africa celebrates it. I would doubt that many Africans have even heard of it.

Hanukkah has been around a lot longer and is observed by a lot more people but it is not nearly as important as Christmas. It is a minor festival. We light candles, say prayers, go about our business. There is no reason to artificially inflate its importance just because it is usually at around the same time as Christmas. Our most important days are usually around September or October. It is ok if you do not know what they are. We do not need everybody to go crazy over them.

I have never met a single Jew who was offended when people wished each other a Happy Christmas. There is nothing about our culture that tells us to resent other cultures. Quite the opposite in fact. Jews have a long history of adapting to other cultures.

We are more than capable of surviving one month of the year when shopping centres decorate their windows and public buildings put stables on their lawns. We can even survive all of those Christmas songs knowing that there are not any Hanukkah songs. It is quite alright. I am sure most Americans are not heartbroken that there are no good Columbus Day songs.

If you want to wish me a Happy Christmas I will not mind. But I do not celebrate it. If you want to wish me a Happy Hanukkah I will not mind that either. But that is like me wishing you a Happy Columbus Day. If you never notice the Yamim Noraim I will not mind. I probably never notice May Day.

The purpose of political correctness is to include everybody and not offend anybody. But trying to include one of our minor festivals with your most important festival is actually a little offensive. It says that you do not know anything about our most important days and assumes that we all think your most important days are more important. The politically correct thing to do in late December would be to say Happy Christmas to everybody.

Slippery When Wet

Some people say that we should not give any attention to fanatical clerics. If it is some schmo bloviating in an online chat room or a winsome young woman ranting in the wind then I would agree. Present company excluded.

But extremists like Marion Robertson have large followings. A frightening number of people listen to this man and take what he says seriously.

In my mind any sensible person can see that Marion Robertson, who calls himself Pat because he thinks Marion sounds too gay, is not the sharpest spike on the rail. But the people who listen to people like him probably think my views on accepting people as they are, turning the other cheek, and forgiveness are dangerous and sinful. Ironically.

I understand the world is made of a wide

variety of people and it takes different strokes for different folks and so on and so on. But how does your brain have to work for you to rationalise your agreement with insanity?

I hate homos so it is all true.

Fair enough. You are homophobic. But does your hatred for different people shut off your frontal lobe? Does hate override reason? Where is the sagacity?

Marion has some logical dysentery that should make even the most hateful homophobe blink.

> *"How can we rule that polygamy is illegal when you say that homosexual marriage is legal? What is it about polygamy that's different?"*

What is it about marrying one person that is different from marrying multiple people? Kindergarten math. I can accept that most people are not especially good at math and maybe homophobes are worse so I will point out the obvious. One is one and two or more is two or more. They are different numbers.

> *"Well, polygamy was outlawed because it was considered immoral according to biblical standards."*

According to what bible? Half of Marion's bible is based on mine and my bible has lots of polygamy. There are entire rules about the hierarchy of different wives.

> *"But if we take biblical standards away in homosexuality, what about the other?"*

I think both should be held to the same standard but Marion and his kind do not treat all of Moses' laws equally. Not even close.

> *"And what about bestiality and ultimately what about child molestation and pedophilia? How can we criminalize these things and at the same time have constitutional amendments allowing same-sex marriage among homosexuals."*

If you are a Marionite have somebody who can read look up the word incommensurable and explain it to you.

An adult human marrying another adult human and having messy anal sex until they become bored with each other and turn their attention to reality TV has as much to do with beastiality and paedophilia as purple. There is also the pesky issue of animals and children having neither the understanding nor legal capablilites to sign a marriage contract. Marion needs his boyfriend's consent if he wants to marry him. But he can rape his dog any time he wants and few people will notice anything.

"You mark my words, this is just the beginning in a long downward slide in relation to all the things that we consider to be abhorrent."

One man's abhorrent is another man's Saturday night. Or two other men and an underaged donkey apparently. As for marking Marion's words, he has a poor track record on prophecy. He was the prophet who said the world would end in the 1980s. That is when Bon Jovi was popular so maybe he was right.

Come on, feel the boyz.

And not for nothing but marriages between two men have been successfully consummated throughout recorded history without the destruction of all life as we know it. I have never heard of any place where it was ever legal to marry your dog. This must be the slowest slippery slope ever.

In 2011 a group of rabbis, rashei yeshiva, educators, and Jewish community leaders got together to address homosexuality in Judaism. They spent a great deal of time talking amongst themselves and researching the issue. Then they published their report, giving it the blockbuster title *Statement of Principles on the Place of Jews with a Homosexual Orientation in Our Community*.

Amongst the authors were Rabbi Yitzchak Blau, rosh kollel of Yeshivat Shvilei Hatorah in Jerusalem, Rabbi Nathaniel Helfgot of Yeshivat Chovevei Torah in New York, and Rabbi Aryeh

Klapper of the Center for Modern Torah Leadership in Boston. I do not remember if it bumped Danielle Steel from the bestseller lists but I read it anyway.

The report concluded that everybody is created in God's image and deserves to be treated with dignity and respect.

> *"Embarrassing, harassing or demeaning someone with a homosexual orientation or same-sex attraction is a violation of Torah prohibitions that embody the deepest values of Judaism."*

It also said that whether homosexuality is a choice or genetic is irrelevant.

I agree that everybody should be treated the same no matter who is in their bed. But I simply cannot see how homosexuality is a choice. Did anybody choose heterosexuality? I do not recall ever making that choice.

Ask a homophobe if they chose to be heterosexual. If they say yes does that imply that they could go either way? I have often thought that being a lesbian would be much easier. Why would I choose to be attracted to men? They are a royal pain in the tuchas.

The report says that heterosexual marriage is "the ideal model". Heterosexuality is the ideal model because the model was written by heterosexuals. Imagine if Moses, Jesus, Mohammed were homosexual. Being gay would today be like being left handed.

As an aside it is interesting to note that if you hypothesise a homosexual Moses, most Jews would make a joke about a burning bush. The idea of a homosexual Jesus would bring calls of censorship and boycotts from Christians. And even imagining the very idea of a homosexual Mohammed would bring death threats.

The report points out that while halakha generally prohibits homosexual acts it does not prohibit homosexual attraction or emotional feelings. Prohibiting homosexuality makes sense in its own tiny way when you are trying to build up your religion. Heterosexuals were the only people who could go forth and multiply before adoption and in vitro fertilisation. Sex without procreation is pointless if you are trying to fill the seats. That is why Catholics are not supposed to use birth control and why Mormons used to go polygamous.

But today there are plenty of Christians, and Islam is growing by the minute. You could argue that we need more Jews, and a lot of people have, but nothing anywhere says that being the Chosen People means having the most people. Several very good arguments have been made that maybe God always wanted us to be in the minority. That is one thing about Judaism that many Christians and Muslims will never understand. We are not trying to be the biggest or most popular kids on the block. There is nothing in our religion that treats it all as a competition.

The rabbi report rejects the idea that homosexuals can be "cured" with therapy, and "affirms the religious right of those with a homosexual orientation to reject therapeutic approaches they reasonably see as useless or dangerous".

If you can give somebody therapy to make them heterosexual then you can give them therapy to make them homosexual. Homophobes should think about that for a minute.

My biggest complaint about Judaism and almost every religion is its attitude toward homosexuality. I understand that controlling sex is a great way to control people but I do not see religion as controlling. We all choose to believe in whatever faith we believe in. We did not all choose to live where we live.

The state has far more control over you than any religion. The state can come into my home, arrest me, and have me killed. Theoretically. My rabbi can, at most, make me feel unwelcome at shul.

The report rejects the concept of "outing" homosexuals, and states that the individual has both the moral and ethical right to determine how open or private their sexuality is known within the community.

I would add that no homosexual should feel the need to live in any closet. But there are many places where openly being who you are can get you killed. Even in the so called civilised countries you can lose your job and friends if they know the truth. If I were homosexual I would never deny it. But I have the luxury of living in a community that treats people as people.

The only thing that needs to be changed for everybody to feel comfortable with everybody is education. We do not need to loosen any rules for homosexuals to hold leadership positions in the community. We simply need to teach everybody that God loves those people over there just as much as he loves us over here. And since it would be extremely inappropriate to discuss a heterosexual hazan's sex life during tefillot it should also be extremely inappropriate to discuss the sex life of a homosexual hazan.

The rabbis say that all Jews are supposed to fulfill mitzvot as best they can, regardless of sexuality.

> *"The attitude of 'all or nothing' was not the traditional approach adopted by the majority of halakhic thinkers and poskim throughout the ages."*

I could not agree with this more. I have taken a lot of shit over the years from the frummest of the frum who take issue with my lax attitude toward some mitzvot. It is like the Jewish equivalent of love it or leave it. If I can love God without saying every single prayer on every single day of all the hundreds of praying days then so can any man who likes men as much as I do.

An interesting point is that most Jews who have problems with homosexuals are really only afraid of male homosexuals. They have been mostly ambivalent toward female homosexuality historically. There is some debate about whether lesbians were ever prohibited at all. None of our books even mention it.

Christians are often the same. Males are an abomination but if it is women, bring a camera. And Islam has absolutely no prohibition toward lesbians according to some. It was common for harem wives to enjoy each other's company whilst the shared husband was with somebody else. Pasolini even made a movie about it.

As for the Christian concept that homosexuality is an abomination, where does it say that? Leviticus 18:22 reads, "V'et zachar lo tishkav mishk'vey ishah to'evah he." The actual translation, as opposed to the Hebrew to Greek to English translation, is "And with a male you shall not lie down in the bed of a female, for it is unclean." Leviticus 20:13 reads, "V'ish asher yishkav et zachar mishk'vei ishah to'evah asu shneihem mot yumatu d'meihem bam." "And a male who lies down with a male in the bed of a female are both made unclean and their blood is on them." To'evah does not mean "abomination". That is an English translation taken from a Greek translation.

A lot of things are ritually unclean according to halakhah. I am ritually unclean every month. That does not mean my lack of pregnancy is an abomination. Only my mother would think that.

Some people have even said that both of those passages only prohibit male homosexuality in a woman's bed. And that you should not have sex with a man and pretend that you are having sex with a woman, thus denying your own nature. It has also been pointed out that when they were written there was a lot of ritual sex and prostitution in the pagan temples that Jewish leaders wanted to keep their people away from.

If homosexuality is "an abomination" then so is eating pigs, rabbits, reptiles, rodents, shellfish, insects, blood, fruit from a young tree, mixing fabrics, mixing crops in the same field, tattoos, piercings, working on Saturday, charging interest on a loan, adultery, insulting your parents, insulting deaf or blind people, sex with a married slave (single slaves are ok), sex during menstruation, even menstruation itself according to the English version.

All of these are to'evah and most Christians do most of them. Have you heard about the woman in Iran who may or may not be stoned to death for adultery? How barbaric is that? Imagine if we in the "Judeo Christian" world executed people for adultery, vegetable gardens, wearing polyester, working on weekends. How barbaric would that be?

Anybody who does not protest the "abomination" of cheeseburgers but protests homosexuality is a hypocrite. According to the Word of God they are equally to'evah.

Jews are supposed to keep 613 mitzvot. Most of us do not. If you are not Jewish then you are not required to keep kosher. So if eating a pork chop is not an abomination for you then what difference does it make to you whom I sleep with?

If you are morally outraged by homosexuals then you have to be morally outraged by everybody who breaks every other mitzvah. Homosexuality may not be a choice but eating a rare steak most definitely is. Of the 613 mitzvot, 365 are prohibitions. Christians ignore almost all of them, as is their right since they are not Jewish. But they put a great deal of weight on two mistranslated verses in Leviticus.

And if you are one of those extremist hypocrites who want to kill homosexuals then you are out of luck. The mitzvot are a covenant between God and Israel. They established the state of Israel and its civil laws. The Christian New Testament is between God and the Christian church. It is international. It has nothing to do with any particular state and its civil laws. So capital punishment, or any other state punishment for any crime, is not applicable for Christians.

The "Statement of Principles" states that homosexual marriages should not be recognised but that any children of such a couple should always be as accepted as anybody else. I disagree with this completely. Not the part about children. That is spot on.

I try to see the point the other side is trying

to make in any argument. If I can see it from their point of view then maybe I can come up with a better argument from my point of view. Or maybe I will even switch sides. If everybody is just screaming at each other and not listening to anything then absolutely nothing is accomplished. You might as well have an American TV programme.

But the insistence that a marriage between homosexuals will somehow destroy heterosexual marriages just makes no sense to me at all. Homosexuals can marry legally in several countries. I have never heard anything about any of the heterosexual marriges in any of those countries being damaged in any way. And how could they? Unless we both have our eye on the same man how can my relationship hurt your relationship?

Some say that a homosexual marriage cannot create children. That is simply not true anymore. But even if it were, so what? Does a childless heterosexual marriage hurt all marriages? Personally I think you have to have an extremely weak marriage for it to be hurt just because the couple next door has sex in a different way than you do.

But I agree completely that all children should be welcome. Any community that rejects its children is doomed to extinction.

The report goes on to state that homosexuals should never be encouraged to marry somebody of the opposite gender, "as this can lead to great tragedy, unrequited love, shame, dishonesty and ruined lives". I agree with this completely.

If I married a woman we would have hot sweaty sex for the first few years and then I would look around for a man to leave his dirty dishes out, wear a t-shirt that should have been burnt years ago, not bathe as often as he should. Because sacrificing my need for dirty man sex just to feel the unconditional love and support of a woman would be an abomination.

The report concludes by stating that God loves everybody. I think this is a big message that most religions tend to forget about when they get wrapped up in destroying religions that are different from their own. We all believe in essentially the same thing. We simply show it in different ways. The things that make us different are minor compared to the things we all have in common. Unfortunately, we enjoy focusing on the differences and using them as an excuse to wipe each other off the map.

An Open Letter to Homophobes

If people choose to be homosexual, when did you choose to be heterosexual? Why did you make that choice? Could you have gone either way?

Would you rather have sex with the most repulsive person of the opposite gender or the most attractive person of the same gender?

How weak does a heterosexual marriage have to be for it to be damaged by a homosexual marriage? If your neighbours have sex in a different way than you do will it damage the way you have sex? And how do you know how they are having sex?

If God hates homosexuality, why did he wait for the English mistranslation of the Greek mistranslation of the original Hebrew to say so? There are plenty of homoerotic euphemisms in Hebrew. Was God waiting for somebody to invent an online translator?

What did Moses, Jesus, Mohammed say about homosexuality? If it is such a horrible sin against God and nature then they must have preached volumes about it.

If homosexual sex is unnatural because it produces no children, does that make the heterosexual sex I have been having for sixteen years without producing children unnatural? Are infertile couples unnatural? Should old people be allowed to have sex?

Is menopausal heterosexual sex an abomination?

Are anal and oral sex between heterosexuals unnatural? Some people would actually say yes to this. Can you imagine living your entire life without oral sex? That is not only unnatural, that is an abomination.

Is there any rational reason to fear homosexuality? Is it contagious? If you use the same toilet as a homosexual will you become homosexual yourself? If two men kiss in the woods and nobody is around will it shatter your glass house? Is homosexuality a gateway sexuality? Does it lead to zoophilia or necrophilia? If you say yes, does that mean heterosexuality leads to paedophelia?

Most paedophiles are heterosexual. Are most necrophiliacs homosexual?

If you can criminalise and deem unnatural people who are unlike you, how hard would it be for somebody to criminalise and deem unnatural people like you?

Why have I never met a single homophobe who could answer any of these questions?

An Open Letter to Homophones

Eye prey to the profits in this guy that wheel never halve such bad whether that covers hour planes with enough reign too tern the aisles in two the see and blank it all the sandwiches hear.

The tail of the arc is weigh to discreet fore hour thyme. It wood never bee maid in the sage. Eye bass this moron a song guy herd from a wrapper then a tail of bear cerial killers and there knead too dye bye fowl pane.

Four egg sample, mini of the euthanasia knead grate idles four patients. If your mail may bee ewe think cow herds are week. An other's ex mite deep end on a heroin with a suite presents four peace of mined.

Some mothers real eyes that if weed sighed with the semen than great things mite bee aloud too poor down from the son.

Eye can knot carrion. There are fork handles near buy and the ceiling is leeking. An dye knead too go two the maul any weigh and by some see salt four two knights' bank wet.

How to Be Antisemantic

Somebody asked me if it was ok to call me a Jew. I responded that it is perfectly acceptable because I am a Jew. The question was based on a common belief amongst some goyim that calling somebody a Jew is a bad thing.

Some people in some circles only hear the word "Jew" attached to "dirty" or "dog" and assume that it must be a bad word. That would make sense if it were universally true. Does calling somebody an "American pig" mean that "American" is a bad word? I would think just the opposite. The reason they have to add "dirty" or some animal is because "Jew" or "American" is not insulting. At least not to most of us.

There is also an issue of grammar at play. "Jew" is a noun while "Jewish" is an adjective. This is different from "Christian" or "Muslim" which can be either. You can say "she is Christian" and "he is a Muslim" but you cannot say "she is a Jewish" or "he is Jew". Unless you are Chinese and do not use articles. There actually is no difference between "Jewish" and "Jew" in Chinese.

Obviously if you want to use "Jewish" as an adjective to describe a noun then by all means do so. "She is the first Jewish president of Saudi Arabia" is perfectly acceptable. Maybe not so much to the Saud family.

I have read that it is best to say "Jewish person" to avoid the issue altogether. But that is redundant. All Jews are people. There are no Jewish lobsters. That would not be kosher. It is like not saying "Happy Christmas" to avoid offending people who are not offended by Christmas.

If you say "Christian" instead of "Christian person" or "Muslim" instead of "Muslim person" why not simply say "Jew" instead of "Jewish person". None of them are insulting but I have always found it best to keep these things simple. And "Jew" rhymes with a lot more than "Jewish person".

A Jewish person, a citizen of Poland, and a female with light coloured hair enter an alcoholic beverage establishment. That is simply not funny.

Some American journalists like to use "of the Jewish faith". There is nothing inherently wrong with that but many Jews are not particulary faithful. You can be the most frum Jew in the world or you can be Jewish and a raging atheist. Again unlike Christians and Muslims, being Jewish can apply to your religion, your ethnicity or both. If you are Christian or Muslim you are probably not an atheist.

Most Jews are ethnically Jewish but not all are. If you convert to Judaism that will not change your ancestry. Not everybody who is ethnically Jewish follows any religion. I read an article in the *New York Times* a long time ago that said most American Jews were not religious. I cannot say if that is true, and I think the writer was an atheist, so it could be wishful thinking.

This is also why Jewish and Israeli are most definitely not mutually inclusive. When I talk about Israelis I specifically mean citizens of Israel, regardless of religion. The international media are often only referring to Jews when they mention Israel but that is factually incorrect.

When I talk about Jews I mean Jewish people, regardless of nationality. Most Israelis are ethnically Jewish. Whether they are religiously Jewish or not is a matter of debate. Something like twenty percent of Israelis are Arab. Most are Muslims while some are Bedouin, Christian, Druze, something else. Another million or so Israelis are neither Jewish nor Arab. They and their ancestry are mostly from Africa and East Asia.

There is no Christian or Muslim ethnic group. While most Arabs may or may not be Muslim, depending who you talk to, most Muslims are definitely not Arab. There are more Muslims in Indonesia and Pakistan than all Arab states combined. And Christians can be pretty much anything. They are certainly not all Italian.

This also makes it easier to discriminate against Jews. Racial discrimination is much easier than religious discrimination.

A Jew born in an Arab state is not considered Arab. A Jew born in a western democracy will be considered a citizen of that country but will always be Jewish rather than white, black, Latin, miscellaneous. History has plenty of examples of discrimination against Christians but it is much harder today since most Christians in any given country are probably in the same racial group as whoever is doing the discriminating.

Christians in modern Iran are killed more than Christians in other Muslim countries probably because most Iranian Christians are not Persian while most Christians in countries like Bahrain are as Arab as their neighbours. How often do you hear about discrimination against Bahraini Christians?

Discrimination against Arabs in the United States is almost always racial. Most American Arabs are Christian so it is unlikely that Americans are targeting their religion. But most Americans probably do not know that most of their Arab neighbours are Christian so it could be attempted religious discrimination. But with their long history of racial problems I would say it is more about race than anything else.

White American Christians do not have to worry too much since most of their leaders will always be white males. Unless there is a black Muslim in office. In that event they can always refresh the tree of liberty by shooting white Christian congresswomen and holding tea parties.

Why Jesus Was Not the Messiah

I have had this discussion many times so there is no original research here. If you are Jewish then you will read this and think it all obvious. But most people on this planet are not Jewish. They never had much interest in or understanding of our Messiah. Then the Christians came and decided that we should adhere to all the new rules that they invented long after we invented our rules. Most goyim with whom I have spoken only know about the Christian idea of the Messiah.

I shall try to provide biblical references if I can remember them. I will probably have to look them up but you do not need to know that. All book names and numbers will be from the Tanakh and might not necessarily match the Christian Bible versions.

I know a lot of Christians. Maybe not as many as people who live in Christian countries but I have plenty of Christian friends. I talk to them all the time. I have lived in a predominantly Christian country. Even in countries where they are a minority I tend to run into them. They seem to be everywhere.

I talk to Muslims a lot. One of my absolute best friends in the world is Muslim. I have never lived in a predominantly Muslim country. I also talk to Jews a lot. There are plenty around here. There always seem to be a few Jews most places I have lived.

The major Abrahamic religions have a lot in common. And a lot of differences. Jews and

Muslims are monotheistic. Christians say that they are too but I do not think they are. Every Christian in the world will disagree with me on this. Jews and Muslims worship a single divine God. Christians worship God, some kind of ghostly spirit god, and Jesus, who seems to drift between divine and human depending on context. That is idolatry to most of us. Having God take on human form makes him small. It lowers him to our level. That is pretty insulting.

Some Christians also worship Jesus' mother, who is not a god but has some kind of divine power depending who you talk to. She is sometimes called the mother of God, which completely goes against monotheism. God, by definition, does not have a mother. Some Christians also worship the pope but I do not believe that they are supposed to. A few Christians worship Joseph Smith but that is not really germane to the topic at hand.

Christians and Muslims share a belief that the world around us is inherently evil. Physical pleasure should be avoided at all costs. Jesus and Mary have to be virgins. Christian priests and nuns have to be celibate. Monks should isolate themselves from the outside world and live like monks. Muslim women should hide from men. Muslim clerics should elevate themselves above the people and not be amongst them.

Jews believe that pleasure was created by God for our pleasure. The world around us is not here to test our restraint and abstinence.

We are supposed to enjoy the wide world of beauty around us. Not to hide from it but to revel in it. Sex in Judaism is not a sin. It is a good thing. Why would God create a means to create life that felt very good and then tell us that if we do it we shall burn in Hell for all eternity. Rabbis and religious leaders are neither removed from the community nor above it. They are given their positions by the community. No organisation tells us who are rabbis will be. We hire and fire them at will.

Christians are supposed to convert as many people to Christianity as they can. Anybody who is not a Christian is a sinner and will burn in Hell for all eternity. Muslims are discouraged from proselytising. They are told that some people who are not Muslim might not be so bad but that most are evil. Jews are supposed to discourage others from converting at all. You do not have to be Jewish to be good or bad. We neither want nor need the entire world to do things our way.

Christians say that only Christians can get into Heaven. Muslims say that only Muslims can get into Heaven. Jews say that any good person can get into Heaven.

Another major difference between Judaism and the others is the word of God. We all say that God passed on his laws to us and told us what we needed to know but we differ greatly on how. Christians and Muslims have some guy who said that God's original version was ok but they happen to have a newly revised edition. I guess God could not get it right the first time. They have no proof that God gave them the updates. You will just have to take their word for it.

Jews say that God gave his original rule book to all the Jews at Sinai. Not just Moses but thousands of witnesses. Men, women, children, believers, heretics, movie critics. Everybody. This is an important point. Muslims and Christians have to take a tremendous leap of faith. Bless them if they can. I would not be able to. I would be inclined to doubt anybody who says that God gave all the answers to them and only them. I have met a few people like that and they are always raving lunatics. Jews only have to believe the testimony of thousands of eyewitnesses. That is sometimes harder when you consider how crazy mobs can get but I think it is more logically sound. It also makes more sense, to me at least, that if God wanted everybody to follow a set of rules that he would give his rule book to an entire nation rather than just one guy and hope everybody believes him.

Chrisitians and Muslims put a great deal of weight on the "miracles" performed by Jesus and Mohammad, most of which were done in the presence of very few witnesses. Jews do not care about any of the "miracles" that Moses performed. They were out of necessity, not to impress anybody. The Tanakh clearly states that people who perform miracles are probably false prophets. Deuteronomy 13.

One of the key aspects to Judaism is the

concept of our Messiah. He is our knight in shining armour who can save us from what has been a brutal run so far. People have been trying to kill us since we brought the concept of good and evil as opposite forces into religion and decided that there was only one God. That really upset a lot of folks. The Messiah is our emotional security.

Jews invented the Messiah. Jews decided who the Messiah should be and what he stands for. The Messiah is to Judaism what The Beatles are to England. Americans can like The Beatles all day but that does not make them American. And it certainly does not make Elvis a Beatle.

Everything about the Messiah is a Jewish concept. Christians and anybody else can enjoy our ideas and take whatever they want from our scholarship. But they cannot change a core concept in our religion any more than Muslims can change Christianity. Everybody can try to change everybody else. But that never works.

The Messiah is supposed to bring one thousand years of peace, end disease and suffering, unite humanity. Not eventually, someday, but immediately and without fail. That "second coming" business was created by Jesus' fans, not Tanakh. The Messiah can get it right the first time. Isaiah 2, 25, 52.

The Messiah is supposed to be a direct paternal descendant of King David. Joseph may or may not have been a direct descendant of David but if Mary was a virgin then Joseph was not Jesus' biological father. If Joseph was his father then Mary was not a virgin. You cannot have it both ways. This virgin business is also a Christian idea. Nowhere is the Messiah's mother supposed to be a virgin. The idea of mortals being impregnated by gods is from pagan mythology and was popular when Jesus' people wrote his biography. It has nothing to do with Judaism. Isaiah 11, Genesis 49, 1 Chronicles 22.

The Messiah is not God. The word messiah comes from moshiach, which means one anointed by God. Jesus clearly said many times that he was either God or the son of God, according to his followers. There is no need for God to anoint himself. The Messiah is supposed to be a human born from human parents who will live, do his thing, die. He is not immortal. He is not meant to be worshipped. Isaiah 11.

The Messiah is supposed to be a military king that other kings go to for counsel. Jesus was the king of twelve outcasts with less military power than modern Palau. People might read his teachings all over the world today but in his lifetime he did not have world leaders flocking to his mount for advice. Isaiah 2.

The Messiah is supposed to be accepted by Jews. During Jesus' time Jews were desperate for the Messiah to take them away from Roman oppressors. They were eager to follow almost anybody. Yet Jesus was overwhelmingly rejected by Jews, so much so that they let him die. Or killed him, depending on your point of view. Isaiah 11.

All Jews will return to Israel when the Messiah comes. Jews were spread out across Africa, Europe, western Asia at the time of Jesus. Far less than half of all the world's Jews live in Israel today. Most Jews did not even start going back until the 19th and 20th centuries, quite a few years after Jesus. Isaiah 11, 43.

All nations will recognise and atone for the wrongs committed against Israel when the Messiah comes. We have more than a few wrapped around our fingers, and of course there is all that controlling the world's banks and film industries, but there are still plenty of holdouts. Jesus never made that happen. If there was ever a time when this happened then I really need to study more history. Isaiah 52, 53.

Some Christians say that Isaiah 53 shows that Jesus was the Messiah. They should read Isaiah 52 again. It is about Israel and the suffering of Jews. Some have argued that if there is any prophecy in Isaiah 53 it is about the torture and murder of Jews at the hands of people who followed Jesus.

Ruined cities and temples of Israel will be restored when the Messiah comes. Jesus never did that. In fact, modern Israel and Islam have made it very difficult for anybody to do that. Ezekiel 16.

All people of the world will look to Jews for spiritual guidance when the Messiah comes. I am pretty sure Jesus never made this happen.

The Romans were more or less at war with Jews during most of Jesus' lifetime. They had a problem with all of that one God talk. Time has not changed that much. I know quite a few Jews today who do not even look to Jews for spiritual guidance. Isaiah 2, Zechariah 8.

The Messiah is not supposed to be a prayer intermediary. Jewish prayer is a private affair. There is that commandment about not having any gods before God. It is important enough to be up at the top. Jesus said that you cannot get to God except through him. Catholics confess their sins to God through a priest. Jews deal with God directly. Psalms 145, Isaiah 2, Zephaniah 3.

All of the world will believe in God and there will be no more illness, hunger, tyranny or evil in the world when the Messiah comes. There will be no more weapons of war. There were lots of wars in Jesus's lifetime and more than a few after he died. Man's weapons of war have improved greatly since Jesus. And I am sure there was never a time before or after Jesus that all of the world believed in God. Isaiah 2, 25, Zechariah 14, Ezekiel 39, Zephaniah 3.

The Messiah is supposed to rebuild the Holy Temple. The Second Temple was built hundreds of years before Jesus was born and was destroyed by Romans 40 odd years after his death. Having the Messiah come while the Temple existed almost negates the purpose of the Messiah. It simply would make no sense to have the Messiah come during Jesus' lifetime. Today that spot is occupied by one of Islam's most important mosques. No new temple can be built without enraging about a billion Muslims. The promise of Judaism cannot be fulfilled unless the Muslims voluntarily take their mosque down. Tearing it down would require a Messiah. Ezekiel 37, 40.

The Messiah is supposed to reestablish the Sanhedrin. That never happened. Like the Temple it was fully functional in Jesus' time. In fact, Christians claim it was the Sanhedrin that condemned Jesus to death. It seems unlikely that the Messiah would restore something that already exists and that it would kill him. It is also interesting to note that the Sanhedrin was strictly forbidden to operate during Pesach, which is when Christians claim they condemned Jesus. And it was the highest court, not a lower court that would normally handle such a case. This is also the only place in the Christian Bible where Jesus publicly claims to be the Messiah, so the factual discrepancies are relevant. Isaiah 1.

All the animals of the world are supposed to live together in peace when the Messiah comes. They did not have Animal Planet when Jesus was around but I am pretty sure animals were still killing each other. Did you see that Youtube video of those lions at Kruger? That was definitely pre-Messiah. Isaiah 11.

Those who believe in God will see eternal happiness and joy when the Messiah comes. I am mostly in a good mood but not eternally. I know a lot of people who believe in God and they are never happy all the time. I have to assume the same was true when Jesus was alive with all the wars, famine, destruction.

Millions of people who believe in God have been persecuted, tortured, murdered since Jesus. Most of them were persecuted, tortured, murdered by people who believed in God. Many were persecuted, tortured, murdered in the name of Jesus. That is not his fault, and it is unfair to blame everything that people do in his name on him, but it is completely contrary to the Messiah. Isaiah 51.

The Messiah is supposed to make barren land fruitful and fertile. Ever been to Southern Israel? There is a whole lot of nothing there. Every Jesus movie I have ever seen takes place in a desert. This tells us that if Jesus sowed the land then Hollywood never heard about it. Isaiah 51, Amos 9, Ezekiel 36.

God's children, particularly Jews, will know the Torah without study when the Messiah comes. When I was in school I would have gladly accepted Jesus if he made that happen. I would have followed Ozzy Osbourne if he could do that. Jeremiah 31.

The Messiah is supposed to faithfully observe the Torah. The Torah clearly identifies anybody who tries to challenge mitzvot as a false prophet. The Christian Bible has many stories of Jesus contradicting the Torah and challenging mitzvot. Jesus declared himself above the law, not a faithful servant of the law. Tanakh also says that such a false prophet will be put to death. That is not prophecy. That was the penal code. Deuteronomy 13, Isaiah 11.

The Messiah is supposed to give all worthy people all that they desire. I am not entirely sure how that works, especially if what you desire contradicts everything else the Messiah is supposed to do. And it seems too greedy to me. But I am sure that Jesus never did it. Psalms 37.

Everybody who has died will be resurrected when the Messiah comes. Whether that sounds creepy or not Jesus never made it happen. Christians say he brought Lazarus back but not everybody. And there is no evidence for Lazarus. I am sure that if he had brought back everybody then there would be some historical records. Resurrection of the entire human race is the sort of thing historians tend to notice. Isaiah 26.

Not all Jews believe all of this, of course. Some say that you cannot take it too literally. Some say that it is just what we should all aspire to do ourselves and not wait around for some miracle worker to change the world. Some even say that the Messiah already came but we were not deserving so he did nothing. That could help the Christian view but I think that if he looked around and said never mind then he was not a very good Messiah. Understandable but lazy.

According to the Christian Bible written by his followers, Jesus fulfilled their obtuse definitions of prophecy. According to the definitions of the Torah, Jesus was clearly a false prophet, a heretic, and really not a very good Jew. And he fulfilled absolutely none of the Messianic requirements.

More than a few Christians have told me that biblical prophecy is difficult to understand. It is if you bend over backward to make it all apply to somebody that you want it all to apply to. It is all very straightforward if you simply read it as is.

Christians inevitably say that Jesus was a prophet and could therefore declare his own prophecies. Unfortunately, none of them are the requirements according to Tanakh. There cannot be any prophets unless most Jews live in Israel. Prophecy ended about 400 BCE. Long before Jesus was born. Historically, Jesus fulfilled absolutely no prophecies. Technically he cannot claim prophet status even if he wanted to.

It is also very important to understand that Tanakh was not written in English or Greek or Latin. The Hebrew text often differs widely from the translations, and when the Christians decided to incorporate it into their books they changed even more. "Like a lion they are at my hands and feet" from Psalms 22 becomes "they pierced my hands and feet" in the Christian version. The translation can easily refer to Jesus. The original Hebrew has no special significance to Jesus. And that passage has nothing to do with the Messiah.

I think that if a group of people decide to write down their own code of conduct and then another group comes along a thousand years later and rewrites it to fit their own agenda they do not get to tell the first group what the original books said. You are more than welcome to worship Jesus or any other Jew as much as you want but when you tell us that he is our Messiah, and we have our books and your books telling us otherwise, you can expect us to change our beliefs as much as you change yours whenever Muslims tell you the new versions of your books.

And if you could stop killing people in the name of Jesus that would be great. I have listed what Jesus was not. I think he also was not the kind of person who wanted his followers to kill everybody. His message was about love. As far as I can tell. If you think enough of him to edit our most sacred books in order to make him look better then you should think enough of him to follow his main principle. He said "love one another", not "kill 'em all and let God sort it out".

The Catholic church has a long history of distorting Jesus' message for their own personal gain. Jesus welcomed women, the poor, the sick, pretty much anybody into his club. Church leaders quickly realised how much easier it was to retain power if they demonised women, the poor, the sick, pretty much anybody who did not tow the party line.

Mary Magdalene is an excellent example. She was easily the most important of Jesus' followers. Many say she was supposed to lead the gang after Jesus. But there was no way the men in charge were going to let a woman lead. Mary Magdalene became the sacrificial lamb for weak men who needed to subjugate women.

Her history was rewritten enough to confuse enough people into believing that she was a common whore. How would Jesus feel about that?

Christians have told me that other religions have also had power struggles and corruption. That is very true. But Judaism, Buddhism, Hinduism have never made any attempt to rule the world. We have all had power hungry men who try to distort our texts to suit their agendas but we never forced the world to convert to our ways under threat of death and torture.

I would doubt that Jesus ever wanted any of that. The popes who invoke his name live very differently than he ever did. As far as I know Jesus never lived in a palace, sat on a gold throne, wore a jewelled crown, directed armies into battle. Today's popes have little hope of waging war but they used to do it more than frequently.

Imagine a world where Christian leaders actually followed the teachings of Jesus. You may say I'm a dreamer but I think the world would be a much better place if the people who followed him saw him as he was rather than how they want him to be.

By trying to claim that he was the Messiah they are making him into something that he was not. I understand why he needed to be a demigod for people to join up two thousand years ago but that stopped being necessary a very long time ago. The history of the world would have been far more peaceful if people saw him as a human who said some good things. As a human his followers could have looked up to somebody who never hated people for being different. According to the New Testament he was very inclusive.

Our planet is full of people from different cultures with different ways of thinking. There is no single issue on which everybody will ever agree. Attempts to force others to believe something they do not have always been problematic.

I often criticise Christianity, Islam, Judaism. But that does not mean that I hate Christians, Muslims, Jews or want everybody to pray my way. I regularly criticise American, Israeli, South African politicians. But that does not mean that I hate Americans, Israelis, South Africans and want everybody to vote my way. I want to live in a world where I can pray and vote my way, and you can pray and vote your way. Or not pray or vote at all.

Too many of us see any criticism and interpret it as hostility. Sometimes that is fair. Sometimes it is not. If I hated you and your people then I would never mention you at all. There is a recent tradition in Judaism to never say the names of some of the murderers responsible for the Shoah. I think that is the right idea. Giving sociopaths publicity only makes them stronger. We cannot ignore what they did but we can certainly deny them their fame.

If I thought Americans were stupid I would never discuss their politics. Deriding American hyperbole is not anti American. If I thought

Muslims were terrorists I would never discuss their religion. Excoriating Arab apathy toward terrorism is not anti Arab. Nor do I see disapproval of Israeli actions as anti Israeli. I see the people who want to kill all Israelis as anti Israeli. My disapprobation of Arab apathy is not comparable to the terrorist view that all Jews must die for the simple fact that I do not want all Arabs to die.

Criticising media bias is not anti media. It is something that I think we should all do. It should never matter if the bias I oppose is the opposite of the bias that you oppose.

Criticising people and places I hate would be a phenomenal waste of time. Who in their right mind would devote their time and energy into something they hate? I absolutely loathe gherkins. Consequently, I never talk about them.

A carrot, a gherkin, and a penis were discussing their lots in life. "My life is hard," the carrot said. "When I get big and fat they cut me up and cook me." "My life is harder," the gherkin said. "When I get big and fat they cover me in vinegar and lock me in a jar." "Well, my life sucks," the penis said. "When I get big and fat they pull a plastic bag over my head, shove me in a dark room, and bang my head against the wall until I vomit and pass out."

NOTES

Wasted Seed on the Ground

Mohandas Gandhi quote is from *The Story of My Experiments with Truth*, originally published in *Navjivan* between 1925 and 1929.

> *"When I despair, I remember that all through history the way of truth and love has always won. There have been tyrants and murderers, and for a time they seem invincible. But in the end they always fall. Think of it. Always. What difference does it make to the dead, the orphans, and the homeless, whether the mad destruction is wrought under the name of totalitarianism or the holy name of liberty and democracy? There are many causes that I am prepared to die for but no causes that I am prepared to kill for."*

The Protection of State Information Bill was formerly the Protection of Information Bill. It was passed by the National Assembly of South Africa on 22 November 2011 with 229 to 107 votes. Every opposition party voted against, and two ANC members who abstained, Gloria Borman and Ben Turok, were subsequently subject to the ANC Disciplinary Committee. Amendments were added by the National Council of Provinces on 29 November 2012 with 34 to 16 votes. The bill passed on 25 April 2013 with 189 to 74 votes.

Like Crimson Curtains Slowly Rising

"Everytime I Dream" by Yusuf Islam, from the album *Roadsinger*, Ya/Island 2009.

World Leader Pretend

"World Leader Pretend" by Bill Berry, Peter Buck, Mike Mills, Michael Stipe, from the REM album *Green*, Warner Bros 1988.

This Has Nothing to Do With Andy Kaufman

"Man on the Moon" by Bill Berry, Peter Buck, Mike Mills, Michael Stipe, from the REM album *Automatic for the People*, Warner Bros 1992.

American Idol

Barack Obama quotes are from his 2012 State of the Union Address, 24 January 2012.

North to the Future

Sarah Palin's Alaska was produced by Mark Burnett Productions for Discovery Communications, and aired on The Learning Channel beginning in November 2010.

Take a Cruiser With All Hands

Benjamin Netanyahu quotes are from his address to the United States Congress, Washington, DC, 24 May 2011.

Moshe Ya'alon quotes were originally published in *Yedioth Ahronoth*, 14 January 2014.

"Get Your Filthy Hands Off My Desert" by Roger Waters, from the Pink Floyd album *The Final Cut*, Harvest Records 1983.

Disproportionate Response

Benjamin Netanyahu quote is from *Fighting Terrorism: How Democracies Can Defeat Domestic and International Terrorists*, originally published in 1995.

The Cost of Freedom

Some information was provided by Israel Ministry of Foreign Affairs and Israel Security Agency.

"Find the Cost of Freedom" by Stephen Stills, from the Crosby, Stills, Nash and Young album *4 Way Street*, Atlantic Records 1971.

Commands Met

Quotes from Asereth Ha'dibroth were originally published in the *Book of Exodus* attributed to Moses, circa 1200 BCE.

History of the World, Part I was written and directed by Mel Brooks and distributed by 20th Century Fox 1981.

Always From Now Until Then

Concluding observations on the second periodic report of the Holy See was published by the Committee on the Rights of the Child, Office of the United Nations High Commissioner for Human Rights, 5 February 2014.

"Hope of Deliverance" by Paul McCartney, from the album *Off the Ground*, Parlophone 1993.

Slippery When Wet

Marion "Pat" Robertson quotes are from *The 700 Club*, an American basic cable television programme, 7 May 2009.

Statement of Principles on the Place of Jews with a Homosexual Orientation in Our Community by Rabbi Nathaniel Helfgot of Yeshivat Chovevei Torah in New York, Rabbi Aryeh Klapper of the Center for Modern Torah Leadership in Boston, and Rabbi Yitzchak Blau of Yeshivat Shvilei Hatorah in Jerusalem was originally published in July 2010.

Slippery When Wet by Bon Jovi, Mercury Records 1986.

ABOUT THE AUTHOR

Meira bat Erachaim was born and raised in South Africa, went to university in the United States, and lived and worked in China before settling in Israel.

She has worked as a helicopter pilot, documentary filmmaker, English teacher, and is currently a casualty extraction and medical evacuation combat support officer with the Israeli Air Force. In her spare time she climbs mountains, swims naked, and irritates her mother.

Her first published book, *Letters To Friends*, received high praise from the five people who read it. Her second book, *Fortnight in the Philippines*, details search and rescue operations in the aftermath of Typhoon Haiyan.

The controversial *Venom of Asps* was followed by *Her Whole Darkness in Motion*.